Due Diligence
Techniques and Analysis

Due Diligence Techniques and Analysis

Critical Questions for Business Decisions

GORDON BING

QUORUM BOOKS
Westport, Connecticut • London

Library of Congress Cataloging-in-Publication Data

Bing, Gordon.
  Due diligence techniques and analysis : critical questions for
business decisions / Gordon Bing.
    p. cm.
  Includes bibliographical references and index.
  ISBN 1–56720–029–X (alk. paper)
    1. Business enterprises—Purchasing—Handbooks, manuals, etc.
  2. Investment analysis—Handbooks, manuals, etc. I. Title.
  HD1393.25.B56 1996
  658.1'6—dc20   95–51411

British Library Cataloguing in Publication Data is available.

Library of Congress Catalog Card Number: 95–51411
ISBN: 1–56720–029–X

First published in 1996

Quorum Books, 88 Post Road West, Westport, CT 06881
An imprint of Greenwood Publishing Group, Inc.

Printed in the United States of America

The paper used in this book complies with the
Permanent Paper Standard issued by the National
Information Standards Organization (Z39.48–1984).

To my wife, Alice: She conceived the concept for this book, and her advice, suggestions and assistance have made it possible.

Contents

Preface

Businesses are complex institutions consisting of many interrelated functions and activities. Potential acquirers or investors must be able to identify, understand, and evaluate the pros and cons of each aspect of their investment as efficiently as possible. But few individuals have the background or could even remember all the possible questions that could be asked, along with how to ask them in the appropriate manner. This book fills that gap by providing a proven, systematic approach to performing due diligence, along with a comprehensive list of possible questions.

To write the book, I conducted an extensive study of how corporations, professionals, and investors actually perform due diligence. I also applied myself to the task of gathering every relevant question that should be asked, and every necessary document that would be needed in performing adequate due diligence.

It became clear to me that most due diligence conducted today is cursory and inadequate, and largely overlooks critical areas, especially in nonfinancial matters. We see daily evidence of this in the business press in the form of failed acquisitions, initial public offerings with collapsed prices, loans in default and investment scandals. Most of these events can be connected, some of them directly, to the due diligence (or lack of it) performed by investors.

The result of my research is the longest and most comprehensive list of questions and relevant information ever developed for publication. Although I have drawn some of the relevant questions from my reviews of other checklists used privately in mergers and acquisitions, most of them come from years of experience in gathering these questions and refining them through actual practice.

Serious consequences can result from the failure to perform due diligence.

On the other hand, knowledge and a strong negotiating position can be drawn from effective and comprehensive due diligence. My hope is that those who use this book will never feel that, "If we had known that, we would have (or never would have) invested."

Acknowledgments

The contributions of James Ryan and Robert Beasley of the law firm of Ryan & Sudan, Houston, Texas, have been invaluable. Their writing of Chapter 4, "Due Diligence from a Legal Perspective," and the legal questions provides an authoritative and essential part of this book.

The review, advice, and comments of Sid M. Shaver, Jr., CPA, CFM, president of S.M. Shaver & Co. P.C., Houston, Texas, have been most helpful in the chapters on accounting issues.

Trent Price of Executive Excellence, Provo, Utah, has made important suggestions and assisted in the production of the manuscript.

Introduction

The analysis of financial statements is important for many reasons, and for those people who routinely check the pulses of their companies, many of these reasons are obvious. But when the analysis relates to the acquisition of, or investment in, a new business, most investors would agree that numbers alone are entirely inadequate.

Financial statements provide thumbnail sketches of a business and its history, supplying a few clues and insights into the company's present, and may possibly offer a reasonable guess about its near-term future. But general and specific conditions and events relating to the business's future, and the ramifications of past events and conditions, will determine its eventual success or failure. Using only past results to forecast the future is folly.

Financial statements do not tell about some of the most critical factors that impact businesses, such as management competence and continuity, market trends, production capability, quality, potential litigation, employee turnover, the status of supplier contracts and a host of other items. These "non-financial" factors, more often than not, determine the future structure and viability of a company. For this reason, potential investors must carefully study these factors during the due diligence phase, before a final agreement is reached.

This book will help you describe, evaluate, and understand an existing or proposed business in which you plan to invest, in terms of both financial and non-financial concerns. It may also be useful in preparing information for potential investors or buyers. It provides a full explanation of the due diligence process, including a systematic method for determining what information is needed, why it is needed and how to gather it. It also explores some of the legal ramifications of performing (or failing to perform) necessary due diligence.

But this book is not designed only for potential investors and buyers.[1] It may assist anyone involved in any phase of the due diligence process or in the general study and analysis of businesses. In fact, most people in business would probably make better decisions if they had more of the important facts, and obtaining these facts can be simplified by knowing what questions to ask. Adequate due diligence is appropriate and applicable to investors and buyers in any type of business, whether large or small, manufacturing or service oriented, existing or proposed.

- Corporate investors and their teams must perform due diligence to comprehensively evaluate both the financial and non-financial aspects of proposed investments or new ventures before making decisions.

- Intermediaries, such as brokers and investment bankers, must apply due diligence to quickly and adequately understand the businesses they represent or target for acquisition, restructuring or refinancing.

- Lending institutions and their loan officers must apply basic due diligence questions to properly evaluate loan requests, especially in the frequently neglected non-financial areas.

- Business appraisers must be able to defend their appraisals with adequate due diligence on all significant aspects of businesses they evaluate.

- Venture capitalists must be able to systematically analyze proposed new ventures with due diligence.

- Corporate attorneys must prepare sound advice and cases based on their knowledge of their clients' businesses, obtained through due diligence. (This book can also help in litigation to determine which questions were asked in due diligence procedures.)

- Accountants must have a complete understanding of every aspect of a business, financial and non-financial, to prepare accurate financial statements and reports, and many perform due diligence for their clients.

- Managers and directors can better fulfill their responsibilities if they know what questions to ask. They can also evaluate the quality and extent of due diligence performed by those who report to them.

- Newly hired managers and directors can reduce their learning curves by supplementing their training with due diligence-style questions.

- Students can gain greater insight into the businesses they study by learning how to ask relevant questions.

Portions of this book may also benefit government regulators, insurance providers, trust and investment fund managers, major customers and suppliers, auditors, securities analysts and management consultants. It also offers assistance, suggestions and insights into the gathering and evaluation of important investor information, such as how to recognize unusual or highly negative responses that may cause you to rethink your position. But keep in mind that, since each business is unique, so are the resources, standards and objectives used in evaluating them. For instance, an acceptable condition in a small business may be totally unacceptable in a large one, and vice versa; an unsatisfactory financial ratio in one industry may be excellent in another, and so forth. Therefore, you must cultivate your own ability to both quantify and qualify the attributes, defects, and finally your conclusions relating to the due diligence you perform.

Chapters 1 and 2 discuss how to plan, organize and conduct due diligence. Chapter 3 explains how to construct and modify a comprehensive checklist of essential information and documents for each business studied. Chapter 4, prepared by James W. Ryan and Robert C. Beasley of Ryan & Sudan, experienced in areas of mergers and acquisitions, describes the legal aspects, responsibilities and perils associated with performing or failing to perform due diligence. The remainder of the book covers the specific groups of questions necessary for due diligence, and how to approach your investigation in those areas of focus. A checklist of all questions is available in the Appendix for easy reference and for use in constructing checklists for individual businesses.

Although this book is designed primarily for the study of American companies, it can also help you establish a starting point for the analysis of any business worldwide. Each country has its own customs, taxes and legislation governing business activities. This book can help you develop questions that will allow you to begin your due diligence in foreign countries. Although you will need the help of people skilled in the analysis of companies in those countries, you will probably find that foreign businesses have more similarities than differences with their American counterparts.

In order to simplify the text, most of the questions and documents described are generic and designed to cover the most common conditions in business. Before you begin your evaluations, make sure that you tailor your requests to the specific industry and type of business you are considering. You may find that you need to add some questions that are specific to certain industries. Remember that anything you consider to be important should be asked before you make your investment. Nevertheless, you will probably find very few questions to add, and your main concern as you construct your list of questions will be to determine whether or not every question in this book will be relevant to your own analysis.

NOTE

1. For the purposes of this book, anyone involved in buying or evaluating a business is an "investor" and anyone involved in selling is a "seller."

Due Diligence
Techniques and Analysis

CHAPTER 1

Planning Due Diligence

Due diligence is one of the procedures we use to study, investigate and evaluate a business opportunity. It normally occurs after the parties to a deal have decided the deal is financially feasible and after a preliminary understanding has been reached (or appears reachable), but before a binding contract is signed. The term came into common business usage during the 1980s. While the term is new, the activity itself is not. Studying and investigating before buying and investing is as old as trading itself. While the term was originally used in the context of studying a potential acquisition or merger, it has been broadened to cover the study of almost all business transactions, including the issuance of securities and private placements, real estate sales, appraisals and commercial lending.

Due diligence can be accomplished successfully if it is preceded by careful planning. Such planning includes the assessment of available resources, the estimation of risk, selection of management, the recognition of the consequences of failure, the identification of possible obstacles to the deal, the definition of the deal's scope—all of which lead to the crucial decisions essential to produce the results one wants to achieve. All of these major planning elements are essential and must be included in the planning process. Establishing clear objectives is of highest priority. To proceed without them would be like setting out on a trip to an unknown destination.

The objectives and results one hopes to attain must be equated with the number of people and the amount of money one has. The scope of the due diligence is also influenced by other resources one has and by the level of risk one will accept. There will always be some risk, but how much there actually is should be carefully assessed. The investor may find it impossible to learn everything about a business. Historical and current information may be useful, but as a sure predictor of future performance they are unreliable. Plans and decisions must include selection of management and individuals for their implementation. Whether the due diligence is conducted by one person or a team, somehow the work must be done.

PURPOSES AND OBJECTIVES

The first step in planning a due diligence program is to define its objectives. There may be multiple objectives, of course, and various individuals participating in your investor group may have various—and different— priorities. Some of the more common objectives are:

• Verification that the business is essentially what it seems to be. (Determining this, by means of interviews, document study and on-site inspections, is the fundamental objective of due diligence.)
• Verification that the investment complies with investors' criteria.

Many investors, investment funds and lending institutions have essential criteria for businesses in which they will invest. Typical criteria involve historical earnings, financial ratios, projected earning potential, tangible book value in relation to price, quality of management and type of business. These criteria reflect what investors hope to get for their money, such as income to offset losses, new facilities or an increased market capability. If criteria are not met, the deal may just not "fit." It could also mean there are easily correctable deviations, or perhaps that the criteria themselves are unreasonable and should be ignored or reconsidered. An interesting situation arises when investors are presented with an opportunity superior in terms of one set of perfectly valid criteria, but not in terms of the investors' set. Will they proceed anyway? Maybe.

Investors should not hesitate to apply one set of standards to their existing investments, yet a different set to new investments. It may just be in their best interest to improve the performance of their existing investments and set higher standards for the new. The standards for new investments can also be used to define new objectives for the old investments. (During negotiations, alert sellers might point out differences in performance between their company and the potential investors to justify their asking price. Investors, in turn, can counter that they have initiated programs to boost their business's performance.)

It's essential that investors gain information that will provide for a profitable business relationship and a smooth, rapid transition after the deal closes. A prudent transition plan identifies actions and positions to be taken and notes their sequence. This task can be greatly facilitated if the investor fully understands the details of the target business.

Securing sufficient information to write an accurate and defensible private placement memorandum, registration statement, prospectus, business plan or appraisal may be an objective. A systematic approach will provide the information required and avoid overlooking key elements. Failure to provide complete and accurate information, or "full disclosure," can lead to costly litigation. Regardless of legal obligations, the information is essential for those involved to describe the business and make wise decisions.

Identifying defects in the business is a primary objective. Since the attributes are nearly always known prior to commencing due diligence, emphasis tends to be placed on what is wrong with the business, not with what is right. Past experience, excessive caution, concerns over legal obligations and unfamiliarity with the industry all encourage a search for potential pitfalls. While misleading or negative information not originally disclosed can often be used to negotiate price concessions, it also can be used by unenthusiastic participants within an investor's group to discourage the investment.

Attorneys, accountants, investment bankers, loan officers and other professionals involved in securities transactions have an obligation to conduct independent due diligence. Full disclosure is not just their clients' responsibility. Attorneys and accountants may be required to provide formal opinion letters regarding the business. Investment bankers and others routinely write "fairness opinions" outlining their view of the transaction. Their objective is not just to provide competent professional service to their clients but to establish a record demonstrating they conducted adequate due diligence under the circumstances. Chapter 4 contains detailed information on their responsibilities.

Definitive acquisition contracts and other investment contracts require the seller or borrower to verify that all pertinent information has been provided and that the business's condition is indeed as it appears. These sections often are the most contentious and difficult to negotiate. Therefore, the more information available, the easier, or at least more rational, will be the negotiations. An objective of due diligence should be to provide on a timely basis the information needed for the investor to formulate his positions (see Chapter 4 for more information).

The objective of the due diligence process should be to quantify major items and monetary values, not simply to identify assets, liabilities, defects or problems. If an asset is improperly valued, is it valued over or under market value? If benefit plans are underfunded, how much will it cost to fund them? Is additional costly equipment needed? Are there any environmental problems that require costly cleanups? Only if major items such as these are quantified can perspective be maintained and rational decisions made. Quantifying these items helps maintain perspective and avoid a "halo effect" in which the presence of an outstanding asset or defect blinds investors to other facets of the business. Avoiding the halo effect and maintaining objectivity is a common problem and challenge.

Another due diligence objective should be to preserve all notes, records, information and documents. They should be readily available for reference during final negotiations and retained to resolve any disputes that might arise later with disgruntled investors or unhappy sellers. Due diligence files can be an invaluable source of information to reconstruct conditions and events during and prior to the transaction's closing. Unfortunately, they also can surface during litigation and may contain damaging information.

Since attorneys writing the definitive contracts and other documents to conclude the transaction must have accurate information for the agreements, part of the due diligence process is to efficiently supply them with the data they need. Attorneys forced to locate data on their own have their meters running all the time and tend to duplicate the efforts of others.

If the due diligence desired is to be only perfunctory in nature, it is best to recognize that as a fact. There are occasions where the transaction is a "done deal" that will close regardless of what due diligence uncovers. In these situations, the objective should be to hold the cost and effort to a minimum or not bother at all.

RISK ASSESSMENT AND SCOPE

While planning the scope and nature of a due diligence program, an investor must determine the degree of business and legal risk he will accept. Scope in this context consists of the depth of questioning on any subject and the quantity of original documents to be reviewed. There are no satisfactory alternatives to a comprehensive and systematic due diligence program because risk multiplies when all aspects of a business are not objectively reviewed. However, one must balance the amount of due diligence against the cost, time and resources available. Investors must recognize that any reduction or restrictions in due diligence activity increase the probability that significant aspects of the business will be overlooked or misunderstood.

An intense, well-run due diligence program cannot guarantee success for the investor, but it can most assuredly improve the odds. Conversely, no amount of data evaluation will totally eliminate risk or generate certainty that the contemplated transaction will succeed. Recognizing that there will always be some risk is not an excuse for conducting little or no due diligence. The only way to avoid any chance of making a bad deal is to make no deal at all.

What constitutes adequate due diligence? No precise answer exists, but there are certain elements that can lessen the investor's risk and possibly justify reducing the scope of due diligence:

- Stable and proven management.
- Audited financial statements with short, easily understood notes.
- History of consistent earnings.

- Few subsidiaries, divisions or joint ventures.
- Strong market position.
- Absence of material litigation.
- No real estate or operations with potential environmental problems.
- Earnings primarily from operations.
- Not dependent upon one or few customers or clients.
- No intangible assets.
- No intercompany transactions.
- No discontinued operations or restructuring.
- Little or no extraordinary income or expenses.
- Strong internal controls.
- Few and readily accessible locations.

Increased due diligence would be signalled by the absence or antithesis of the above factors, which are by no means an all-inclusive list. It would be indefensible not to conduct extensive due diligence if a number of significant adverse risk factors arose.

Whether the due diligence proves adequate will only be known with certainty in hindsight. However, reducing its scope can arguably be justified if key elements of the business are in favorable condition. Of course, if the deal goes well, regardless of risk factors, it is likely the due diligence program will be forgotten soon after the closing.

It's a mistake to balance the scope of due diligence in relation to the size of the transaction. If the potential loss from failure of the investment can be contained to an amount insignificant to the investor, due diligence often is less aggressive. A $10 million loss to a $1 billion corporation may damage a few careers but be financially immaterial. A comparable situation can occur prior to a deal involving numerous subsidiaries, divisions, factories or other business units in which only the larger ones are fully studied. The fallacy in placing the scope of due diligence in proportion to the size of the transaction, or restricting it only to major units in a large deal, is that financial exposure usually cannot be neatly limited. The search by plaintiff attorneys for "deep pockets" has produced corporate horror stories. Anyone considering shortcuts should review the defendants' agony in the infamous asbestos litigation.

A factor influencing risk assessment and the scope of due diligence is the involvement and potential personal exposure of those providing information. Key managers whose own net worth is at risk are more likely to be convinced of the viability of the deal and truthful with investors. A criterion of investment for many investors is that management has both the potential for great financial reward and knowledge that failure could bring personal financial pain. Continued management involvement can reduce the scope in many situations, but it would be unwise for an investor to totally rely on management. Regardless of management's enthusiasm and commitment, they have only their own viewpoints and objectives in a situation where other opinions are valuable.

Investors often act like sheep when they are part of an investment group that has a lead investor. This is particularly true in venture capital and loan syndications led by prestigious individuals or institutions. However, complete reliance upon lead co-investors, rather than independent due diligence, has brought grief to many. While lead co-investors may have their own variety of due diligence, they may lack the long association or knowledge comparable to a committed management. The scope and intensity of co-investor due diligence is often unknown and reliance on others does not eliminate legal responsibility, nor monetary losses, from a bad deal.

Excess due diligence and irrational risk concerns go hand-in-hand. Exactly what is "excess" and what is "irrational" in this context are as difficult to define as pornography. But their effects can be recognized and guarded against during the due diligence process. Excesses produce subtle and insidious psychological effects that tend to discourage completion of even the most desirable transactions. Since there are no perfect businesses, the longer an investor studies the business, the larger the warts become. As a result, more and more study is conducted and information sought. The investor tends to talk himself out of the deal by dwelling on what is wrong rather than what is right. An attitude of boredom and weariness of the deal can set in. While the investor's enthusiasm is lost in data, the seller or borrower becomes impatient, loses respect for the investor and begins to evaluate alternatives. Well-planned and rapid due diligence, coupled with quantification of defects, is the best defense against excesses.

Problems in past or existing investments will affect the scope of due diligence. An investor burned by bad management, product liability suits, environmental surprises or other significant problems will be exceptionally sensitive to issues that in the past have caused difficulty. If the investor is an institution, all executives involved in the review and approval process will expect due diligence to be performed in great depth in these sensitive areas. No one wants to be in the position of making the same mistake twice.

TIME AND COST

It's crucial when planning due diligence to determine how much time can be allotted for the work. Many preliminary agreements define a time period in which a definitive agreement must be signed. During this period the investor is given the opportunity to conduct due diligence. The actual time for due diligence is somewhat less than the full time allotted prior to the closing date, since time must be reserved for review and decision-making.

The parties, based on what they know and expecting no surprises, want to complete the deal, and recognize that delays are opportunities for something to go wrong. Tight time schedules for closing are generally desirable, but they can conflict with the due diligence timetable. Those negotiating the time schedule should have some understanding of the due diligence process. While a very short time schedule occasionally can be compensated with additional manpower, there are instances when due diligence may become confined to major issues and dangerously abbreviated.

Some deals call for closing only after due diligence has been satisfactorily completed. Investors simply take the conservative position not to proceed until they are fully satisfied with the business's condition and outlook. Even in these cases it is wise to set a timetable for completion, as it tends to facilitate planning and prevent procrastination, particularly by those with other pressing duties and interests. With time schedules, the reasoning "If I have to get it done, I will" can be made to prevail.

Due diligence covering aspects of the business subject to the warranty and representation sections of the definitive contract should preferably be completed before negotiations commence and definitely before the negotiations are concluded on these sections. This requires internal coordination between those conducting due diligence and the negotiators and attorneys. Since the warranty and representation sections are frequently contentious and difficult to negotiate, they may remain the last to be settled, giving those studying the business a little more time.

Tight time schedules for due diligence may also prevail for those writing registration statements, prospectuses, private placement memorandums, business plans and loan or financing agreements. The circumstances controlling time for completion can vary widely with each situation, but in most cases there emerges a practical, if not formal, deadline.

Timing is a key factor when the buyer elects to conduct comprehensive due diligence before price negotiations commence. Because of the expense of due diligence, most buyers rely on the seller's financial statements, offering memorandums and other readily available information to negotiate a price contingent upon future satisfactory due diligence. However, some buyers accept the cost of early due diligence in the belief that they will be better able to evaluate the business and negotiate. They definitely are better informed, but if price agreement proves impossible, or another buyer makes a deal while the due diligence is under way, the money spent is wasted. When conducting early due diligence, speed helps reduce the risk of intrusion by other potential buyers and placates the seller. Sellers generally are not happy with the inconvenience and loss of secrecy associated with a buyer's team gathering information prior to agreement on price. By conducting costly early due diligence, a seller may assume the asking price is acceptable, which may or may not be true.

Once the scope and timetable are established, an estimate of the due diligence cost should be made and budgeted. Whoever is making the final decisions should be aware of the estimate. Conditions that tend to influence and greatly increase costs are the employment of outside accountants and consultants, the number and location of facilities and business units, existence of foreign operations and the complexity of the business. Investors have been known to abort a deal when confronted by the enormous cost of adequate due diligence. However, for most the cost will be an essential expense both small in relation to anticipated benefits and minuscule compared to the unacceptable risks of not performing due diligence or having a disorderly transition of ownership.

STAFFING

Management, gathering and evaluation of information may be handled by one person or require a team with well-defined responsibilities. The size of the transaction, legal requirements and time to complete will largely determine the number of individuals from within or outside the investor's organization. In any event, someone or a team has to be responsible for gathering information directly from the business. While the ideal person is unlikely to be readily available, if he or she did exist, these would be essential characteristics:

1. *Possesses broad knowledge of the industry.* With such knowledge the investigator can avoid asking questions a seller would consider demeaning, will know when to pursue subjects in depth, and can engage in "shop talk" and industry gossip that will help build a rapport with those providing information.

2. *Possesses in-depth knowledge of the investor and is an effective advocate of the investor.* While the investor's representatives are gathering information, executives of the target business usually are seeking as much information as possible about the investor. The investor's representatives should expect information gathering to be a two-way street. The ability to speak knowledgeably about the investor, extol his virtues and present as favorable a picture as is honestly possible is highly desirable. The investigator is a de facto salesman for the investor.

3. *Understands accounting and finance.* Since much of due diligence involves review of financial records, the ability to read financial statements and understand accounting and financial systems is essential. A strong accounting knowledge enables the investigator to know what he is looking for and when to pursue subjects in depth.

4. *Is not intimidating.* The investigator who is not overbearing, almost shy in demeanor, but very persistent in securing the desired information will be effective. As a guest at the business being studied, he should be as unobtrusive as possible.

5. *Keeps opinions to himself and avoids being outwardly judgmental.* A quick way for an investigator to discourage the flow of information is to voice harsh

judgments relative to the business to those providing information. Negative views and second-guessing of management errors and follies may be warranted, but an investigator should contain himself until he returns home.

6. *Cannot commit the investor.* Negotiations should be separate from due diligence so investigators should not be allowed to make final decisions concerning the transaction. However, the investigators are at the business and readily available, hence they easily become conduits to relay positions or hints of positions regarding open issues. This is unavoidable and even desirable as long as the investigator's role is limited to "messenger."

7. *Understands corporate politics, power structures, cultures and how employees relate to each other.* A perceptive investigator should be able to determine how the business functions. This is critical information useful in negotiations and essential in planning the transition. Simply recording answers as given will deny an investor the advantage of broader insight into the business. A better picture will emerge as the result of a study by one who can discern from both direct information and obscure clues how the business really operates.

8. *Is totally loyal to the investor.* Loyalty will be reflected in the manner by which the investigator conducts himself. A conviction that the investor is outstanding will help promote the transaction. Loyalty will prevent the investigator from confiding to the business's executives the investor's less perfect traits or voicing doubts about the desirability of the deal.

9. *Has the traits of persistence, perceptiveness and patience necessary to secure details.* Investigators unable to pursue details thwart the major activity of ferreting out obscure but highly significant assets, defects or business problems. Reliance upon intuition and business sense, combined with a big ego, can result in a cursory job of due diligence. The investigator must have the patience to pursue tedious detail.

10. *Has a mature appearance and demeanor.* While many exceptions prevail, if all other factors are essentially equal, an older, experienced investigator can be more effective than a bright, highly educated younger one. The older individual is likely to be gathering information from people his own age or younger and maturity does create confidence and receive some respect. While credit may be given an older investigator for more wisdom and perception than actually exists, a mature demeanor can be helpful.

11. *Is open-minded, and neither his career nor his net worth will be affected by the outcome of the due diligence.* A constant problem in due diligence is how to avoid conflicts of interest that could, or appear to, influence objectivity. The greater the benefits individuals will enjoy or lose if the transaction proceeds, the more questionable will be the thoroughness and reliability of their due diligence. Regardless of how well the due diligence is conducted, the actual objectivity will be in doubt in the presence of conflicts of interest.

Whenever possible, qualified employees of the investor are preferable in due diligence investigations. Employees can represent their employer with authority and have a better grasp of important areas to emphasize. They will be available to answer questions and take responsibility after the deal is complete, unlike an outsider who completes a report and departs upon its issuance. While there probably is no such thing as a "typical" employee, employee investigators will be viewed as typical and representative of the investor's employees.

Lack of available employees, special skills, distant locations or other factors may make it necessary to turn to outside professionals. Their assignments may consist of conducting all due diligence, including assisting the investor during negotiations, or may be limited to a portion of the program or even a specific issue.

The most commonly used and readily available professionals are teams from public accounting firms representing their audit or consulting sections or both. Major accounting firms have offices or affiliations with other firms worldwide and can quickly assemble personnel to review operations. If the target business has diverse and international locations, an international accounting firm can be retained to conduct some or all of the due diligence. When these conditions prevail, there are few comparable alternatives for completion on a timely basis. Accounting firms can conduct all aspects of a due diligence investigation and analyze the data. They are able to establish the scope of the due diligence when the investor wants a complete program or is unsure of what should be done. Sophisticated investors tend to decide themselves upon the scope of the assignment and may limit the accounting firm to specified financial aspects.

Normally, both the investor and accounting firm will want an engagement letter defining the scope of the assignment. Accounting firms can be particularly helpful in exploring in-depth aspects of the business troublesome to the investor or matters about which suspicions of improprieties, misrepresentations or concealed failures exist. Public accounting firms are prepared to give formal opinion letters regarding their work. They should provide cost estimates or even fixed-price bids before starting their work.

Consultants with special expertise often are essential, and in many cases invaluable, in the due diligence process. Their use and value is primarily in evaluating specific aspects of a business rather than conducting complete due diligence programs, although some of the larger firms will accept full responsibility. Environmental engineers, engineers to evaluate products and R&D programs, marketing experts, actuaries to calculate pension liability, attorneys to evaluate litigation and other legal problems and tax experts are some of the more frequently utilized consultants. They are appropriate whenever an investor lacks the expertise within his organization or wants an additional opinion.

Professional societies, recommendations from business associates, trade associations, even the Yellow Pages, are sources for consultants. In all cases, interviews to verify experience, capability and cost are in order.

Investment bankers conduct due diligence, but usually as a part of a broader assignment. They prepare prospectuses and offering memorandums, arrange financing, write fairness opinions, serve as financial advisors and underwrite securities. Their due diligence is primarily a necessity conducted to accomplish some objective rather than an exercise limited to information gathering and evaluation.

A problem that occurs with regularity with due diligence conducted by public accounting firms, consulting firms and investment bankers is that the actual data gathering is assigned to younger employees long on education, intelligence, enthusiasm, ambition and confidence but lacking in experience. This deficiency tends to manifest itself in limited ability to ask appropriate follow-up questions, perceive obscure defects and maintain objectivity. Claims that younger professionals are supervised by a senior partner do not completely solve the problem.

MANAGEMENT AND ANALYSIS

Someone must be in charge. The complete due diligence program may be conducted by only one person when the investor is an individual or small business and the transaction is not large or complex. However, when the investor is a large business someone must assume or be assigned the responsibility for managing the due diligence program. For businesses of any size the due diligence management responsibility may be retained by the CEO, but usually it is delegated to the chief financial officer, the executive responsible for planning and acquisitions, or an operating executive who will oversee the business if the transaction is completed. Accounting firms, law firms and investment bankers usually have a partner who is responsible for their activities. Lending institutions typically have the loan officer in charge of the account responsible for the due diligence.

It is best for one individual, not a group, to manage and coordinate all due diligence activities. The primary activities for the manager are:

- Plan the entire program.
- Oversee the systematic compilation of a list of information and documents to be sought. Decide what data are needed.
- Select employees to serve.
- Select, employ and make assignments to outside professionals.
- Manage all activities to meet time schedules.
- Provide data to negotiators of contracts.
- Oversee preparation of business plan.
- Coordinate development of a transition program.
- Maintain and preserve records and file all data.
- Condense and summarize raw data.

- Review and analyze all data received, including reports of professionals.
- Quantify or value assets, liabilities and problems.
- Secure opinions from all appropriate parties involved.
- Present data to whomever makes final decisions.

These are the essential elements of a due diligence program that must be overseen to ensure that they happen. Most investors realize that a potential deal large enough to justify a due diligence effort requires a carefully managed program. This can best be accomplished by a manager with the experience, stature and authority to make commitments and demand performance. He also must read all pertinent information and be able to view the investment in its entirety, balancing the good and bad. The manager will automatically be involved in evaluation of information and influence or make the decision to complete the deal.

Cooperation from personnel in other segments of the investor's organization is essential. Those who will oversee and be responsible for the business, once acquired, should be fully involved. They should suggest subjects for the due diligence study, help write and approve the business plan and plan the transition. Their enthusiastic support is essential. Executives administering loan covenants must know their terms and believe compliance is possible. Technical employees must furnish opinions and planning in their areas. Opinions on individual aspects, as well as the whole transaction, must be received on a timely basis during and at the program's conclusion.

A rather mundane but essential management task is to collect the data and documents accumulated during due diligence. This information, all of which must be studied page-by-page, should be organized in a central location and available for ready reference and preserved indefinitely. Data as collected must be available to those negotiating, writing business plans or making decisions prior to closing the transaction. In larger organizations this information eventually should be summarized or condensed into a more readable form and ultimately assembled into a final report.

A critical task of the manager is to ensure the proper evaluation of all information. The due diligence is largely wasted if a superb job of collection is then not properly evaluated or is ignored. In fact, disregarding highly detrimental information may void any future misrepresentation claims of the investor against the seller. The manager will be in a position where his opinions will be important and possibly deciding, but he also should have the role of gathering all other necessary opinions and approvals. If controversy exists over the wisdom of the transaction, he may have to mediate differences.

FREIGHT TRAIN EFFECT AND CONFLICTS OF INTEREST

Once set in motion, an acquisition or other transaction requiring due diligence can be like a freight train roaring down the track. It has great momentum and is very difficult to stop. The train is fueled by ambition, status, self interest and opportunity for financial gain, which all can be thwarted if highly negative information emerges. All too frequently, the last thing the parties want is unwelcome information that clearly says, "Stop the train."

The opportunities for personal gain are so prevalent and enticing that the tendency to ignore or rationalize defects and problems flourishes. There can be enormous incentives to complete the deal, with many of the benefits and fees payable immediately upon completion, regardless of its long-term success. An investor's long-coveted ambition may be realized. Careers can be enhanced and executive responsibilities expanded. Options can be exercised and golden parachutes opened. Owners can cash out. Attorneys' fees are largest if the deal is completed. Investment bankers and others working on a contingent basis will receive extraordinary fees. Accountants log more billable hours and may pick up a new client. Acquisitions executives and CEOs can carve another notch on their guns and add another line to their resumes. Loan officers, at least temporarily, are appreciated for bringing in business. Just because generous compensation and other rewards can accrue to the participants and their advisors, one cannot automatically assume their judgments will be flawed. However, it can be, and the condition occurs with such frequency that everyone associated with a due diligence program should be aware of the possibility. Its existence can be open or subtle and insidious.

Personal relationships that have existed or which develop during the courtship and negotiation of the deal are more fuel for the train. A prelude to any deal is creating confidence and a degree of trust with positive relationships. However, this can make it very difficult to say "no" regardless of the information discovered. Even renegotiation can be difficult for some.

If possible, a counterweight should be built into the due diligence process. A devil's advocate can be invaluable to counter biased opinions resulting from self-interest or excess enthusiasm. In some organizations the proposed transaction may be so controversial that one or more vocal opponents may arise without any prompting or selection. They may very effectively challenge data, assumptions and conclusions, forcing a greater level of objectivity. In other investor organizations, someone is designated to play the role of devil's advocate who is not necessarily an opponent but who can force greater attention to detail, well-reasoned, balanced views and discourage irresponsible business decisions.

CHAPTER 2

Conducting Due Diligence

Investors must be objective, able to maintain an open mind and avoid premature conclusions and yet react quickly to significant adverse information. There is no point in continuing a due diligence program once defects of a "deal killer" magnitude arise. The most common evidence of a biased mind-set at one extreme is to be awed by a management that seems all virtuous, rarely makes bad decisions, is highly efficient and has total concern for the employees and shareholders. If prominent people or celebrities are involved in the business or promoting the transaction, due diligence investigators should be even more wary and not attribute to the business virtues that do not exist.

An opportunity to acquire a long-coveted business can place blinders on the potential investor. It can be equally erroneous to start with an assumption that the management is evil, solely concerned with short-term personal enrichment and has survived in spite of itself. A Pollyanna view of looking only at the positive aspects of a business is as much indicative of a closed mind as exclusively concentrating on defects, characterized by the attitude of, "We are going to find out what is wrong with it."

An objective approach free from ill-conceived prejudices, one that quantifies defects, can result in a rational evaluation of the business. Those involved in due diligence soon learn that more often than not what first appears to be a major problem or defect can be explained. Or there may be solutions under way and the problem is of lesser magnitude than first believed. An alarming first impression should only dictate that more study is necessary before conclusions are drawn. However, when critical problems arise, or the full dimensions of others known or suspected are revealed, the investor should reassess his position and might even want to suspend further due diligence. False financial statements, product failures, serious environmental problems, and litigation of uncertain and potentially costly outcome all can bring due diligence to a halt.

PRELIMINARY DUE DILIGENCE

The product of a due diligence program can be strengthened if an investor begins amassing information long before there is any certainty of an agreement or need for comprehensive due diligence.

Data collection and evaluation commences when the business opportunity first arises and continues throughout the talks. There often are numerous meetings before a preliminary agreement is reached and the investor initiates a due diligence program. Information from these meetings can, with some forethought, be systematically captured and preserved. By arriving at meetings well organized and with a checklist of needed information, some due diligence information can be secured informally with minimum cost and effort. A prospectus, business plan or descriptive brochure can be very helpful to investors, but the information they convey must be verified. The basic information accumulated prior to reaching a preliminary agreement should be made available to those involved in the due diligence.

The documents to request and questions associated with Chapter 5, "Business Description and Basic Information," and Chapter 6, "Critical Early Questions," consist of most subjects and data that should be discussed, evaluated and reviewed while considering a business opportunity. This information, much of which will eventually be required, constitutes a preparatory checklist of critical data necessary for a preliminary agreement. The individuals having contact with representatives of the business can use this checklist for information to be requested in early meetings. Before each meeting, the participants should identify the information needed and not be shy with their requests.

Preservation of data, impressions and any other information can prove invaluable. Information received orally should be promptly recorded in notes and memos. Descriptions and impressions of offices and facilities should be made by each visitor. Preferably, detailed notes are written immediately after meetings if note-taking during meetings intimidates or inhibits anyone from speaking freely. All notes, documents, data and impressions are best accumulated and kept together in one central location for ready use. Because of increasing volume of information, it's advisable to organize files by subject matter. In larger organizations someone should be responsible to plan, coordinate and collect reports of meetings and exercise the discipline essential to accumulate a central file. Participants should not create their own private files.

A central file of information tracking the due diligence program helps avoid duplicate requests for information already in hand and thus reduces time, cost and embarrassment. The data in these files become a baseline used to measure improvements or declines in the business. They allow for in-depth attention to be given problem areas. With the data, the due diligence team can identify areas in which little or no information exists. The file also can point to potential problem areas where information is missing or has been withheld. Conversely, it can be used to note areas where no further study or verification is necessary. Finally, the file can be used to brief those assigned to conduct the formal due diligence.

The due diligence team must remember that initial information received by an investor prior to conducting due diligence may be misleading or dated. Financial statements record only history, not the present. Similarly, promotional brochures or offering memorandums should be viewed with skepticism. Sales documents also often contain "recast" reports in which prior financial statements are rewritten to eliminate unusual expenses or charges. They may even add income that should have occurred but didn't. Don't forget that the purpose of these documents is to present a rosy picture of the business and imply the future will be even better. Such recast financial reports are often miracles of imagination, with any future results based on the contrived past. Such "massaged" documents are useless without all the assumptions that they were based upon, along with copies of the actual reports that were modified.

A variety of other financial statements are also of limited value. Pro forma financial projections volunteered by a seller or borrower or his professional advisors are always suspect. These are developed primarily for promotional purposes and should be viewed skeptically. The investor who relies totally on financial projections other than his own is a fool. Those prepared by the investor near the conclusion of the formal due diligence and reviewed by executives of the business are most likely to be reliable. They at least will be defensible.

The presence of only dated or unreasonably old financial statements is generally an indication that the current reports show a major decline in the business and have been intentionally withheld. Old financial statements indicate that the first priority in due diligence is to secure the latest statements. Summarized financial statements also indicate there is something to hide. Recast, old or summary statements are given in hopes of generating such strong interest in the business that when bad news finally emerges, it will be overlooked. Professed concerns over confidentiality to delay providing full information are often a smoke screen. Business executives proud of their results are usually eager to give a serious investor current financial statements.

Among the first non-confidential documents received that can be misleading are descriptions of products and services in the form of sales brochures, advertising and press releases. Their purpose is to promote the product, not indicate sales revenues. Advertising, brochures and press releases that precede actual sales illustrate the skills of advertising and PR personnel rather than reflect results or financial importance. Due diligence investigators should coldly focus on actual sales and profits-to-date from each product line, secure realistic projections for the products and avoid being swayed by creative marketing.

Just reviewing a central file of material already in the investor's possession and comparing it to established criteria and objectives may be sufficient to decide not to proceed. A final review by all involved just prior to negotiating a preliminary agreement and commencing the full due diligence program is an appropriate time to reconfirm the suitability of the investment. If the decision is to proceed, task assignments with timetables can be made and the in-depth study of the business commence.

APPROACHING THE TARGET

The investor should describe the desired extent of due diligence very early in discussions with representatives of the prospective acquisition. This will essentially consist of stating that at the conclusion of the due diligence, there will be no secrets. Disclosure that the scope of the due diligence may involve hundreds of questions and a review of all key documents should not be withheld or minimized. Individuals sophisticated in business transactions will not be surprised, but to those who have never sold a business, borrowed substantial funds, been involved in the issuance of securities, or who have limited experience in such matters, a comprehensive due diligence investigation can be a shock. They may have a vague understanding that the investor has the right to inspect the business but seldom realize the depth of such study. Little more may have been expected than a cursory "kick the tires" review. A wise investor will assume the other party has less sophistication than claimed and explain the due diligence program in detail. An explanation of the scope and purposes of due diligence planned may elicit confessions of defects or problems not previously disclosed or even conclude discussions, but for most the program will be accepted as necessary and unavoidable. A candid explanation of the reasons for the due diligence and reassurance of its confidentiality, including non-disclosure of the results beyond the investor's organization, and particularly to the IRS or any other government agency, will be helpful. Many business owners have an irrational fear of the IRS and for some there is ample reason for concern.

The targeted business should be informed by the investor of the names, titles and affiliations of those conducting the due diligence. Their arrival and estimated duration of stay should be presented. Whom they wish to meet, what information in general they are seeking and what they will want to see should also be explained. The business being studied should appoint someone with whom to coordinate activities. The investor will benefit if he can gather information from several individuals and so permit greater exposure and the opportunity to cross-check opinions. Unless the business is small, it's unlikely one person would have all the answers and documents requested.

It is decidedly best for the business under study to candidly inform its employees who will provide the information of the nature of the due diligence and its purpose. If left unexplained, they likely will figure it out for themselves and have a lower regard for their management. If, during preliminary stages, confidentiality is necessary to conceal the visitors' identities, ruses that have had some success are to declare them bankers, tax auditors, insurance inspectors, friends of key shareholders, or to just say nothing at all. Those concerned with secrecy should ask themselves exactly how important it is and if there are any serious consequences if others know.

Due diligence is difficult if not impossible in a hostile environment. Advance notification of the program's scope and who will be involved will often help pave the way to cooperation. However, if the business's owners and executives are not fully in accord, or there are deep divisions over the wisdom of the deal, something less than full cooperation may be given. Those opposed or who will be adversely affected by the transaction may be openly hostile and refuse cooperation, withhold or, worse yet, provide misleading data. Those favoring the transaction can be helpful by identifying opponents and individuals who believe they will be adversely affected. Knowledge of who they are will make it possible for the due diligence investigators to avoid or minimize contact with them.

In hostile situations, there may be opportunity to question former executives or employees. While many are dispassionate and objective, caution should always be exercised with former employees. By their very status, their information may be dated. Senior executives may try to rationalize past decisions and performance. Mid-level personnel may only have knowledge of limited aspects of the business. Former employees at any level may have axes to grind, perceived grievances to be redressed or even be looking for an opportunity to recover their positions. Still, they may be a source of information attainable no other way, which by itself may be invaluable or a warning to investigate specific areas. They also may identify neglected assets and confirm positive features of the business. Any discussions with former employees, whether the deal is friendly or hostile, are likely to be considered an insult and offensive by present owners and executives.

Opponents will seize upon and exaggerate any alleged rudeness or indiscretions displayed by an investor's representatives, in an effort to prevent the deal. All such charges should be quickly investigated. Whenever a hostile atmosphere prevails, the principals behind the deal should meet promptly to resolve whatever obstacles exist to conducting the due diligence. There should be no delay in eliminating problems because of the high probability that matters could further degenerate.

Comprehensive due diligence includes a visit to every location of the business and visual inspection of all major assets. The business's owners should permit arrangements to be made and make available key executives and employees on agreed dates. In larger transactions with multiple locations, scheduling may be difficult, but it is a mistake not to visit even the smallest. Only with a visual inspection can one ascertain its precise nature.

The business executives should be informed that those conducting due diligence are limited to gathering information and will not be evaluating data while at the business or voicing opinions or conclusions. The due diligence team's job is to secure information as rapidly and unobtrusively as possible and depart to evaluate it later.

Executives of the business under study should be reminded that an objective will be to fully understand the financial statements, and far more detailed information may be required than they anticipated. The lack of uniformity in financial statements is a constant source of confusion, misunderstanding and erroneous conclusions. Recognition by all parties at the onset that this problem may exist will lessen the chance of complaints of excess due diligence. Each party is accustomed to its own accounting format and policies and the tendency is to assume the other party employs the same system and chart of accounts. For example, the composition of "Cost of Sales" can vary widely and any conclusions based upon percentage comparisons of operating profit without full knowledge of included expenses can be fallacious. Financial ratios can result in totally misleading conclusions if the underlying account's composition is misunderstood. Some sophisticated investors recognize that their own organizations' executives are accustomed to a certain type of accounting format, and they instruct their due diligence personnel to gather the necessary details to restate the financial statements into that format.

In approaching the business to be studied, investors must be realistic and realize that most information given is believed accurate and decisions made by sellers or borrowers are rational and explainable, not part of some devious plot. Inaccuracies and exaggerations are far more likely to be attributable to excess enthusiasm, sellers' hype and the very human tendency to confuse actual with hoped-for performance. Executives have ample motivation to present the business in the best possible light and may feel little compunction to volunteer all possible negative information about the business or industry. They also may be unfamiliar with some business details and seek answers from subordinates, or worse, make unfounded estimates that may result in less-than-accurate information. Regardless, the investor should avoid imputing significance to this unless a pattern of deceit evolves. It's unrealistic to assume an owner or executive of a substantial business would know every detail about the business or its industry.

In his approach, the investor should not assume anything done differently in the business is automatically suspect or inferior to his own methods. All too often an irrational attitude of "we are the investor, so we are the best" blinds the investor and can sour relations. Any investor impressed enough to reach a preliminary agreement and conduct due diligence should realize the business is more likely a gold mine of ideas for use in other businesses. Unfortunately, many investors' egos do not permit them to look at a successful business with different methods and systems in a favorable light and, consequently, they lose many possible benefits.

REQUESTING DATA

In requesting data the investor must keep in mind that this phase of the due diligence program is designed to gather as much information as quickly as possible without irritation or disruption. The objective is to innocuously gather data for evaluation at a later time. The investigator should take advantage of a response to a specific question that includes not only the answer but information answering one or more other questions on the checklist.

An investigator displaying most of the ideal traits described in Chapter 1 can be most effective and efficient when well organized. A checklist of all information and documents required will help avoid repetitious questions and reduce the need to return, both of which can become extremely irritating to those providing information. Poorly planned, lengthy visits and return visits give the investor an appearance of being disorganized and uncertain.

Whenever information is received, it is best accepted as factual. It may not be accurate, which can be determined later, but initially, it is better to accept all at face value. Tentative acceptance will not impede production of additional material nor prevent one from challenging the validity at a later date. Information the investigator considers incomplete, misleading or even false should be accepted with minimal comments, although the investigator may be tempted to voice an opinion to demonstrate he is not a fool. Acceptance of dubious information is not a bar to immediate follow-up questions or requests for supporting documents. Confrontations over unreliable data are a matter for the principals and not the data-gathering investigators.

Investigators should take not only what is requested but everything offered and anything of possible interest known to exist. The investigators should be real "pack rats" and readily accept copies or originals of internal reports, business studies, consulting reports, industry studies, litigation or whatever else may appear. Internal reports of the business's operation or financial position should be requested when they are known to exist. If, in response to a question, the information giver takes a report from his desk to reply, this is an opportunity to ask for the entire report.

Sincere compliments on successes and innovations of the business are appropriate and may lubricate the flow of information. When negative information is provided and the giver wants to discuss the bad news and provide explanations, the investigator should listen to all being volunteered but limit comments to sympathy and understanding. Rarely do managements knowingly make bad decisions. They may turn out bad and are painfully obvious to everyone including the decision-makers, so there is little value in belaboring the subject. The temptation always exists to be critical of what in hindsight was a blunder. While criticism may be satisfying, it tends to impede the flow of information, or places the investigator in an overly partisan position.

If a degree of hostility exists toward the deal and/or the investigator and there is little chance of building rapport with the information giver, then the fewer comments the better. Don't waste time with compliments and definitely avoid criticism. Request information in a precise and businesslike manner. In this environment, the parties will want to conclude the information gathering quickly, since it is not a pleasant experience for the participants.

Any question or request for information should be viewed as a means to broach a subject and not just secure a narrow answer to a specific question. The more experienced and perceptive the investigator, the more easily he can conclude a response is adequate or that follow-up questions are necessary. Such questions may simply be to gain a full understanding of a complex subject, or may result from an answer perceived to signal a significant problem. The necessity for follow-up questions precludes any tendencies toward shyness on the part of the investigator. The best time to ask follow-up questions is when the subject first is discussed, rather than to return at a later date when further questions will imply serious concern by highlighting the subject.

The stakes are so high in due diligence that few, if any, questions can be considered inappropriate as long as the subject is directly or indirectly related to the business. Even personal questions barred by law in employment, selection and promotion procedures are acceptable for an investor trying to understand the business. However, one variety of question is inappropriate and causes irritation and disrespect. That is the question that has been previously asked. It may have been asked by someone else or a mistake was made to not record the answer, but duplicate questions are not appreciated. Requests for financial statements or other documents previously given are equally vexing. The embarrassment of duplicate requests can be avoided with planning, management and creation of a central file.

Responses to questions involving tangible assets are more complete and accurate when supplemented with visual inspections. There are no substitutes for visual inspections to confirm assets exist and their condition. Visual inspections of all facilities and major assets should be a basic part of due diligence. By inspection, one can see if an office has active employees or is partly shut down. An inventory largely covered with dust will confirm a slow-moving or obsolescence problem. Idle machinery may indicate many areas of inquiry are in order.

MISLEADING INFORMATION AND SURPRISES

Is it a misunderstanding, ineptitude, deceit or fraud? This is the question whenever information received turns out to be all or partially misleading or false. Misunderstandings can occur whenever the investor's questions are unclear. Ineptitude is the cause whenever an investor is given information or documents believed to be accurate but eventually proved otherwise. The information, although inaccurate, was the best the business's executives possessed, and they relied upon it themselves. Deceit usually occurs in sales documents and private placement memorandums with half-truths, significant omissions and clever wording. Little of the information is exactly false, but it can be very misleading. Fraud occurs when false information is deliberately supplied or the business has engaged in practices such as inflating inventory value or recognizing phantom income.

In any due diligence study, when facts do not ring true, the last possible cause to consider is fraud and the first is a misunderstanding. Few businessmen will intentionally provide false information and not many will rush to volunteer unfavorable information to correct an investor's overly enthusiastic misconceptions. More often than not, inaccurate data can be attributed to reasons other than deliberate lying. Incorrect information appearing on financial reports or other internal reports used by management usually is the result of human errors and system failures rather than an attempt to deceive. Those preparing and relying on the information believed it to be correct or the best attainable and probably accurate. Another cause of misinformation is the tendency of those providing it to guess or make quick estimates rather than admit they do not know. The investigator should advise those being questioned not to guess, and be sufficiently perceptive to know when guessing occurs.

An investor's enthusiasm for the business can be so great that it clouds his views. The longer the business has been coveted, or if it represents a key component in a strategic plan, the greater can be irrational enthusiasm, creating a reluctance to be objective. Due diligence can have a sobering effect when illusions are shattered. An example of a financial illusion can be a large amount of cash correctly appearing on the balance sheet that excited an investor. However, much of the cash may be restricted as compensating balances, backing for performance bonds, or may periodically evaporate as in a highly seasonal business. If the investor had asked early, he would have known the true cash condition because executives of the business would willingly have told him.

Inaccurate data due to ineptness and faulty systems is not normally cause in itself for terminating due diligence unless an uneconomically large effort is necessary to produce corrected data. The task to construct accurate information and the magnitude of post-investment systems work may indicate the investment would be imprudent. Incomplete or inaccurate financial statements are so prevalent in privately held businesses and subsidiaries or divisions of public companies that it is reasonable to start with the assumption they are inaccurate but hope they are not.

Intentionally deceptive information is another matter, and the investor has to decide how much will be tolerated before walking away. Sales brochures, offering memorandums and early conversations often contain sales hype involving recast financial statements, extremely optimistic forecasts, exaggerations of assets or omissions of important liabilities. This is to be expected and a sophisticated investor will look at it as such. However, once due diligence commences, the sales hype should stop and factual, complete information should be presented.

Regardless of the cessation of sales hype, if the due diligence reveals a pattern of programs and practices to make the business appear better than it is, with the purpose of deceiving an investor, the investor should be extremely wary. Liberal accounting policies designated to inflate income, withholding of capital expenditures, cosmetic actions to improve appearance of facilities and delaying payment of invoices are examples of practices that, while not illegal, are designed to deceive. The cumulative effect of incidents and practices designed to deceive at some point should cause the investor to consider terminating the due diligence and forget the investment opportunity. How much, if any, effort should be expended to learn true conditions depends on how desirable the investment appears and whether cooperation can be secured. The degree of forbearance is a judgment call.

Discovery of any deliberately false data or documents is ample reason to cease due diligence and walk away. Fabrication of data most commonly occurs as part of schemes to reduce taxes or mislead shareholders; the repercussions, if and when discovered by the deceived, cannot be ignored. The investor should assume discovery will occur. Existence of one falsified document is an indication that many more may exist, yet to be discovered, and that whoever was associated with creating the document is untrustworthy.

Suspicions of criminal offenses unearthed during due diligence can best be handled by the investor withdrawing while actual knowledge of the offense is limited to a strong suspicion. It is hardly practical to ask individuals, during the due diligence, in a straightforward fashion if they are dishonest, and expect a candid reply. Probably the most common offenses that may be discovered are security fraud, skimming (pocketing cash receipts without recording), price-fixing and kickbacks. Since failure to report a crime can under certain conditions be a crime itself, there is particular merit in walking away at the suspicion stage. If the criminal acts are clearly without the knowledge of senior management or the owners, the suspicions can be reported to them to investigate and handle, after which the investor may agree to return. How those informed react and respond can be illuminating. In all cases, suspicions of, or actual discovery of, criminal acts should prompt an investor to discuss the facts with his own attorney.

Another serious problem is when information or documents are said not to exist, are claimed to be lost, or are not forthcoming. For the investor this is intolerable and he should assume the data is very negative. The investor has no choice but to demand the information or walk away from the deal.

Due diligence is a search for surprises and few businesses are viewed exactly the same after due diligence. Surprises that may be good, bad or both can add to the value of the business or constitute serious defects. Any list of potential surprises would be endless and unpredictable, but an investor can be certain surprises are likely to surface. Unexpected characteristics of the business or surprises are so probable that an investor should assume some will surface. An investor should have doubts if none are brought to light and even question the calibre of his due diligence. When surprises surface, the most rational first steps are to gather sufficient additional data to fully understand their nature and then evaluate their impact. After quantifying, the impact on the contemplated deal can be rationally assessed.

CHAPTER 3

Constructing the Checklist

Once an investor decides to seriously consider a business opportunity, a list of information and documents that eventually may be required should be compiled. It should contain all essential data yet avoid the superfluous. Such a large quantity of information on so many subjects is needed that an effort must be made to circumvent matters of little importance or those that are irrelevant. Superfluous data will overburden, confuse, delay and distract analysts already confronted with a voluminous amount of data. Overly burdensome demands for information could jeopardize the potential transaction by antagonizing a seller or whoever provides the data. As a result, the belief that the more information one has about a business, the more likely a shrewd investment decision will result, is not always true.

The objective of data collection is to obtain enough information to make an informed business decision. No precise definition exists as to what is "sufficient," but the following questions can help develop your questionnaire:

- Is the information necessary to understand the business?
- Is it necessary for negotiations and to write the contracts to conclude the deal?
- If the information is not requested now, will it be needed at a later date?
- Could mistakes be avoided by obtaining the information?
- Is the information necessary to affect a smooth transition and for those managing the investment to be effective?
- Since it's impossible to predict which subject or document will prove to be of great importance, it's better to include a subject than to delete it.

A due diligence checklist is a memory crutch on a grand scale; it records answers and identifies what is missing. The checklist is not only recognition of the fact that an extraordinary amount of information and documents on many diverse subjects is required; it also helps you remember what to request.

HOW TO DESIGN

This book's Appendix is a systematic compilation of subjects relative to requisite information and documents. The subjects usually are written in question form to help initiate discussions on each subject. Additionally, the Appendix is organized by general categories of business activity, such as Ownership, Marketing, Legal, and so on, for convenience and planning purposes.

Effective due diligence requires questions to be presented orally with the investigator recording the answers when the response is understood. How questions are posed or whether they're used to broach a subject is not as important as ensuring that subjects are adequately explored. Since an investigator's task is to learn what is important about a subject, his own words may be better received than a prepared question.

During the selection of questions and subjects from the Appendix, there may be some uncertainty as to their nature or purpose. In such cases, reference can be made to the appropriate chapter where the nature of a subject and its importance are explained. The commentaries are relatively brief, but additional books, papers and articles exist on most subjects, to provide further background.

A separate checklist should be prepared for each business and each of its major segments to be studied. The first step in constructing a list of needed information is to review the questions and documents in the Appendix and delete those that are irrelevant. The remaining questions will contain nearly all subjects in Chapter 5, "Business Description and Basic Information," and Chapter 6, "Critical Early Questions," and at a minimum the first questions appearing in each section of the Appendix. The sections' initial questions are either of great importance or designed to secure an overview from which decisions can be made relative to the depth of questioning in a subject area. Other questions should be selected as deemed appropriate and applicable.

For areas of special concern to the investor, all or nearly all questions in a particular section should be included. For example, if the quality of receivables is suspect, most questions on receivables would be appropriate. If marketing is an unknown, include questions in that field. Any business area in which the investor has experienced problems in prior investments will definitely require intense questioning, even though problems may not be apparent.

The selected questions should be used to create a separate list. Adequate space should be left between questions for answers or to refer to where the information, if lengthy, is located. The checklist should be used as a means to conveniently record and organize information. A checklist becomes expendable after its data have been added to the permanent central file on the deal.

INDUSTRY QUESTIONS

Each checklist should contain questions specific to the industry of the business being studied. These may be developed by the investor and knowledgeable people in his organization or, if the investment is a diversification move, outside consultants may be necessary to help with the questions and to educate the investor. These questions should be couched in terminology readily understood by those supplying answers.

Don't confuse units of measure with dollars when constructing industry questions. This can easily occur with those unfamiliar with an industry's jargon. Also, data contained in internal business reports often are in units other than dollars. As a result, an investigator may expect answers in dollars but receive them in other units. Cases and barrels in the beverage industry, tons in the iron and steel industry, board feet in the lumber industry and pounds in specialty chemicals are all examples of units commonly used in measuring productivity. The units are also used in industry studies to make comparisons between companies—something in which an investor should have a keen interest.

USING AND MAINTAINING CHECKLISTS

Once the checklist has been developed, review information already obtained on the business and record the data on the checklist prior to seeking more. Note partial answers or those that need verification but do not record information from outdated documents. This procedure not only reduces duplicative efforts but refreshes the memories of those involved in the due diligence.

The Appendix, by guiding creation of a checklist organized by general topic or business activity, develops a convenient means to plan and assign tasks for the due diligence team. Those making assignments should recognize that team members may have limited experience in some areas but are highly knowledgeable or even experts in their own fields. They must be instructed as to the minimum, but specific, information sought. Presenting each with a section of the checklist requiring answers and documents to be secured is an easy way to define and give assignments. For instance, an attorney can be assigned legal questions while a tax manager handles tax questions and a manufacturing manager tackles manufacturing.

Selecting questions and subjects to create a checklist is a formidable task. While a questionnaire is expendable for each business unit studied, there is no reason copies cannot be retained for use in studying very similar businesses where few modifications will be required. However, for totally different businesses in different industries, it is advisable to construct new questionnaires tailored to the business and industry.

If the business being studied has multiple units, such as divisions and subsidiaries, there should be a separate checklist for each. Some may be abbreviated because information on many subjects will be received when reviewing the parent company. The independence, size and diversity of each business unit will influence the checklists' content.

An investor should never be satisfied with his checklist but should continually strive for improvement. After each use, notes should be made for practical revisions to be incorporated into a new questionnaire prior to conducting the next due diligence. All of the questions and subjects found in the Appendix constitute a broad foundation upon which an investor can construct his own due diligence program.

You'll find that an original central file that may have been only a few inches thick prior to due diligence explodes in volume as material is collected and organized. If the due diligence program is well-organized, frantic searches for information and documents can be avoided during the stressful period prior to closing. Organization by topic simplifies preparation of reports by making all data on a specific topic readily accessible and reducing the chance of material information being overlooked. Reports may be a summation of information for decisions by loan committees, executives or boards of directors that may or may not demand supporting data retained in the files. Due diligence files for registration statements or other activities involving securities will be referred to frequently to verify full disclosure of all material information. They also may be considered necessary by those involved in the transition or management after the closing.

___ CHAPTER 4 ___

Due Diligence from a Legal Perspective

James W. Ryan and Robert C. Beasley

INTRODUCTION

"Due diligence" will be involved in almost every type of business transaction and all business persons, including the professionals representing them or otherwise involved in the transaction, should be interested and concerned about conducting proper due diligence. Proper due diligence rewards a cautious person and increases the opportunity to avoid a problem situation. Failure to conduct proper due diligence could lead to other implications, such as liability to third parties or criminal liability. Attorneys, accountants, broker/dealers, appraisers and other professionals may also find themselves being sued by their clients or by third parties asserting the failure to have conducted proper due diligence.

By being alert to the need for due diligence and focusing on the proper issues at the beginning of any transaction, a person can avoid a bad business transaction or unwanted liability. For example, early due diligence in a business acquisition may alert the purchaser to the need to structure the transaction in such a way as to avoid unassumed liabilities. Proper due diligence may also serve as a legal defense to third-party claims after a transaction closes. Finally, part of the due diligence process in many transactions includes the drafting of contracts and other documents (such as acquisition agreements and loan documents) that contain appropriate representations and warranties that elicit information and identify and address the transaction's risks. The information obtained from proper due diligence will also be critical to negotiating the terms of a business deal.

LEGAL CONSEQUENCES OF FAILING TO CONDUCT DUE DILIGENCE

Bad Business Transactions and Unexpected Liabilities

One obvious reason for conducting thorough due diligence is to help avoid a bad business transaction, but due diligence also helps an investor avoid unassumed and unexpected liabilities that may accrue to a person in a transaction. The lack of due diligence can affect any number of transactions, including the acquisition of a business, lending money, investing in a company, or raising capital through a stock offering.

Buyers of Businesses

By conducting proper due diligence, a buyer of a business is better able to: evaluate the strengths and weaknesses of a business and determine whether the business is compatible with the buyer's business; identify issues that need to be addressed to ensure an orderly transition; identify liabilities and obligations of the business so, if possible, to avoid assuming unwanted liabilities and obligations; and to identify any unexpected or unforeseen risks or business problems.

Although an investor will want a carefully drafted acquisition or loan agreement containing appropriate representations and warranties and indemnification, such provisions are no substitute for careful due diligence. Indemnification is, of course, only as good as the financial resources of the indemnifying party. Even if the indemnifying party is financially sound, it is always better to know about problems *before* wading into the transactions. The problem may be such that the purchaser would not have entered into the transaction if it had known about the problem beforehand. In addition, there will be the additional direct and indirect costs of dealing with the problem and possibly litigation to obtain indemnification from the indemnifying party. Some problems, such as lack of valid title to essential assets, cannot be cured by indemnification.

In analyzing the legal consequences that could flow to a purchaser who has not conducted adequate due diligence, it is helpful to consider the two sides of the seller's balance sheet: the "asset" side and the "liabilities" side. Obviously, due diligence will help a purchaser uncover and avoid unwanted liabilities, as discussed below. But due diligence also allows a purchaser to "know what it's buying," and thus it will be better able to negotiate the terms of the transaction. In addition, the transition to new ownership may require certain steps to be taken to ensure the purchaser gets good title to all of the seller's assets. A discussion of the due diligence required of a seller's assets is beyond the purview of this chapter, and the reader is directed to Chapter 3, which contains detailed questions regarding due diligence.

In addition to providing a thorough review of the asset side of a seller's business, proper due diligence helps to avoid unknown and unassumed liabilities to third parties. This can be illustrated by the types of liabilities that purchasers of businesses often unknowingly assume:

Environmental Liabilities. One source of potential liability that probably causes the most concern today for purchasers, lenders, officers and directors, professionals and other business persons is environmental liability. For a purchaser, one serious concern is potential successor liability for environmental problems of the seller. A purchaser of a business can incur environmental liability in a number of ways, including:

1. The purchaser may be held strictly liable, jointly and severally with others, under federal and state environmental laws for any cleanup costs, damages or other environmental response costs with respect to any real property it acquires in a transaction. In light of the fact that the average cost of cleaning up a site deemed contaminated by the Environmental Protection Agency (EPA) is estimated to be $26 million,[1] this liability is of grave concern to purchasers of real property.

2. In addition to being liable for cleanup costs, the property acquired may decline substantially in value or become worthless as a result of the environmental problems.

3. The business acquired may be liable to the government or third parties for its wrongful actions in disposing of or transporting hazardous waste, or it may have toxic tort liability for injuries to persons or damage to property caused by elements in the seller's building or under the real property.

The types of environmental hazards that cause concern for purchasers are numerous. For example, a seller's building may contain asbestos, and if the asbestos is "friable" and inhaled by the seller's employees over a period of time, it can cause various fatal diseases, such as lung cancer, gastrointestinal cancer and mesothelioma, a cancer of the lining of the chest. Friable asbestos can be enormously expensive to remove, and obviously reduces the value of any building. For example, the sales price of Exxon Corporation's headquarters building in New York was reportedly reduced by $100 million because of the presence of asbestos.[2] The Arco Plaza in Los Angeles was sold at a $50 million discount because it contained asbestos.[3] Other hazardous elements include polychlorinated biphenyls (PCBs), which often leak from transformers, capacitors and other electrical equipment. In 1981, an 18-story office building in New York, including its PCB-containing electrical transformer system, ignited, spreading PCB-contaminated smoke throughout the entire building. The building was vacant for more than six years. Although the building's original cost was only $15 million, the cleanup expense was $30 million.[4]

The primary federal statutes that impose liabilities on owners and operators of real property are the Comprehensive Environmental Response,

Compensation and Liability Act of 1980 (CERCLA), as amended by the Superfund Amendments and Reauthorization Act of 1986 (SARA),[5] also known as "Superfund"; the Resource Conservation and Recovery Act (RCRA);[6] the Clean Water Act;[7] the Clean Air Act;[8] and the Toxic Substances Control Act (TOSCA).[9] CERCLA imposes strict joint and several liability for: (1) all costs of remedial or removal action by the United States or a state; (2) all response costs incurred by private parties; (3) damages for destruction to natural resources; and (4) the cost of studies to evaluate the effects of contamination.[10] CERCLA imposes strict liability on "owners" or "operators" of real property contaminated by hazardous substances. Owners and operators who will be found liable include not only owners or operators who owned the property at the time the hazardous substances were released or disposed, but any current owner or operator of contaminated property. Thus, purchasers of businesses must be acutely sensitive to environmental liability whenever the seller's business has any real property or has operated on third-party premises. Similarly, even if the purchaser leases real property from the seller or from some third party, the purchaser may still be liable for cleanup responsibilities as an "owner."

In addition to the federal regulations, the states have also adopted extensive environmental regulations. Although most state environmental laws are fairly uniform and similar to federal environmental laws, the law of the particular state where the property is located should be reviewed in connection with the due diligence process. For example, the New Jersey Environmental Cleanup Responsibility Act absolutely prohibits the transfer of any contaminated property until it is cleaned up, and New Jersey can void a sale if the owner does not submit a proper cleanup plan.[11]

By understanding the importance of due diligence and by conducting proper due diligence at the early stages of the acquisition process, the purchaser may be able to structure the transaction to avoid potential environmental problems. For example, if the seller's business has violated environmental laws (such as on-site or off-site disposal of hazardous substances), or if the seller's properties contain potentially hazardous substances subjecting it to toxic tort claims (such as asbestos in the seller's building), any remaining liability for those violations would flow to the surviving corporation in a merger, or would remain intact in the purchase of stock. In contrast, a purchaser may be able to avoid certain liabilities for past environmental violations if it purchases only certain assets of the business. For example, a purchaser of contaminated property may be able to raise as a defense to any liability that it was an "innocent purchaser" of the property.[12] Also, if possible, any contaminated property could be excluded from the acquisition. By focusing at the early stages of the due diligence process on whether there are any potential environmental problems, the purchaser may be able to take other actions to ameliorate its risk, including obtaining appropriate indemnification from the seller, establishing available defenses to third parties, or avoiding the transaction altogether.

Employee Benefit Plan Liability. Another type of liability a purchaser may unknowingly assume arises from unfunded employee benefit plans. If the seller has any employee benefit plans, the purchaser will need to review each to quantify any potential unwanted liability. For example, the purchaser would want to ascertain that any defined benefit pension plan of the seller is fully funded. If the seller has been unable to pay the benefits under a defined benefit pension plan, or if the funding available for the plan does not meet certain statutory requirements, the plan may be terminated by the Pension Benefit Guaranty Corporation (PBGC).[13] Whenever a defined benefit pension plan is terminated, if the assets of the employer are insufficient to pay guaranteed benefits, the PBGC will make such payments, but the employer, and each member of the employer's "controlled group," will be liable to the PBGC for the amount necessary to pay the guaranteed benefits.[14]

Product Liability. The purchaser should also be concerned about potential successor liability for any product liability claims arising from the business prior to acquisition. If the seller is a manufacturing concern or otherwise makes products for which there may be potential product liability, the purchaser may want to consider structuring the transaction as an asset sale. Even if the transaction is structured as an asset sale, the attorney for the purchaser will want to ensure that the purchaser will not be subject to the laws of certain states that impose successor liability, even in asset sales. Certain states, such as California,[15] have expanded the liability of successor corporations in asset transactions by establishing what has come to be known as the "product line" theory of liability. Under this theory, if a purchaser acquires the assets of a business and continues the manufacture and production of the products of the seller, it assumes strict tort liability for defects of the same product manufactured and distributed by the predecessor corporation before the sale of the business. Although originally adopted in California, other states, including New Jersey[16] and Pennsylvania[17] have also adopted the "product line" theory of liability. One important issue for purchasers to consider is that it may be difficult for the parties to specifically agree which state law would apply. For example, in *Hickman v. Thomas C. Thompson Co.*,[18] a plaintiff was injured by copper enameling products manufactured by a corporation that sold its assets to another corporation. Both companies had their operations in Illinois and the contract of sale was signed in Illinois. Illinois is a state that has rejected the "product line" theory. Nevertheless, the plaintiff, who was a resident of Colorado and was injured in Colorado, brought suit in Colorado. The federal district court in Colorado applied Colorado law and concluded that Colorado would adopt the product line exception. Thus, it is important that proper due diligence is conducted to determine, among other things:

(1) the product liability history of the seller to determine, if possible, the extent of potential product liability; and (2) where the seller has distributed products that may be defective.

If there is any possibility that product liability will transfer to the purchaser, it may want to reduce the purchase price or consider other methods to ameliorate the risk. Such methods include contractual indemnification by a financially responsible party or deferring payment of a portion of the purchase price by establishing an escrow fund or by issuing the seller a promissory note that the parties would agree could be offset by any product liability claims made against the purchaser involving products produced prior to the acquisition.

Other Liability Concerns. Of particular concern to any purchaser is whether the seller's business is involved in litigation, either as a defendant or as a plaintiff. Similarly, a purchaser needs to know if the business is being investigated by any governmental agency, is subject to various fines or penalties, or whether it has been prohibited by the government, by court order or by agreement from engaging in any activities. In addition, the purchaser will want to probe whether the business's operations meet all legal and regulatory requirements. A purchaser does not want to find itself investing in a company that, shortly after closing, is fined millions of dollars by a government agency, such as OSHA, or subject to a large jury verdict.

The purchaser will want to know of and review any lawsuits in which the business is involved, for obvious reasons. Not only might the business be liable for the underlying claim, but even if the claim is without merit, the business will incur costs to defend against or settle the lawsuit. The lawsuits or claims may also indicate a trend in claims of a particular nature that may be foreboding for the business or its industry.

In disclosing litigation to the purchaser, the seller may try to describe the litigation in the best possible light. It may also, either intentionally or inadvertently, fail to disclose issues that the investor may deem important. By obtaining copies of the actual pleadings and other important documents and interviewing the attorney representing the seller, the investor will be able to more accurately determine the essential facts of the case, the status of the case and the possible outcome. In addition, because the majority of litigation is eventually settled, it is important to obtain copies of all settlement agreements. Although a particular litigation matter may have been settled, the settlement agreement may require the business to do certain things or it may prohibit the business from engaging in certain activities. In fact, the terms of a settlement agreement may have a significant impact on the business's operations. The purchaser also should obtain drafts of any proposed settlement agreements.

One of the best sources to obtain an objective summary of pending litigation is from copies of the letters sent by the business's attorneys to the business's independent public accountant for purposes of the audit of the business (the so-called "audit response letters"). A letter of audit inquiry to the business's lawyer is the auditor's primary means of obtaining corroboration of the information furnished by the business in its financial statements concerning litigation, claims and assessments. The auditor will generally request that the attorney disclose all material "loss contingencies." A loss contingency is defined in the Statement of Financial Accounting Standards No. 5 as "an existing condition, situation or set of circumstances involving uncertainty as to the possible loss to an enterprise that will ultimately be resolved when one or more events occur or fail to occur."[19] The standard of what is material will generally be agreed upon by the business and its auditor, and will be set forth in the attorney's letter. In the letter, the attorney will provide information as to the nature of the claim, the progress to date, and the position taken by the business. Under the American Bar Association's Statement of Policy Regarding Lawyers Responses to Auditors' Request for Information (ABA Statement), Paragraph No. 5, a lawyer should also furnish information to the auditor on unasserted claims if the business has determined that it is probable that a possible claim will be asserted, that there is a reasonable possibility that the outcome will be unfavorable, and that the resulting liability would be material to the financial condition of the business. Under the ABA Statement, the lawyer should provide an evaluation of the outcome of the case in those cases where it appears that an unfavorable outcome is either "probable" or "remote." Further, the attorney should provide an estimate of potential loss if the probability of inaccuracy is slight.[20] With all these standards in mind, the purchaser should be able to obtain an objective summary of the litigation against the business from the audit response letters, followed up by personal interviews.

Lenders

With the ever-increasing liability for environmental problems and the growth of environmental legislation, lenders should be particularly sensitive to their borrowers' environmental problems and conduct appropriate due diligence. One obvious risk to a lender is that if a borrower is required to clean up contamination on its property or otherwise is subject to environmental liability, the borrower might default on the loan; however, that is only the surface of the problem for lenders. If environmental problems exist on land that serves as collateral for the loan, the collateral's value could be greatly reduced, either from the contamination itself or from market reaction to the knowledge of the contamination. In such case, the lender will be left with an under-collateralized loan. Even if the borrower's land is free from contamination but is in close proximity to property that is contaminated, the borrower's land may still decrease in value. Furthermore, under a number of state environmental statutes, cleanup costs incurred by the government create a "superlien" on the property that is remediated.[21]

Such a superlien will take priority over *prior* recorded liens, including mortgages, thus leaving the lender with a loan that is subordinated to the state's right to reimbursement for cleanup costs. In some states, this lien even applies to all property of the owner in the state, not just the contaminated property.[22] In addition, if the borrower defaults and the lender has to foreclose on the contaminated property (which is often the case whenever there are environmental problems), the lender may be considered an "owner" of the property, requiring it to clean up any environmental problems.[23]

A lender may be liable under additional legal theories for a borrower's environmental problems. For example, a lender has recently been held liable as an aider and abettor of its borrower's Clean Water Act violation, where the lender knew or should have known about the violation at the time the loan was made.[24] Furthermore, lenders could be liable for cleanup costs under various state environmental statutes.[25]

Liabilities to Officers and Directors

Officers and directors of companies often do not realize that they can be personally liable to their shareholders and to investors under a number of situations. Directors and officers owe a fiduciary duty to their corporation and to the stockholders thereof.[26] This fiduciary duty generally involves the duty to exercise that degree of care that an ordinarily careful and prudent person would use under the circumstances. Until the mid-1980s, most directors were confident that they were not violating this duty as long as they did not partake in some egregious activity. However, two factors contributed to shocking directors, particularly outside directors of public companies, into being extremely concerned about liability to shareholders. The first was the difficulty, beginning in the mid-1980s, in obtaining adequate director and officer liability insurance. The second was the decision of the Delaware Supreme Court in the case of *Smith v. Van Gorkom*,[27] in which the Delaware Supreme Court held directors personally liable for actions that many, with hindsight, felt did not support the amount of the liability. In 1980, Trans Union Corp. merged with a subsidiary of the Marmon Group, Inc. In this transaction, the Trans Union shareholders were paid a premium of approximately $20 over the market price of the stock. Trans Union's chairman, an experienced chief executive officer and a substantial stockholder, had put the transaction together and had more or less presented it to the board as a "done deal." The board, which was an impressive group consisting of deans and chancellors of universities and chief executive officers of companies, approved the transaction in just two hours, without the advice of an investment banker. Although the transaction appeared to be an excellent transaction for the company, some shareholders thought the share price was too low and sued directors. The Delaware Supreme Court held the directors liable, basing its decision primarily on the fact that the directors had failed to inform themselves fully of the circumstances surrounding the transaction that they had approved.[28]

In the ensuing years, courts have looked at various aspects of decisions made by directors to determine if they have adequately exercised their duty of care. The factors the courts have focused on include: (1) whether a majority of outside directors approved the transaction, and whether a special committee existing solely of outside directors was created to approve the transaction; (2) whether there was consultation with financial advisors and legal counsel retained by either the board as a whole or separately by outside directors as a group; (3) if the outside directors actually asked questions of management and investment bankers and legal counsel; (4) if there was a timely distribution of relevant documents before the actual board meeting to approve the transaction; (5) did the directors actually read and carefully review the documents; (6) was there a thorough discussion of the proposed transaction at a lengthy meeting and maybe more than one meeting; and (7) was there adequate documentation of the due diligence process.[29]

With the increased governmental and private sector scrutiny of environmental concerns, officers and directors may be subject to environmental liability. For example, in *Wisconsin v. Rollfink*,[30] the Wisconsin Supreme Court held that the chief executive officer of a waste facility was personally liable for forfeiture and penalties assessed against the corporation for violating state hazardous waste laws, even though he had no personal participation in the illegal acts. In another recent case, the president and vice president of a Houston company were convicted of hazardous dumping under the Texas Solid Waste Disposal Act, and were sentenced to three years in prison and fined a total of $25,000.[31] The EPA has also sought to hold officers and directors personally liable for environmental cleanup costs.[32] In light of such decisions, officers and directors have an additional reason to ensure that their corporations conduct adequate environmental due diligence prior to the acquisition of property as well as implementing ongoing environmental compliance procedures.

If a company decides to go "public," its officers and directors will be held strictly liable for any material misrepresentation or omission in the prospectus that is distributed to investors. Section 11 of the Securities Act of 1933 (the Securities Act)[33] imposes liability for *every* material misrepresentation or omission in the prospectus against (1) the company offering the security, (2) the underwriters of the offering, (3) any member of the board of directors of the company at the time of the offering, (4) officers of the company who sign the registration statement (the chief executive officer, the principal financial officer, and the principal accounting officer are required by SEC rules to sign the prospectus), and (5) any expert who has prepared any segment of the registration statement and consents to being named as an expert, which will include the independent public accountants who certify the company's financial statements. Officers and directors often do not realize that each officer signing the prospectus and each director of the company at the time of the prospectus is personally liable for the accuracy of every statement in the prospectus. Directors, and particularly outside directors, often merely skim the prospectus prior to signing it. As one commentator stated: "Resolutions approving registration statements have come to be adopted with about the same amount of deliberation as a resolution opening a bank account."[34] In particular, outside directors, who usually have jobs elsewhere, do not have much time to spend reviewing the prospectus. Furthermore, because the "window of opportunity" in a stock offering is often so short, the time pressure to complete the prospectus and file it with the SEC is enormous. Thus, the liability of officers and directors is not at all commensurate with the type of due diligence often undertaken, and the liability can be astronomical. Officers and directors are personally liable for the entire amount of the stock offering, which could wipe out the net worth of such persons. In addition, plaintiffs in these cases often add other theories of liability, such as Rule 10b-5 claims under the Securities Exchange Act of 1934 (the Exchange Act) and common law fraud, seeking further damages. Because these actions are often highly complex and usually involve conflicts among various officers and directors necessitating separate counsel, the legal costs alone in defending the claims may be staggering. Although most officers and directors have indemnification contracts with their companies, this may be of little comfort if the company is not financially able to fulfill those contracts. On top of all this, directors' and officers' liability insurance is becoming increasingly difficult for companies to purchase, even at extremely expensive premiums.[35]

Liability under Section 11 can be imposed on a director no matter how long he or she has held the position. In *Escott v. BarChris Construction Corp.*,[36] two outside directors who were elected less than a month before the Registration Statement took effect were held personally liable under Section 11. The court stated:

Section 11 imposes liability upon a director, no matter how new he is. He is presumed to know his responsibility when he becomes a director. He can escape liability only by using that reasonable care to investigate the facts which a prudent man would employ in the management of his own property.[37]

As alluded to in *BarChris* and as discussed further below, officers signing the Registration Statement and directors can assert a "due diligence" defense to liability under Section 11. Section 11 divides this due diligence defense into two categories. As to the portions of the prospectus that are "expertised" (such as financial statements or engineering reports), the officer or director will have to show that he had no reasonable ground to believe and did not believe that the statements made were untrue or omitted to state a material fact. As to the other, "non-expertised" portions of the prospectus, the officer or director will have to show that he had, after reasonable investigation, reasonable ground to believe and did believe that the statements made were true and that there was no omission to state a material fact necessary to make the statements made not misleading.[38]

Liabilities of Professionals

Attorneys, accountants, appraisers, broker/dealers and other professional advisors must also be concerned about conducting proper due diligence, particularly in the current litigation climate. In the wake of the savings-and-loan debacle, the government and the public are looking increasingly to professionals to uncover and disclose the misconduct of their clients and third parties, and to be financially responsible if they are negligent in that process. The oft-quoted statement by Judge Stanley Sporkin in the Keating/Lincoln Savings and Loan case reflects the attitude of the times:

There are . . . unanswered questions presented by this case. Keating testified that he was so bent on doing the "right thing" that he surrounded himself with literally scores of accountants and lawyers to make sure all the transactions were legal. The questions that must be asked are: Where were these professionals, a number of whom are now asserting their rights under the Fifth Amendment, when these clearly improper transactions were being consummated? Why didn't any of them speak up or disassociate themselves from the transactions? Where also were the outside accountants and attorneys when these transactions were effectuated?[39]

Accountants

Plaintiffs have particularly been asking these questions of accountants, as is evidenced by the wave of litigation against accounting firms since 1990. For example, Ernst & Young agreed to pay $400 million to settle government claims arising from the S&L industry.[40] Coopers & Lybrand recently lost a jury verdict of $200 million in the *Mini Scribe* case.[41] Price Waterhouse recently overturned a $338 million jury verdict in connection with the sale of United Bank.[42] A Houston jury recently awarded $77 million in punitive damages against Deloitte & Touche.[43] *Time* magazine reported in April 1992 that the six largest accounting firms had paid over $300 million in claims in the previous 12 months.[44] More lawsuits have been pursued against accountants in the last 15 years than in the entire previous history of the accounting profession.[45] Litigation has been one of the primary causes for the collapse of Laventhol & Horwath, with substantial personal assessments being charged against its partners.[46] Smaller accounting firms are similarly subject to potential exposure. Because of such liability claims, many accounting firms are limiting the services they offer and many are abandoning audits of public companies altogether.[47]

One reason for expanded liability of accountants is that the courts are expanding the persons to whom accountants owe a professional duty of care. Recent cases are tending to hold accountants "accountable" to the entire investing public. This is in contrast to the traditional rule. The traditional rule, beginning with the New York Court of Appeals decision in 1931, in *Ultramares Corp. v. Touche*,[48] was that an accountant only owes a duty to its client. In that case, Touche, the accounting firm, was aware that the certified balance sheets would most likely be used by the client to obtain financing, but it did not know the identity of the lenders to whom the certified balance sheets would be distributed. The court required that the plaintiff establish that there must be either "privity" of contract between the accounting firm and the third party, or there must be a bond so close as to "approach that of privity." Because the accounting firm did not know exactly which lenders would be receiving and relying on the balance sheets, there was no duty owed to the lenders.

Although this had been the traditional approach, courts have expanded accountants' liability by adopting three other theories of liability. The first of these is an approach based on Section 552 of the Restatement (2d) of Torts, which allows someone to recover if the accountant knows that that person will rely on the audit opinion or other document. In *Ruch Factors, Inc. v. Levin*,[49] the court stated that accountants will owe a duty of care not only to the client to whom the financial information or audit reports are provided, but also to "the person for whose benefit and guidance the accountant intends to supply the information or knows that the recipient intends to supply it."[50] At least 16 jurisdictions have adopted some version of the Restatement position.[51]

Another approach, adopted in California, balances a variety of factors to determine liability, including: (1) the extent to which the transaction was intended to affect the plaintiff; (2) the foreseeability of harm to the plaintiff; (3) the degree of certainty that the plaintiff would suffer injury; and (4) the closeness of the connection between the defendant's conduct and the injury suffered.[52]

The most extensive approach adopted by courts would hold an accountant liable to all persons the accountant "reasonably should have foreseen" might obtain and rely on reports. At least four states have adopted this approach.[53] This approach is dramatic in that accountants could be liable to any member of the general investing public if they are found negligent in performing their duties.

Although accounting firms are being faced with unprecedented legal actions from a variety of plaintiffs, one recent decision is encouraging. In *Security Pacific Business Credit, Inc. v. Peat Marwick Main & Co.*,[54] the court held that Peat Marwick was not in "privity" with, and thus not liable to, a lender of the client, even though the accounting firm knew that the client was engaged with the lender in negotiations for financing, and the lender had telephoned the accounting firm to advise it that it would be relying upon the audited report and received assurance from the firm as to its comfort with the forthcoming unqualified opinion. The "privity" issue addressed in this case should concern accountants as well as other professionals in analogous fact situations and roles. In situations where the financial statements may be presented to identifiable third parties, the first "due diligence" step for the accounting firm is to ensure that those third parties in the transaction clearly understand that the certified opinion is being delivered only to, and can be relied upon solely by, the client. This relationship is commonly referred to as "privity" between the parties.

Whenever the audited financial statements and certificates are included in a prospectus filed with the SEC, the accountants could be determined to be liable under Section 11 of the Securities Act for any material misrepresentation in the audited financial statements; in such case, the accountants would have to prove that they had no reasonable ground to believe, and did not believe, that the financial statements were untrue or contained a material omission.[55]

Once it has been determined to whom the duty of care is owed (who they are in privity with), the accountants must be aware of exactly what is expected of them. The accountants generally satisfy the duty of care required of them in an auditing context when they perform the audit in accordance with generally accepted auditing standards (GAAS) and the financial statements present fairly the financial position, results of operations and changes in financial position in conformity with generally accepted accounting principles (GAAP). It is well-established that the auditors do not guarantee the absolute accuracy of the client's records and its financial statements. The auditors can only guarantee that it followed GAAS in performing the audit, applied GAAP to the client's records and detected no material errors.[56] However, there has been a strong push to expand the responsibilities of accountants. The U.S. Supreme Court even characterized accountants as "public watchdogs" who owe their "ultimate allegiance" to the investing public.[57] This attitude is reflected in the wave of litigation against accountants arising out of the failure of many transactions of the 1980s.

In responding to this pressure, the American Institute of Certified Public Accountants (AICPA)[58] has recently tightened its professional standards to require accountants to actively search for fraud by a company. Because GAAS and GAAP incorporate the professional standards promulgated by the AICPA,[59] the standards are important in determining the duties of accountants. In 1988 the AICPA adopted ten Statements on Auditing Standards (SAS) that, in effect, require auditors to design the audit to detect fraud.[60] Whereas under the previous standards the accountants had a duty to plan the audit examination to search for material errors and irregularities, now they have an additional duty to "design the audit to detect" material errors and irregularities.[61] In addition, the new standards also: (1) increase the accountants' responsibility to detect and report illegal acts of clients; (2) discuss the accountants' consideration of a company's ability to continue in business; and (3) address variances in the accountants' standard report. The accountants are required to actively search for material errors and irregularities and are required to exercise enough "professional skepticism" to make it more likely that any such material errors and irregularities are detected and to resign under certain circumstances. In addition, the accountants may be required to notify governmental authorities if fraud or illegal activities are detected.[62]

To assist accountants in addressing the increased standard of care being imposed on them, a group of accounting firms and other professional organizations developed a list of "audit red flags" designed to assist accountants in detecting client fraud.[63] These red flags include such items as: rapidly decreasing operating cash balances; insufficient working capital; inadequate lines of credit; potential violations of debt covenants; pressures to obtain a budgeted objective; commitment of major resources to a single division or a single product; management compensation based on operating results; extensive and/or material related-party transactions; significant quarter-end or year-end transactions; the use of creative accounting; delays in beginning the audit, followed by pressures to complete the audit; problems in gathering audit evidence; lack of documentation to support recorded transactions; lack of management cooperation; evasive responses by management to auditor requests; and uncorrected major weaknesses in internal controls.[64]

In a recent case discussing the duty of care owed by accountants, the SEC sought injunctive relief against Price Waterhouse (PW) for violations of the antifraud provisions of the Securities Act of 1933 and the Securities Exchange Act of 1934 in connection with PW's audit of the financial statements of AM International, Inc.[65] The court adopted the following rule of liability in that case:

The SEC must prove that the accounting practices were so deficient that the audit amounted to no audit at all . . . or "an egregious refusal to see the obvious, or to investigate the doubtful" . . . or that the accounting judgments which were made were such that no reasonable accountant would have made the same decisions if confronted with the same facts.[66]

Thus, it appears that, at least in SEC injunctive proceedings, accountants will be liable only if an audit is so below standard that "no reasonable accountant" would have made the same decisions.[67]

Attorneys

As is the case with accountants and other professionals, attorneys are increasingly being sued by their clients and by third parties, and the claims against them have been enormous. Five legal malpractice claims over the last three years resulted in payments of over $20 million for each claim.[68] For example, the New York firm of Kaye, Scholer, Fierman, Hayes & Handler agreed to pay $22 million to the government.[69] In addition, in 1990, Kaye, Scholer, Fierman, Hayes & Handler agreed to settle two class actions for $20 million.[70] Chicago's Sidley & Austin entered into a $7.5 million settlement of a malpractice claim brought by the Resolution Trust Corporation on behalf of Lincoln Savings & Loan Association and earlier settled for $4 million in a class action case with similar allegations.[71] The Philadelphia firm of Blank, Rome, Comisky & McCauley paid $50 million to the government in connection with claims relating to its improper representation of a Florida S&L.[72] Juries have also found law firms liable in recent decisions, as evidenced by a $17.4 million legal verdict against a Houston law firm.[73]

In light of these events, the conduct of proper due diligence has become increasingly important to attorneys. One primary way that attorneys are exposed to liability, and therefore must conduct careful due diligence, is in rendering legal opinions. Attorneys are called upon from time to time to render legal opinions in various transactions, such as loan transactions, business acquisitions and securities offerings. The opinions generally cover topics such as the client's existence and good standing, the corporate power and authority to enter into the transaction, the due authorization and validity of the transaction, the execution and delivery of the transaction documents, absence of any conflicts with other agreements or applicable laws, absence of material litigation, absence of any required consents and the valid and lawful issuance of stock if stock is being issued in the transaction.

As in the case with respect to the liability of accountants, the courts have been struggling with determining to whom an attorney owes responsibility. It is clear that if a legal opinion is addressed to its client and/or a particular third party, the attorney will owe a duty to its client and/or that third party. It is less clear to what other third parties the attorney will owe a duty. The traditional rule is that only third parties named in an opinion have privity with the attorney;[74] however, various courts have adopted more liberal standards. Certain courts have adopted the "third-party beneficiary" theory.[75] Under this theory, when the client, with the attorney's knowledge, intends to confer the benefit of the opinion to a specified third party, the third party may sue the attorney for damages that may be caused by the lawyer's defective opinion. For example, the attorney for an oil and gas limited partnership drilling program rendered an incorrect opinion. The drilling program was financed in part by a lender that loaned funds to the limited partnership, and the loan was secured by promissory notes payable to the partnership by the limited partner investors. These promissory notes were guaranteed by surety bonds issued by a surety company. The opinion was addressed to the third-party lender, but it stated that it could be relied upon by the third-party lender and its assignee. The lender assigned the loan to Crossland Savings FSB, which was unable to collect on the loan according to its terms. Crossland Savings then sued the surety company that issued the surety bonds guaranteeing the investor notes. The surety company argued that it was subrogated to the rights of Crossland Savings against the law firm and that it was therefore entitled to sue the law firm. The court, in denying the law firm's summary judgment motion against the surety company, stated that when a lawyer, at the direction of its client, prepares an opinion letter addressed to a third party or which expressly invites another third party's reliance, the attorney has engaged in a form of limited representation of the other third party.[76]

Other courts have adopted the California "balancing factors" standard.[77] In one case,[78] a law firm prepared an opinion letter to a client, knowing that the letter was to be shown to the plaintiff, a prospective lender, in connection with a loan to the client by the plaintiff lender. The letter expressed the law firm's professional opinion that the client was a general partnership, but it failed to disclose that certain of the general partners believed the client was a limited liability entity and that they did not have personal liability. When the client defaulted, the lender sued the law firm. The lender argued that it would not have lent the money if it had known that the partners believed that their liability was limited, which forced the lender to incur legal costs to establish the general partners' liability. In holding the law firm liable, the court stated that the opinion was rendered for the purpose of influencing the lenders to make the loan, and thus it was "clearly foreseeable" that the lender could be harmed by the attorney's negligence.[79] The court stated it had no difficulty in determining that the issuance of a legal opinion intended to secure benefit for the client, either monetary or otherwise, must be issued with "due care, or the attorneys who do not act carefully will have breached a duty owed to those they attempted or expected to influence on behalf of their clients."[80] In view of this expansion of persons to whom a duty is owed, attorneys should realize that a lack of due diligence may also make them liable to persons in addition to their clients.

Once it has been determined to whom the duty is owed, it must be determined what duty is owed. The general duty requires a lawyer to perform both the legal research and the factual investigation necessary to form an appropriate basis for the opinion. The California Supreme Court has stated:

A lawyer is expected to possess knowledge of those plain and elementary principles of law which are commonly known by well-informed attorneys, and to discover those additional rules of law which, although not commonly known, may readily be found by standard research techniques. Even with respect to an unsettled area of law, we believe an attorney assumes an obligation to his client to undertake reasonable research in an effort to ascertain relevant legal principles and to make an informed decision as to a course of conduct based upon an intelligent assessment of the problem.[81]

In rendering opinions, the attorney will need to investigate not only the applicable law but also the underlying facts. The facts of a situation are often so closely connected to the legal issues as to be determinative of what the legal conclusion will be.

In addition to liability under common law principles of negligence, corporate/securities attorneys may have additional liability in connection with the opinion that is contained in a securities prospectus. Attorneys may be strictly liable under Section 11 of the Securities Act when the attorneys' opinion, with the attorneys' consent, is contained in a registration statement, if the opinion includes a material misstatement or omission.[82] In such a case, the attorneys will have a "due diligence" defense if they can prove that after reasonable investigation, they had reasonable grounds to believe, at the time the registration statement became effective, that the statements they made were true and that there was no omission to state a material fact.[83]

Attorneys may also incur liability under Section 12(2) when the opinion is deemed part of the "prospectus," provided that the lawyer acts in such a way as to be a "seller" of the security and the lawyer has not exercised "reasonable care."[84] A "seller" under Section 12 generally includes: (1) one who owned the security sold to the purchaser; (2) an agent for a vendor (such as a broker) who successfully solicited the purchase; (3) one who solicited the purchase with the intent to personally benefit thereby; and (4) one who, without financial benefit to oneself, solicited the purchase to serve the owner's financial interest.[85] The recent Supreme Court decision of *Pinter v. Dahl*, interpreted Section 12(1) to mean that, as a general rule, attorneys will not be liable as a "seller" simply by rendering an opinion without other factors being involved.[86]

In addition to liability for a defective opinion, attorneys may also be liable to their clients and, ever-increasingly, to third parties for failing to exercise reasonable care. Possibly the greatest amount of potential liability can be incurred by a securities lawyer. It has been stated by courts that: "The duty of the (securities) lawyer includes the obligation to exercise due diligence, including a reasonable inquiry, in connection with responsibilities the lawyer has voluntarily undertaken."[87] In particular, in connection with the issuance of stock by the attorney's client, it has been stated that the attorney must make a reasonable, independent investigation to detect and correct false or misleading materials.[88] Most of the cases under the federal securities laws where the attorney has been held liable involve facts where the attorney is also either a director or is acting as an officer of the company. In *Escott v. BarChris Construction Corp.*, one director-defendant was also serving as the issuer's counsel. Because of his role as counsel, the court placed a higher burden of due diligence upon him compared to other outside directors.[89] In *Feit v. Leasco Data Processing Equipment Corp.*, the court categorized a director who was also counsel for the issuer as an "inside" director, and stated that such persons have an extremely high duty to require accuracy in the prospectus:

BarChris imposes such stringent requirements of knowledge of corporate affairs on inside directors that one is led to the conclusion that liability will lie in practically all cases of misrepresentation. Their liability approaches that of the issuer as guarantor of the accuracy of the prospectus.[90]

Plaintiffs are also increasingly using state "Blue Sky" and common law claims in securities litigation against attorneys, including claims for negligence, breach of fiduciary duty, fraud and malpractice allegations. In the recent case of *FDIC v. O'Melveny and Meyers*,[91] the FDIC, as receiver for American Diversified Savings Bank, a failed savings and loan, sued the law firm of O'Melveny & Meyers, claiming professional negligence for its part in the preparation of a private placement memorandum distributed by the failed S&L to its investors. The private placement memorandum did not disclose the failed thrift's financial difficulties, which the FDIC claimed were caused in part by the fraud of the thrift's executives. The law firm claimed it was not aware of such items as the overvaluation of thrift assets, and that it was not obligated to search for and discover such alleged misdeeds. The trial court agreed with the law firm and dismissed the suit. The appeals court, however, held that the law firm owed a duty to protect the public and its client, and that attorneys fulfill this duty by performing the legal services for which they have been engaged with "such skill, prudence and diligence as lawyers of ordinary skill and capacity commonly possess."[92] The court also stated that an important duty of securities counsel is to make a "reasonable, independent investigation to detect and correct false or misleading materials."[93] The court noted that a basic fundamental obligation of a law firm in preparing such private placement memorandums would be to contact and discuss the issuer's affairs with its independent accountants and any previous legal counsel in order to determine if the statements being made in the offering materials are accurate.[94]

Lastly, an attorney may be liable under the SEC's enforcement authority, including the SEC's ability to seek injunctive relief.[95] In particular, Rule 2(e) of the SEC's Rules of Practice permits the SEC to suspend, limit or bar attorneys and other professionals from practicing before it.[96] In *SEC v. Frank*,[97] the SEC brought for the first time an injunction action against an attorney based solely on his actions in preparing documents for his client. The attorney had prepared an offering circular that related to an exempt offering. The SEC suspended trading in the issuer's stock and obtained a temporary injunction against the lawyer that prohibited him from drafting misleading offering documents. The court held that the attorney had a duty to realize that certain representations of his client were false.[98] In *SEC v. Spectrum Limited*,[99] the Second Circuit Court of Appeals expanded the liability of attorneys in rendering legal opinions in securities matters, and would allow the SEC to enter injunctions against lawyers only on the basis that the lawyer "should have known" that the issued opinion would be used by a client to further violations of the securities laws.[100] However, since the *Spectrum* decision, the Supreme Court has held that "scienter" is required in SEC injunctive actions under Rule 10b-5.[101] Nevertheless, the SEC has been given increased enforcement authority under the Securities Law Enforcement Remedies Act of 1990, which allows the SEC to impose a cease and desist order on any person who is a "cause" of a securities violation, even those who "should have known" that their conduct "would contribute" to the violation.[102] The SEC may seek to use this authority against securities counsel.[103]

Although claims had previously been brought against attorneys and other professionals under the theory that they were "aiding and abetting" violations of Rule 10b-5 of the Exchange Act, the U.S. Supreme Court has recently held, in *Bank of Denver N.A. v. First Interstate Bank of Denver, N.A.*, that there is no implied right to this cause of action under the Exchange Act.[104]

Appraisers

Appraisers of real estate and businesses increasingly are being held liable to lenders and other persons for negligence in preparing their appraisals. In the case of *Costa v. Neimon*,[105] the Costas had applied for VA financing with a lender, and the lender retained Neimon to appraise the real estate. Neimon appraised the property at $21,500, and the Costas bought the property. Soon after the purchase, the Costas sought to relocate and hired an independent appraiser, who valued the property at $13,000. A few years later, the Costas failed to make payments on their mortgage, and the lender foreclosed. The Costas brought suit against Neimon, and the court held that an appraiser could be liable for a negligent appraisal to a third party like the Costas, even though the lender was the one who retained the appraiser.[106]

In another case, an appraiser was held liable to a lender for preparing an appraisal "negligently, unskillfully, and without due care."[107] The appraiser had been commissioned by the borrower, but the appraisal was addressed to the president of the bank. The appraiser appraised the commercial real estate at $57 million, and the bank made a loan of $37 million based on the appraisal. The Federal Home Loan Bank Board (FHLBB) rejected the appraisal and required the bank to write down the loan to $13 million. The bank foreclosed on the land, which actually had a market value of $9.5 million, and brought suit against the appraiser. The court held that an appraiser could be liable for information negligently supplied to persons or classes of persons whom the appraiser knew would rely on the information, even though there may be no "contractual privity" directly between the appraiser and the party relying on the appraisal.[108]

Appraisers are also bearing some of the blame for the savings and loan debacle. The House Committee on Governmental Operations examined the impact of faulty appraisals on S&L failures, and concluded:

Faulty and fraudulent real estate appraisals have become an increasingly serious national problem. Their harmful effects are widespread, pervasive and costly. They have seriously damaged and contributed directly to the insolvency of hundreds of the nation's financial institutions and have helped cause billions of dollars in losses to lenders, private mortgage insurers, investors, and federal insurance funds.[109]

According to the House Committee, the combined losses attributable to fraudulent or incompetent appraisals are between $750 million and $1 billion as of 1986.[110] A number of cases can be cited for negligent appraisal in relation to the fast-paced lending atmosphere of the 1980s. For example, in the case of Sunrise S&L Association of Florida,[111] a small S&L grew from $3 million in assets in 1980 to $1.5 billion in assets in 1985. These inflated assets were due particularly to inflated appraisal figures. The banking examiners found that large loan appraisals were generally prepared by appraisers unknown to the association's officers. These appraisals generally contained technical deficiencies that violated the regulatory requirements. Reappraisals on many of the Sunrise loans showed an aggregate decline in value of almost 50 percent from the original appraisals.[112] In addition, between January 1983 and October 1985 the real estate loan portfolios of 25 percent of the over 3,000 federally insured S&L associations were found to have significant appraisal deficiencies.[113]

In light of these deficiencies, Congress passed specific provisions of the Financial Institution Reform, Recovery and Enforcement Act of 1989 (FIRREA) establishing standards for the performance of real estate appraisals in connection with "federally related real estate transactions" regulated by government agencies.[114] A "federally related real estate transaction" in effect is any real estate loan made by an insured depository institution.[115] Federally related real estate transactions having a value of $1 million or more must involve a state certified appraiser.[116] FIRREA also requires appraisals to be performed in accordance with "generally accepted appraisal standards" in accordance with the Appraisal Standards Board of the Appraisal Foundation.[117]

Broker/Dealers

In recommending a security to its customers, a broker makes an implied representation that there is a reasonable basis for the recommendation and that the security is suitable for the customer.[118] This implied representation arises under Rule 10b-5 of the Securities Exchange Act and applies to both buy and sell recommendations. As stated by the SEC:

It is a violation of the anti-fraud provisions [which include 10b-5] for a broker-dealer to recommend a security unless there is an adequate and reasonable basis for the recommendations and further, that such recommendations should not be made without disclosure of facts known or reasonably ascertainable, bearing upon the justification for the recommendation. As indicated, the making of recommendations for the purchase of a security implies that the dealer has a reasonable basis for such recommendations which, in turn, requires that, as a prerequisite, he shall have made a reasonable investigation. In addition, if such a dealer lacks essential information about the issuer, such as knowledge of its financial condition, he must disclose this lack of knowledge and caution customers as to the risk involved in purchasing the securities without it.[119]

As the SEC stated, a "reasonable basis" for a recommendation presupposes a "reasonable investigation" of the issuer of the security.[120] Although there is no clear rule as to what is required of broker/dealers, the courts have focused on the following factors: the broker's relation to the issuer; the issuer's size and stability; the broker's access to information about the issuer; and whether the issuer is suffering apparent financial difficulties.[121] Also, the scope of the investigation will depend on the broker/dealer. Brokers who are also serving as underwriters in an offering will be judged with greater scrutiny. Similarly, large brokerage firms will be required to conduct a greater investigation than an individual broker.[122]

The rules of the National Association of Securities Transactioners (NASD) require that broker/dealers, in recommending to a customer the purchase, sale or exchange of any security, shall have reasonable grounds for believing that the recommendation is suitable for the customer upon the basis of the facts, if any, disclosed by such customer as to his other security holdings and as to his financial situation and needs.[123] Although the rule itself does not specifically impose a duty on the broker to investigate the customer's financial situation, the SEC has stated that a broker/dealer is expected to make reasonable inquiry concerning the customer's investment objectives, his financial situation and other necessary data.[124]

In addition, members of the New York Stock Exchange must "use due diligence to learn the essential facts relative to every customer" (the "know your customer rule").[125]

DUE DILIGENCE AS A FUTURE DEFENSE OR AS AN ELEMENT OF A CLAIM

Not only will the appropriate due diligence procedures alert investors and professionals to potential unwanted liability, but proof of proper due diligence may serve as a defense against third-party claims after the transaction is completed. In addition, due diligence may be a necessary element of a plaintiff's claim. Examples of how due diligence may serve as a defense or as an element of a claim are discussed below.

The "Innocent Landowner Defense" in the Purchase of Real Property

A purchaser who buys real property in a transaction must undertake adequate due diligence to avail itself of the "innocent landowner" defense under CERCLA against environmental law claims.[126] The innocent landowner defense is also extremely important to lenders in the event they must foreclose on collateral. CERCLA provides a defense to a purchaser of property if it can show that it did not know and had no reason to know that hazardous substances were on the property at the time of the purchase.[127] In order to establish this "innocent landowner defense," a showing must be made by the purchaser that it conducted all appropriate inquiry into the previous ownership and the uses of the property consistent with good commercial or customary practices, in an effort to minimize liability.[128] In determining whether a purchaser has made a sufficient inquiry to establish the defense, CERCLA requires courts to consider:

1. Any specialized knowledge or experience of the purchaser;
2. The relationship of the purchase price to the fair market value of the property (that is, if the purchase price is unrealistically low, the purchaser may be deemed to have knowledge concerning the condition of the property);
3. Commonly known or reasonably ascertainable information about the property (such as prior use of the property, whether the purchaser contacted adjacent landowners about the condition of the property and general reputation of the property as to its use as a disposal site);
4. The obviousness of the presence or likely presence of contamination at the property; and
5. The ability to detect the contamination by appropriate inspection (which generally entails a Phase I environmental audit).[129]

Thus, for a purchaser to protect itself against potential environmental problems, it will need to conduct at least a Phase I environmental audit as part of its due diligence review. By conducting the proper investigation, the purchaser may be able to avail itself of the "innocent landowner defense" against claims that it did not uncover in the investigation. This process, however, will not be beneficial to serve as a defense to the risk of loss for environmental liabilities such as off-site disposal or toxic tort claims, particularly in a stock purchase or merger transaction.

Lenders should also conduct a Phase I environmental audit on industrial, commercial or farm real estate both before the loan is made and, if the loan goes into default, before foreclosure. An audit before foreclosure should be considered even though one may have been done before the loan, because the conditions of the property may have changed. Lenders will want to conduct audits and take other necessary steps to avail themselves of the "innocent landowner defense" similar to any other landowner.

Due Diligence as a Defense in Stock Offerings

Proper due diligence is of vital concern to officers, directors and the investment bankers of a company issuing stock, as well as to accountants, attorneys and other professionals who provide expert information, opinions or reports and consent to their names being utilized in the prospectus. The failure to conduct adequate due diligence may result in personal liability of such persons. The two primary liability sections of the Securities Act are Section 11,[130] which imposes strict joint and several liability for misstatements or omissions in a publicly filed registration statement, which applies only to public offerings, and Section 12(2),[131] which is a general anti-fraud provision. Under both these sections, due diligence is an affirmative defense. The nature of the due diligence defense under Section 11 depends on whether the omission or misstatement appears in the regular, or "non-expertised," portion of the prospectus, or in the parts of the prospectus prepared by an expert, such as financial statements or engineering reports. As to the "non-expertised" portion, the Section 11 defendant will have to prove that it had, after reasonable investigation, reasonable ground to believe, at the time such part of the registration statement became effective, that the statements therein were true and that there was no omission to state a material fact.[132] With respect to the "expertised" portions, it will need to prove only that it had no reasonable ground to believe and did not believe that the statements therein were untrue or contained a material omission.[133]

In determining what constitutes reasonable ground for belief, Section 11(c) provides that the standard that will be applied is that of a "prudent man in the management of his own property."[134] There is no clear elaboration of what a "prudent man" would do, and the courts have applied a variable standard of due diligence, depending upon a person's role in the registration statement. For example, in *Feit v. Leasco Data Processing Equipment Corp.*, the court stated:

What constitutes "reasonable investigation" and a "reasonable ground to believe" will vary with the degree of involvement of the individual, his expertise, and his access to the pertinent information and data. What is reasonable for one director may not be reasonable for another by virtue of their differing positions. Inside directors with intimate knowledge of corporate affairs and of the particular transactions [are] expected to make a more complete investigation and have more extensive knowledge of facts . . . than outside directors.[135]

In addition, SEC Rule 176 lists eight factors bearing on the question of the sufficiency of a due diligence inquiry.[136] Such factors include: the office held when the person is an officer; the presence or absence of another relationship to the issuer when the person is a director or proposed director; reasonable reliance on officers, employees and others whose duties should have given them knowledge of the particular facts; and when the person is an underwriter, the type of underwriting arrangement, the role of the particular person as an underwriter and the availability of information with respect to the registration.[137]

Over the years, the appellate courts have reviewed various lower court decisions in attempting to determine whether underwriters and other potential defendants have satisfied their due diligence requirement. In *Sanders v. John Nuveen and Co.*,[138] the Seventh Circuit held that an underwriter of short-term commercial paper, who relied on false certified financial statements, failed to make reasonable inquiries that would have led to the discovery of the falsity, and was therefore liable, under Rule 10b-5, to its customers for their losses sustained as a result of the issuer's default. The court focused on the fact that the underwriters did not make a request to examine federal income tax returns, corporate minute books and accounting work papers, and that the underwriters did not review the issuer's contracts, talk with outside auditors or assume there was a fraud to begin with (as it apparently should have as indicated by the court).[139] In *Shores v. M.E. Ratliff Investment Co.*,[140] the underwriter was held liable in connection with the issuance of $1,510,000 in bonds by the Arkansas Valley Environmental and Utility Authority to finance real estate improvements in Prue, Oklahoma. M.E. Ratliff Investment Co. (Ratliff) sold the bonds at a 20 percent discount. Although Ratliff had described Prue as a rapidly growing suburb of Tulsa, Oklahoma, there was actually little development taking place and it was an isolated area. Furthermore, the developer and the operators of the project had no operating experience and no net worth or operating capital when the bonds were sold.

In the recent SEC injunctive action against Donaldson, Lufkin & Jenrette Securities Corp. (DLJ),[141] DLJ served as the underwriter of the initial public offering from Matthews and Wright Group, Inc., a broker/dealer that had engaged in a series of fraudulent underwriting activities immediately prior to its initial public offering. Matthews and Wright had engaged in some municipal bond offerings that they had fraudulently closed in December 1985. The SEC concluded that DLJ should have explored further into the fraudulent bond offerings by Matthews and Wright. In particular, the SEC stated that DLJ at least should have reviewed the bond closing documents.[142]

Underwriters often are adept at implementing due diligence procedures in public offerings. However, directors and officers often are not as versed in conducting their own due diligence. In light of the potential for staggering liability to officers and directors in a registration statement, the due diligence defense becomes crucial. Officers and directors thus should insist that certain "due diligence steps" be taken at the outset of the discussions on conducting a public offering. For example, the company may employ a "due diligence officer" for the purpose of ensuring the accuracy of the statements in the registration statement.[143] The due diligence officer should have unfettered access to all persons in the organization, from the chief executive officer down to the lowest level employees. In fact, the due diligence officer should interview every employee with operational responsibility that relates to a matter discussed in the prospectus. In addition, if any portions of the registration statement involve technical issues, it may be advisable to obtain opinions from outside experts. As is the case with due diligence in all business transactions, the due diligence process should be documented in writing to prove that the due diligence was adequately conducted.

Due Diligence as Prerequisite for Claims

The adequacy of the due diligence by an investor may be critical for it to successfully sue a seller of a security for violation of the civil liability provisions of federal and state securities laws. For example, an investor may be able to sue a seller of stock under Rule 10b-5 of the Securities Exchange Act of 1934 if it can prove that the seller made an untrue statement of material fact or that the seller omitted to state a material fact that was necessary so that the statements that were made would not be misleading.[144] However, various courts have ruled that as part of a Rule 10b-5 claim of an investor, the investor must prove that it was "diligent" in pursuing its investigation with care and good faith,[145] while other courts have held that the seller may be able to raise as a defense the lack of due diligence of the investor.[146] The courts are not uniform on exactly what level of due diligence is required of the investor. The majority of courts have held that an investor will be barred from asserting a Rule 10b-5 claim only if it has been "reckless."[147] To determine whether an investor is reckless in its due diligence, no one single factor is dispositive, but rather, courts will consider all relevant factors. The courts have been guided by the following factors:

1. The sophistication and expertise of the plaintiff in financial and securities matters;

2. The existence of long-standing business or personal relationships;

3. Access to the relevant information;

4. The existence of a fiduciary relationship;

5. Concealment of the fraud;

6. The opportunity to detect the fraud;

7. Whether the plaintiff initiated the stock transaction or sought to expedite the transaction; and

8. The generality or specificity of the misrepresentations.[148]

In the recent case of *Brown v. E. F. Hutton Group, Inc.*,[149] the court held that the investors in oil and gas limited partnerships had failed to perform adequate due diligence when, although they were told orally that the investment was of low risk or of no risk, the written prospectus contained numerous "risk factor" warnings.

It is clear that a complete lack of due diligence, or only a cursory due diligence if there are obvious purchaser concerns, could be viewed as reckless. Furthermore, a thorough due diligence will serve as sound evidence against any claim or defense the seller could raise about the investor's due diligence.

In addition to the concerns raised above regarding the lack of due diligence of the investor as impeding its claims under the federal securities laws, the investor may have the same problem if it tries to assert any state law fraud claims against the seller, or against third-party experts. Generally, in order to assert a state law claim of fraud against the seller or against an expert, the investor will be required to prove that it "reasonably" relied on any misleading statement or omission.[150] Thus, the seller will be required to show that it exercised ordinary care for the protection of its interests, and generally will be charged with knowledge of all facts that would have been discovered by a reasonably prudent person who was similarly situated. Therefore, a thorough due diligence would also serve as solid evidence in any state fraud claim the purchaser may want to assert.

Certain courts have also held that in order to sue sellers of real property or realtors for negligent misrepresentations, a purchaser must show that it exercised reasonable care.[151] The purchaser's duty to investigate is particularly found whenever: (1) defects are obvious; (2) the realtor is acting solely as the seller's agent; and (3) when the realtor's representations are vague.[152] For example, in one case a realtor told a purchaser that a house was "very well built." After closing, the purchaser found numerous defects. The court held that the realtor's comment was not a misrepresentation but was mere "puffery" and could not be relied on by the purchaser.[153]

CONDUCTING DUE DILIGENCE TO ACCOMPLISH
THE TRANSACTION

Consider Due Diligence Early

The key to proper due diligence in any transaction is to begin at the earliest possible time. In the earliest stage of negotiations of any transaction, an investor should be focused on due diligence and the potential legal implications of the findings uncovered by the due diligence. For example, without proper early due diligence, a purchaser of a business will be at a disadvantage in the negotiations with the seller. The more knowledge a purchaser has about the seller's business, the better position the purchaser will be in to negotiate the terms and to elicit appropriately tailored representations and warranties in the acquisition agreement. Due diligence should be addressed in the letter of intent, which should specifically state that the purchaser's obligation to complete the transaction is subject to its satisfactory completion of its due diligence. If the purchaser knows of potential problems with the seller's business or assets, the purchaser may want to address these concerns in the letter of intent. For example, if the seller is a manufacturer, the purchaser will need to make certain that no hazardous materials have been released or deposited on the seller's premises during the manufacturing process. The letter of intent should therefore specifically provide that the purchaser's obligation to buy is subject to the satisfactory results of a Phase I environmental audit, conducted by environmental experts designated by the buyer and paid at seller's expense.

Results of early due diligence in an acquisition context may also motivate the purchaser to restructure the transaction. The parties may have initially structured the transaction as a merger or a stock-for-stock tax-free reorganization to achieve certain tax benefits or a certain accounting treatment (such as pooling of interests), or to continue the business and goodwill of the acquired company. In these situations, however, the surviving corporation remains liable for the predecessor's debts in a merger. Similarly, in a stock purchase, the acquired corporation and its liabilities remain legally intact. If the purchaser's due diligence uncovers liabilities that the purchaser does not want to assume, the purchaser may want to structure the transaction as an asset sale. In an asset sale, the purchaser assumes only certain identified liabilities of the seller's business. Nevertheless, even if the transaction is structured as an asset sale, the law sometimes dictates that certain liabilities flow with an asset sale, even when they are not contractually assumed.[154] Thus, even in an asset sale, the purchaser's attorney should be included early in the due diligence process in order to detect potential liabilities and to provide additional suggestions to avoid unwanted liability or to ameliorate the risk.

Similarly, a lender should address its due diligence concerns at the outset of the loan negotiations. In particular, the borrower should know that the lender will require thorough due diligence with respect to environmental matters.[155] The commitment letter should specifically set forth the due diligence that is going to be required by the lender. The commitment letter should also provide that these environmental studies and expenses will be borne by the borrower.

Beginning due diligence early is also very important in a public stock offering. Time is usually at a premium in a stock offering because market conditions are changing rapidly during the offering process and, normally, due diligence is done hurriedly at the same time that the prospectus is being prepared. However, companies often consider going public or raising capital months before actually beginning the process. Therefore, it is advisable to begin a draft of the prospectus before the actual decision is made to go public. This may facilitate a more thorough and focused investigation of items contained in the prospectus that need in-depth due diligence, and provide enough time to accomplish it.

Coordination of Persons in the Due Diligence Process

A successful due diligence program will require careful planning, guidance and coordination from professional advisors. Professional advisors, such as attorneys, investment bankers and accountants, are experienced in conducting due diligence and the due diligence team should be formed as early as possible. Although the substance of the due diligence examination will vary depending on the transaction, effective due diligence will require the input from all members of the team as well as the client focusing on all aspects of the transaction.

The due diligence team includes a broad range of persons. In addition to the above-named professional advisors, the team should include a person in the company's management who will be the "due diligence" officer and serve on the due diligence team. The team's duties will usually consist of management, which will review operational information and issues; the attorneys, who will focus on key liability issues and will often guide much of the due diligence and the accountants and investment bankers, who will carefully review financial statements and other financial information.

In an acquisition, one of the most frequent due diligence mistakes is for management to leave most of the due diligence work to its advisors and fail to closely examine potential business problems. Although the work of professional advisors in uncovering undisclosed liabilities is extremely important, management should not deemphasize the need to review in depth the potential business issues in the transaction, such as: reviewing the seller's informational systems, the expertise of its management and upper-level employees, its marketing or distribution techniques and its employee relations.

The due diligence team, in consultation with each other, will need to draft a due diligence checklist. The due diligence questionnaires and other materials provided in this book should serve as an invaluable resource in drafting the checklist. The checklist should be tailored to fit the specific business transaction. Input from the investor's management, attorneys, accountants and investment bankers should be obtained to make the due diligence checklist as thorough as possible. In addition, it should be tailored to make sure that it is not so overbearing as to hinder the process of negotiation. For example, in an acquisition, a purchaser will need to be careful not to exasperate a seller with a list that is unnecessarily long or complex. The purchaser should keep in mind that although it is important to review requested documentation, it is also equally, and sometimes even more important, to have access to various personnel of the other party. For example, the purchaser often elicits valuable information by having access to all levels of a seller's employees.

As discussed above, an acquisition that involves real property will require an environmental audit to be conducted. This will obviously necessitate retaining an experienced environmental consulting firm to conduct the audit. As noted above, the environmental audit should be discussed at the earliest possible stages because it may take two weeks, at the earliest, and up to months, to obtain a thorough audit from an experienced firm. The transaction should be conditioned upon the results of the audit, and as stated before, the purchaser should negotiate for the seller to bear the costs of the audit, but the purchaser should determine which firm will be used. Proper environmental due diligence should actually consist of two parts: first, the acquisition audit of the property to determine if it contains hazardous substances; and second, the "compliance" audit to determine if the seller has violated environmental statutes or otherwise may be subject to toxic tort liability to third parties for off-premises matters. This due diligence will thus require the coordination of at least three groups: management (preferably someone with environmental expertise), the environmental audit firm and attorneys with corporate and environmental expertise.

It is extremely important to hire an experienced and qualified environmental audit firm. The failure of a firm to detect environmental problems could be disastrous, and even though it hires an expert, an investor may not be able to rely on the innocent landowner defense if certain more obvious items go undetected. For example, in one case, an appraiser hired by a lender failed to notice evidence of contamination. The court held that the contamination was plainly visible, that the appraiser had knowledge because the photographs attached to the appraisal showed the contamination, and the lender was chargeable with the knowledge of its appraiser.[156]

As with an acquisition, a public offering of stock will require a coordinated effort of management and professionals. Generally, the underwriter and its counsel will take the lead in the due diligence investigation of a public offering. This is true for a number of reasons, including the fact that the underwriter will in effect be purchasing the stock and distributing it to the public, and for the additional reason that the underwriter is incurring potential exposure in its role. Additionally, as previously discussed, officers signing the registration statement and the directors of the issuer can be personally liable for misrepresentations made in the prospectus.[157] Therefore, officers and directors of the issuer must in effect make the due diligence inquiry their own personal inquiry, and should take due diligence extremely seriously. In this regard, the issuer should appoint a due diligence officer with the capability and authority to conduct appropriate and adequate due diligence on behalf of the issuer and its officers and directors.

One important decision that officers and directors of the issuer should make is to hire experts to provide expertise in a subject covered by the prospectus for which issuer's personnel does not have adequate expertise. In *Feit v. Leasco Data Processing Equipment Corp.*, the court held the directors liable for, among other things, failing to retain an outside expert to estimate the amount of the reserves.[158] There may be other subject matter areas requiring the retention of an expert, such as aspects of the issuer's technology, patents, copyrights or other such matters. As one underwriter stated:

Our experience has shown that in addition to our own evaluation of companies, plants, products, and managements and in addition to the due diligence exercised by leading attorneys and accountants, it is extremely desirable to supplement this work by the use of independent experts and specialists in the individual fields which constitute the business of the prospective issuer. We feel that no investment banking firm can expect to maintain on its staff the people who would be qualified to properly and in-depth evaluate the broad spectrum of companies which come before it for financing. We also feel that the objectivity of an independent evaluator provides a balance to an internal staff member's point of view.[159]

Due Diligence and the Transaction Document

A crucial aspect of proper due diligence is representations and warranties in the "transaction document." This document includes such records as an acquisition agreement, a loan agreement, or an underwriting agreement. Representations and warranties in the transaction document are simply statements made by a party about itself or its business. Representations and warranties serve five primary functions:

1. They will elicit the type of due diligence information that an investor needs to determine whether it wants to close the transaction or, possibly, to renegotiate the terms of the transaction.

2. They may assist the investor in understanding what approvals, consents, filings or other actions must be taken before the transaction is consummated.

3. They will assist on certain due diligence defenses. In particular, environmental representations and warranties will give additional assistance to the environmental audits for the "innocent landowner defense."

4. They will serve the invaluable function of allocating the risk of any unknown liabilities, preferably to the other party.

5. They will lay the basis for the investor's remedies, which are generally termination of the transaction before closing and indemnification for any misrepresentation that is not discovered until after closing.

The representations and warranties should be worded so that they will disclose the relevant information prior to closing. For example, in the sale of a business, it is imperative that the representations and warranties cover every conceivable aspect of the seller's business. The purchaser should educate its attorney about the seller's business and about any concerns the purchaser may have about the seller's business so that the representations and warranties can be fashioned to fit the seller's business. Although the acquisition agreement should be well drafted to allow for the purchaser's remedy of indemnification, suing the seller after closing for a misrepresentation is never as favorable as knowing about a problem before closing and either terminating the transaction or negotiating around the problem, such as reducing the purchase price. The acquisition agreement should therefore specifically provide the purchaser a mechanism to terminate the transaction, at its option, if the purchaser discovers any misrepresentations prior to closing or if there are negative due diligence results. In addition, the purchaser should consider incorporating in the acquisition agreement the right to recoup any expenses it may have incurred in the transaction, if a misrepresentation is discovered. For example, the purchaser may have incurred significant time and expenses (attorneys' fees, accounting fees, bank commitment fees) prior to discovering the misrepresentation. If the purchaser wants the right to recoup these expenses, the acquisition agreement should specifically provide for this right.

No matter how thorough the due diligence is, certain unknown liabilities may escape the due diligence review. In addition, an unscrupulous seller may intentionally hide certain facts about the seller's business. Thus, the representations and warranties should be carefully drafted so that the purchaser can pursue the seller through the indemnity contained in the acquisition agreement. It is also important that the seller represent in the acquisition agreement that the representations and warranties are true and correct as of the closing date and that they survive the closing date. Without such a provision, the seller may argue that the purchaser knew of a misrepresentation before the closing, but waived its right to indemnification by closing the transaction.

Lending documents, such as a loan agreement, deed of trust or security agreement, should also contain adequate representations and warranties. Representations in lending documents generally serve the same primary functions as they do in an acquisition. Representations and warranties will not only elicit further information about the borrower, but will in particular establish a record of due diligence for the lender.[160] As is the case with an acquisition agreement, the representations and warranties in the loan documents should specifically address environmental concerns. The representations and warranties should state that there have been no releases of hazardous substances on any properties of the borrower or of any of its subsidiaries. The environmental representations and warranties should also cover specific items, such as the presence of underground storage tanks, PCBs and asbestos. The results of any environmental questionnaire should be specifically incorporated by reference into the representations and warranties.

The underwriting agreement in a public offering should also contain representations and warranties of the issuer. The representations and warranties serve the principal purposes of allowing the underwriter to not close the offering should a material misrepresentation or omission be discovered prior to the closing. The underwriting agreement will in fact specifically provide that the underwriter's obligation to purchase the stock is subject to the accuracy of the representations and warranties. The representations and warranties also assure the underwriters that the issuer, its attorneys and accountants have been diligent in making adequate disclosures in the prospectus. In this regard, the representations and warranties may also serve as a checklist of items about which the issuer should be concerned in ensuring that the prospectus is accurate and complete.

CONCLUSION

As our society becomes increasingly litigious, proper due diligence becomes essential in every business transaction, not only for investors, but for the professionals representing them as well. The failure to conduct proper due diligence may result in civil liability to third parties, with damages reaching into the millions of dollars.[161] In addition to civil liability, investors and professionals may also be exposed to criminal liability if they do not take due diligence seriously. Thus, emphasizing and implementing careful due diligence should become standard operating procedure in all business transactions.

NOTES

1. Ann Burkhart, *Lender/Owners and CERCLA: Title and Liability* 25 Harv. J. on Legis. 317, 318 n. 3 (1988).

2. Jay Gwin, Robin Phelan, Saundra Steinberg and Stacey Griffin, "Dancing the Toxic Two-Step: Corporate Environmental Liability Under Superfund and in Bankruptcy," at Q-3 in *Advanced Corporate and Securities Institute* (University of Houston Law Center,- 1990).

3. Ibid.

4. Ibid. Another common environmental problem is underground storage tanks ("USTs"). Leakage from USTs is probably the most common source of soil contamination. The EPA has estimated that there are more than one million USTs in the United States, many of which are older tanks that either contain or have in the past contained petroleum products. The EPA and, to a large extent state and local governments, require owners and operators of USTs to monitor them, repair leaks or replace them, and remediate any contamination caused by leaking. See Richard May, ENVIRONMENTAL LAWS: IMPACT ON BUSINESS TRANSAC-TIONS, section 1.3.5 (1992).

5. 42 U.S.C., section 9601 et seq.

6. 42 U.S.C., section 6901 et seq.

7. 33 U.S.C., section 1251 et seq.

8. 42 U.S.C., section 7401 et seq.

9. 15 U.S.C., section 2601 et seq.

10. CERCLA, section 107(a); 42 U.S.C., section 9607(a).

11. N.J. Stat., section 13: 1K-6 et seq.

12. CERCLA, section 107(b)(3); 42 U.S.C., section 9607(b)(3); see infra text accompanying notes 127–129.

13. 29 U.S.C., section 1342.

14. 29 U.S.C., section 1341(c) and section 1362(a) and (b).

15. See *Ray v. Alad Corp.*, 560 P.2d 3, 11 (Cal. 1977); *Kaminski v. Western-MacArthur Co.*, 175 Cal. App. 3d 445, 220 Cal. Rptr. 895 (Cal. Ct. App. 1985).

16. *Ramirez v. Amsted Industries, Inc.*, 431 A.2d 811 (N.J. 1981).

17. *Dawejko v. Jorgensen Steel Co.*, 434 A.2d 106 (Pa. Super. 1981).

18. *Hickman v. Thomas C. Thompson Co.*, 592 F. Supp. 1282 (D.C. Colo. 1984).

19. American Institute of Certified Public Accountants' Statement of Auditing Standards, No. 5.

20. American Bar Association's Statement of Policy Regarding Lawyers' Responses to Auditors' Request for Information, Paragraph 5.

21. "Superlien" states include Connecticut, Maine, Massachusetts, New Hampshire and New Jersey.

22. See Davidson, *Environmental Considerations in Loan Documentation*, 106 Banking Law Journal 308, 312 n. 14 (1989).

23. See e.g., *United States v. Fleet Factors*, 901 F.2d 1556 (11th Cir. 1990) cert. denied, 111 S.Ct. 752 (1991); *United States v. Mirabile*, 15 Envtl. L. Rep. (Envtl. L. Inst.) 20994, 20995–96 (E.D. Pa. Sept. 4, 1985); *U.S. v. Maryland Bank and Trust Co.*, 632 F. Supp. 573 (D. Md. 1986); *Guidance v. BFG Electroplating & Mfg. Co.*, 732 F. Supp. 556 (W.D. Pa. 1989). But see *In re Bergsoe*, 910 F.2d 668 (9th Cir. 1990); *Northeast Doran Inc. v. Key Bank of Maine*, 15 F.3d 1 (1st Cir. 1994); *Waterville Industries Inc. v. Finance Authority of Maine*, 984 F.2d 549 (1st Cir. 1993); *U.S. v. McLamb*, 5 F.3d 68 (4th Cir. 1993). In 1992, the EPA promulgated a rule under which, if lenders complied with the "safe harbor" pro-

visions of the rule, lenders which had foreclosed on property would not be considered owners of the property. This EPA rule was struck down in early 1994 by the U.S. Court of Appeals for the District of Columbia in *Kelly v. EPA*, 15 F.3d 1100 (D.C. Cir. 1994). As of the date of publication, the Clinton administration had proposed an amendment to CERCLA, as part of the Superfund Reform Bill, which would give statutory force to the EPA rule.

24. *O'Neill v. OLCRI, Inc.*, 750 F.Supp. 551 (D.R.I. 1991).

25. See e.g., Pennsylvania's Hazardous Sites Cleanup Act, Pa. Stat. Ann. Tit. 35, section 6020.101 et seq., Kansas Environmental Response Fund, Kan. Stat. Ann., section 65-3454(a) (1988 Supp.).

26. See e.g., *Mills Acquisition Co. v. Macmillan, Inc.*, 559 A.2d 1261, 1280 (Del. 1989), citing *Revlon, Inc. v. MacAndrews & Forbes Holdings, Inc.*, 506 A.2d 173, 179 (Del. 1986); *Smith v. Van Gorkom*, 488 A.2d 858, 872 (Del. 1985); *Loft, Inc. v. Guth*, 2 A.2d 225 (Del. Ch. 1938), Aff'd 5 A.2d 503 (Del. 1939); Dennis J. Block, Nancy E. Barton and Stephen A. Radin, *The Business Judgment Rule-Fiduciary Duties of Corporate Directors*, chs. 1, 11 (n.p., 1989).

27. *Smith v. Van Gorkom*, 488 a.2d 858, 873 (Del. 1985).

28. Ibid.

29. See Block, Barton and Radin, *The Business Judgment Rule- Fiduciary Duties of Corporate Directors*, ch. 2. A (4)(c), p. 59 (1989).

30. *Wisconsin v. Rollfink*, Wis. Sup. Ct., No. 89-1908 (Sept. 19, 1991).

31. "Pair Convicted of Hazardous Dumping," *Houston Chronicle*, December 8, 1993.

32. See e.g., *United States v. Northeastern Pharmaceutical & Chem. Co.*, 579 F. Supp. 823, 847 (W.D. Mo. 1984), *aff'd in part, rev'd in part*, 810 F.2d 726 (8th Cir. 1986); Memorandum from Courtney M. Price to Regional Administrators et al., "Guidance Regarding CERCLA Enforcement Against Bankrupt Parties" (May 1984).

33. 15 U.S.C., section 77k.

34. Carlos Israels, *Issuer's Counsel—Advice to My Client*, 24 Bus. Law. 537, 563 (1969).

35. For a good discussion of these issues, see Robert Alan Spanner, *A Litigation Perspective on the Prospectus Preparation Process for an Initial Public Offering*, 16 Sec. Reg. L.J. 115 (1988).

36. *Escott v. BarChris Construcition Corp.*, 283 F. Supp. 643 (S.D. N.Y. 1968).

37. Ibid. at 688.

38. 15 U.S.C., section 77k(b).

39. *Lincoln Sav. & Loan Ass'n v. Wall*, 743 F. Supp. 901, 920 (D.D.C. 1991).

40. Geoffrey Aronow, *Accountants Lead the Latest Charge for Liability Reform*, 7 INSIGHTS 17 (1993).

41. Ibid.

42. Ibid.

43. Nelson Antosh, "Jury Administers $77 million Slap," *Houston Chronicle*, November 3, 1993.

44. "Who's Counting," *Time*, April 13, 1992, at 48.

45. Brian Kirby and Thomas Davies, *Accounting Liability; New Exposure for an Old Profession*, 36 S. Dakota L. Rev. 574, 575 n. 3 (1991).

46. Aronow, supra, note 40 at 17.

47. See Berton, "Legal-Liability Awards are Frightening Smaller CPA Firms Away From Audits," *Wall Street Journal*, March 3, 1992.

48. *Ultramares Corp. v. Touche*, 174 N.E. 441 (N.Y. 1931).

49. *Ruch Factors, Inc. v. Levin*, 284 F. Supp. 85 (D.R.I. 1968).

50. Ibid. at 92.

51. See Gary Lawson and Tamara Mattison, *A Tale of Two Professions; The Third Party Liability of Accountants and Attorneys for Negligent Misrepresentation*, 52 Ohio St. L.J. 1309, 1320 n. 51 (1991).

52. See e.g., *Roberts v. Ball, Hunt, Hart, Brown, & Baerwitz*, 57 Cal. App. 3d 104, 110-11, 128 Cal. Rptr. 901, 905 (1976); *Cicone v. URS Corp.*, 183 Cal. App. 3d 194, 207-11, 227 Cal. Rptr. 887, 895-97 (1986).

53. See *International Mortgage Co. v. John P. Butler Accountancy Corp.*, 177 Cal. App. 3d 806, 810-20, 223 Cal. Rptr. 218, 220-27 (1986); *Touche Ross Co. v. Commercial Union Ins.*, 514 So. 2d 315, 318-23 (Miss. 1987) (relying heavily on a state statute); *H. Rosenblum, Inc. v. Adler*, 93 N.J. 324, 334-53, 461 A.2d 138, 142-53 (1983); *Citizens State Bank v. Timm, Schmidt & Co.*, 113 Wis. 2d 376, 382-87, 335 N.W. 2d 361, 364-66 (1983).

54. *Security Pacific Business Credit, Inc. v. Peat Marwick Main & Co.*, 79 N.Y. 2d 695 (1992).

55. See supra, text accompanying note 38.

56. See *Goss v. Crossley (In re Hawaii Corp.)*, 567 F. Supp. 609 (D. Hawaii 1983); *SEC v. Arthur Young & Co.*, 590 F.2d 785 (9th Cir. 1979); *Rhode Island Hosp. Trust Nat'l Bank v. Swartz, Bresenoff, Yavner & Jacobs*, 455 F.2d 847 (4th Cir. 1972); *United States v. Simon*, 425 F.2d 796 (2d Cir. 1969), cert. denied, 397 U.S. 1006 (1970).

57. *United States v. Arthur Young & Co.*, 465 U.S. 805 (1984).

58. American Institute of Certified Public Accountants, STATEMENTS ON AUDITING STANDARDS (1988) (hereinafter AICPA).

59. AICPA Professional Standards, *Auditing*, section 411 (CCH 1985).

60. AICPA Statements on Auditing Standards (SAS), No. 16.

61. Ibid.

62. Ibid.

63. Weiss, *An Introduction to Concepts of Accountants' Liability*, 57 CPA J., July 1987, at 30.

64. Ibid.

65. See *Securities and Exchange Commission v. Price Waterhouse*, No. 85C 4787, slip op. (S.D.N.Y. June 29, 1992).

66. Ibid. at 80-81.

67. Ibid.

68. See *Keating Lawyers Settle Malpractice Case for $7.5 M*, New Jersey Law Journal (October 31, 1991).

69. Ibid.

70. Ibid.

71. Ibid.

72. See "Rising Malpractice Rates Make Lawyers Victims of Own Success," *Washington Post* (March 4, 1991).

73. *Panaphour v. Sewell & Riggs*, 1991 WL 445354 (LRP Jury).

74. See e.g., *Spivey v. Pulley*, 138 A.D. 2d 563, 526 N.Y.S. 2d 145 (1988); *Simon v. Zipperstein*, 32 Ohio St. 3d 74, 512 N.E. 2d 636 (1987); *Flaherty v. Weinverg*, 303 Md. 116, 121, 492 A.2d 618, 620 (1985).

75. See e.g., *Ogle v. Fuiten*, 102 Ill. 2d 356, 466 N.E. 2d 224 (1984); *Guy v. Liedervack*, 501 Pa. 47, 459 A.2d 744 (1983); *Auric v. Continental Casualty Co.*, 111 Wis. 2d 507, 331 N.W. 2d 325 (1983).

76. *Crossland Savings FSB v. Rockwood Ins. Co.*, 700 F. Supp. 1274, 1282 (S.D. N.Y. 1988).

77. See e.g., *Biakanja v. Irving*, 49 Cal. 2d 647, 320 P.2d 16 (1958); *Roverts v. Ball, Hunt, Ilart, Brown & Bacrwitz*, 57 Cal. App. 3d 104, Cal. Rptr. 901 (1976); *Franko v. Mitchell*, 158 Ariz. 391, 762 P.2d 1345 (Ct. App. 1988); *Jenkins v. Wheeler*, 69 N.C. App. 140, 316 S.E. 2d 354 (1984).

78. *Roberts v. Ball et al.*, 128 Cal. Rptr. at 906.

79. Ibid.

80. Ibid.

81. *Smith v. Lewis*, 13 Cal. 3d 349, 118 Cal. Rptr. 621, 530 P.2d 589 (1975).

82. 15 U.S.C., section 77k(a)(4).

83. See *In re Citisource*, 694 F.Supp. 1069 (S.D. N.Y. 1988).

84. 15 U.S.C., section 77b(10); 15 U.S.C., section 77l(2).

85. *Pinter v. Dahl*, 108 S.Ct. 2063 (1988).

86. Ibid. See also *Abell v. Potomac Insurance Co.*, 858 F.2d 1104 (5th Cir. 1988), judgmt vacated on other grounds, 109 S.Ct. 3236, cert. denied, 109 S.Ct. 3242 (1989).

87. *Felts v. Nat. Account Systems Ass'n Inc.*, 469 F. Supp. 54, 67 (N.D. Miss. 1978).

88. *Escott v. BarChris Construction Corp.*, 283 F. Supp. 643 (S.D. N.Y. 1968).

89. *Escott v. BarChris Construction Corp.*, 283 F. Supp. 643, 683 (S.D. N.Y. 1968).

90. *Feit v. Leasco Data Processing Equip. Corp.*, 332 F. Supp. 544 (E.D. N.Y. 1971).

91. *FDIC v. O'Melveny and Meyers*, 969 F.2d 744 (9th Cir. 1992). The Supreme Court has reversed and remanded this case with respect to issues relating to the FDIC's claims and defenses as a receiver of an insolvent thrift. However, the Supreme Court left intact the holding by the Ninth Circuit that professionals may be liable to their clients for failing to protect them from liability that may flow from disseminating false or misleading information to the public.

92. Ibid. at 748, quoting *Lucas v. Hamm*, 56 Cal. 2d 583, 591; 15 Cal. Rptr. 821, 825, 364; P.2d 685, 689 (1961).

93. Ibid. at 749, quoting H. Bloomenthal, *Securities Law Handbook*, section 27.02, at 1096 (1990-91 ed.)

94. Ibid. at 749.

95. See *Aaron v. SEC*, 446 U.S. 680, 688-89 (1980).

96. 17 C.F.R., section 201.2(e).

97. *SEC v. Frank*, 388 F.2d 486 (2d Cir. 1968).

98. Ibid. at 489.

99. *SEC v. Spectrum Limited*, 489 F.2d 535 (2nd Cir. 1973).

100. Ibid. at 541-42.

101. *Aaron v. SEC*, 446 U.S. 680 (1980).

102. Securities Act, section 8A(a); 15 U.S.C., section 77h-1(a); Securities Exchange Act, section 21C(a); 15 U.S.C., section 78u-3. See Allan A. Martin, Theodore N. Mirvis & Edward D. Herlihy, *SEC Enforcement Powers and Remedies are Greatly Expanded*, 19 Sec. Reg. L.J. 17, 23-24 (1991).

103. See Darrel Rice and Marc Steinberg, *Legal Opinions in Securities Transactions*, 16 J. Corp. L. 375, 423 (1991).

104. *Bank of Denver, N.A. v. First Interstate Bank of Denver. N.A.*, S.Ct., 128 L.Ed.2d 119 (1994). However, legislation is pending that could impact aider-and-abettor liability. Senate Bill 240, the Private Securities Litigation Reform Act of 1995, would expand liability to include "any person who intentionally rendered substantial assistance to the fraudulent conduct of [one who makes a material misrepresentation or omission knowing others are likely to rely on it], with actual knowledge of such person's fraudulent conduct or fraudulent purpose, and with knowledge that such conduct was wrongful." The House of Representatives has introduced the Common Sense Legal Reform Act of 1995, H.R. Rep. No. 50, 104th Cong., 1st sess. (Feb. 24, 1995). While this act would allow recklessness to substitute for actual knowledge in the scienter element of primary liability, the bill would not revive aiding-and-abetting liability.

105. *Costa v. Neimon*, 366 N.W.2d 896 (Wis. App. 1985).

106. Ibid.

107. *First State Savings Bank v. Albright & Associates of Ocala, Inc.*, 561 So.2d 9 (Fla. 1990).

108. Ibid. at 1329, citing *First Florida Bank v. Max Mitchell & Company*, 558 So.2d 9 (Fla. 1990).

109. House Comm. on Government Operations, Impact of Appraisal Problems on Real Estate Lending, Mortgage Insurance, and Investment in the Secondary Market, II.R. Rep. No. 891, 99th Cong., 2d sess. 4 (1988) (hereinafter House Report).

110. House Report at 16.

111. See House Report at 17.

112. Ibid. at 16-23.

113. Frank Vickory, *Regulating Real Estate Appraisers; The Role of Fraudulent and Incompetent Real Estate Appraisals in the S & L Crises and the FIRREA Solution*, 19 Real Est. L.J. 3, 8 n. 11 (1990).

114. FIRREA test. XI, section 110; 12 U.S.C., section 3331.

115. FIRREA tit. XI, section 1121(4); 12 U.S.C., section 3350(4).

116. FIRREA tit. XI, section 1113; 12 U.S.C., section 3342.

117. FIRREA tit. XI, section 1111; 12 U.S.C., section 3340.

118. See Jacobs, *Litigation and Practice Under Rule 10b-5*, Clark Boardman Securities Law Series, section 211.01 (1993).

119. Distribution by Broker-Dealers of Unregistered Securities, Exchange Act Release No. 6721 at 3 (February 2, 1962).

120. See e.g., *Hanly v. SEC*, 415 F.2d 589, 595-96 (2nd Cir. 1969).

121. See *University Hill Found v. Goldman, Sachs & Co.*, 422 F. Supp. 879, 898 (S.D. N.Y. 1976); *Quincy Co-operative Bank v. A.G. Edwards & Sons*, 655 F.Supp. 78, 86 (D. Mass. 1986).

122. See *Jackson v. Bache & Co.*, 381 F. Supp. 71, 89 (N.D. Cal. 1974).

123. Art. III, Sec. 2, NASD Rules of Fair Practice, CCH NASD Sec. Dealers Manual, section 2152.

124. Exchange Act Release No. 8135 (July 27, 1967).

125. New York Stock Exch. Rule 405, 2 CCII New York Stock Exch. Guide, section 2405.

126. CERCLA, section 107(c)(3); 42 U.S.C., section 9607(b)(3).

127. Ibid.

128. CERCLA, section 101(35)(B); 42 U.S.C., section 9601(35)(B).

129. Ibid.

130. 15 U.S.C., section 77k.

131. 15 U.S.C., section 77l.

132. 15 U.S.C., section 77k(b)(3).

133. Ibid.

134. 15 U.S.C., section 77k(c).

135. *Feit v. Leasco*, 332 F. Supp. 544-578 (E.D. N.Y. 1971).

136. 17 C.F.R., section 230.176.

137. Ibid.

138. *Sanders v. John Nuveen and Co.*, 463 F.2d 1075 (7th Cir.), cert. denied, 409 U.S. 1009 (1972).

139. Ibid.

140. *Shores v. M. E. Ratliff Investment Co.*, Paragraph 98, 425 CCH-Fed. Sec. L. Rep. (N.D. Ala. 1982).

141. *In the Matter of Donaldson, Lufkin & Jenrette Securities Corporation*, File No. 3-7863, Release No. 33-6959.

142. Ibid.

143. See Robert Alan Spanner, "Limiting Exposure in the Offering Process," 20 Rev. of Sec. & Comm. Reg. 59, 61 (1987).

144. 17 C.F.R., section 240.10b-5.

145. *Rodriguez v. Montalvo*, 649 F.Supp. 1169 (D. Puerto Rico 1986).

146. *Peil v. Speiser*, 806 F.2d 1154 (3rd Cir. 1986).

147. *Dupuy v. Dupuy*, 551 F.2d 1005 (5th Cir. 1977), cert. denied, 434 U.S. 875 (1977).

148. See Arnold S. Jacobs, *Litigation and Practice Under Rule 10b-5*, Clark Boardman Securities Law Series, section 64.01[b] [iii] (1993).

149. *Brown v. E. F. Hutton Group, Inc.*, 991 F.2d 1020 (2d Cir. 1993).

150. See e.g., *City of Del Rio v. Ulen Contracting Corporation*, 94 F.2d 701 (5th Cir. 1938); *In re Com. Oil/Tesoro Petroleum Securities Litigation*, 484 F.Supp. 253 (W.D. Tex. 1979).

151. See e.g., *Evans v. Teakettle Realty*, 736 P.2d 472 (Mont. 1987); *Hope v. Brannan*, 557 So.2d 1208 (Ala. 1989).

152. See Clarence Hagglund and Britton Weimer, *Caveat Emptor: Realty Purchaser's Duty to Investigate*, 20 Real Estate L.J. 373 (1992).

153. *Williamson v. Realty Champion*, 551 So.2d 1000 (Ala. 1989).

154. See e.g., the text supra accompanying notes 1–20.

155. See, generally, Charles Davidson, *Environmental Considerations in Loan Documentation*, 106 Banking L.J. 308 (1989); see also George Nation III, *Minimizing Risk of Loss From Environmental Laws*, 108 Banking L.J. 346, 368 (1991).

156. *Horicon State Bank v. Kant Lumber Co., Inc.*, 165 Wis. 2d 543, 478 N.W. 2d 26 (1991).

157. See supra text accompanying notes 33–38.
158. *Feit*, 332 F. Supp. at 544, 580–81.
159. Securities Act Release No. 5275 (July 26, 1992) at 9 n. 22.
160. See generally, Davidson, supra note 164 and 326.
161. See supra text accompanying notes 40–47 and 68–73.

CHAPTER 5

Business Description and Basic Information

The business description and basic information enumerated in the checklist associated with this chapter (see the Appendix) constitutes the core reports, documents and data necessary to commence due diligence investigations. Financial reports are important, but at this stage additional information on the organization's structure and the participants is essential. A primary objective of due diligence is to verify, analyze and distill basic information initially accepted at face value. After all, it was this temporary acceptance that spurred some interest or type of agreement to justify the cost of proceeding. It should be an adequate framework within which to plan the due diligence program.

An overview of the business gained from the basic information enables an investor to plan the due diligence. Planning would be impossible without some general knowledge of the business, its structure and names and responsibilities of the participants. Without this information, the program's scope cannot be estimated, assignments made or realistic time schedules developed. Requests for data would be misdirected or irrelevant and result in excessive expense, and needlessly antagonize those interrogated. An objective always should be expeditious completion, something that can only be achieved with intelligent preparation. At this stage, the majority of the basic information for planning the entire due diligence process is probably in the investor's possession.

During the analysis, you should record the time period of the study and the dates and source of documents and information received. Since any business is a moving target, the study is little more than a photograph of a specific time in its history. Business investments usually take considerable time, even when all goes well. The parties may also find agreement impossible or may agree to delay negotiations. Before negotiations do resume after a hiatus, the investor will want to review accumulated data and determine whether it's dated.

Participants' names, titles, addresses and telephone numbers should be recorded. Since investors rarely have enough information, they'll want to return to those involved for more information and opinions or to compliment or criticize. Be sure to record the names of all involved in the questioning, not just those of the principals, for if the investment turns sour there surely will be a review of the due diligence activity and everyone's performance.

All financial information, both public and private, constitutes the most basic information studied in due diligence. While financial reports covering three to five years are desirable, most important are reports for the last fiscal year and the interim statements since year's end. Businesses can change rapidly, making it essential to have the most current data. Interim and monthly statements are particularly important because year-end statements and tax returns are seldom finalized until at least three months after year's end.

Two types of organizational charts are invaluable in due diligence, and if not in existence they should be constructed. One is the typical personnel chart displaying names, titles and reporting relationships of management personnel for the business as a whole and for each subsidiary or division. A second chart applicable for more complex businesses illustrates each legal entity, the ownership and percent of ownership. This would show subsidiaries, joint ventures, partnerships, minority investments and other legal relationships. These charts should reflect and indicate both active and inactive units. The charts are not only invaluable to understanding the business but they assist in making certain that all aspects of the business are studied. What may not initially appear, or what may merely resemble a blip on a balance sheet, can be a disaster waiting to happen or a valuable neglected asset.

An understanding of a business's history also is helpful to understand the present. Businesses often have brochures or other prepared literature describing their history. Questions about the history are an ideal way to begin face-to-face meetings, since they are innocuous and most people enjoy talking about the "early days" and past crises and successes. There are few companies that have been in existence any length of time about which someone has not exclaimed, "Someone ought to write a book about this place." While this often has been done, it's usually in a glorious, sugar-coated form to celebrate anniversaries or long-tenured CEOs. As a result, never assume such books tell the whole story.

As a final piece of basic information, professionals involved should be identified and their fees estimated. An investor must be prepared to accept the costs or abandon the project. The investor should also know if some will claim excessive fees or fees to which they are not entitled. Along with determining fee obligations, it's important to know where each professional's loyalty lies; is it to the seller, the buyer or only to himself?

Professional fees can run into many millions of dollars for large transactions, and on smaller deals they may be so large that the deal's economics are jeopardized. While the percentage of the total transaction committed to fees may be relatively small, the total amount in dollars for actual services performed may be outrageous by anyone's standard except the recipient of the fees. It is a mistake to ever underestimate the rapacious greed that may surface in these affairs. Of course, in most transactions the fees prove to be reasonable and justifiable. But all parties nevertheless should be on guard. For many expecting fees it will be their last opportunity and they will not be concerned with preserving future business.

CHAPTER 6

Critical Early Questions

The responses to questions or topics in the checklist related to this chapter, the preceding chapter, and the initial questions in all ensuing sections of the checklist (see the Appendix) should provide an investor with a comprehensive but not complete understanding of the business.

The ramifications and costs of due diligence require that priority be given to questions, data and analysis most likely to affect an investor's final decision. The answers and analysis may inspire greater interest in the investment's potential, trigger in-depth studies of problem areas or constitute "deal killers" that cause the investor to back out. Pertinent questions or subjects discussed in ensuing chapters should not be neglected nor their relevance minimized if the due diligence continues.

Top priority must be given to a dispassionate evaluation of management, since the success or failure of any business is primarily a function of management. The evaluation should include key executives who have managed or had a major influence on the business during the past five years. They are responsible for the business's current condition. However, the most important executives requiring intense evaluation are those responsible today and in the future. The investor should devote the time necessary and use whatever proven techniques are available to reach valid conclusions. Simultaneously, replacements for existing or anticipated management vacancies must be identified and evaluated.

Management evaluations are both objective and subjective. Announced terminations to retire or take other positions, serious health problems, education and the performance of the business managed are objective factors. Actual results and identifiable accomplishments are of paramount importance. Personality characteristics, management skills, creativity, leadership ability and a myriad of other traits involve subjective evaluations. In evaluation of management, the competence of those engaged in the evaluations is as important as that of management.

Due diligence is a search for trends and anomalies necessary to understand current conditions, identify requirements for remedial action and forecast future performance. Trends in revenues, cash flow, profits at various levels and the entire spectrum of financial ratios provide insight but may mislead without knowledge of definitions and causes of deviations. Management's task is to perceive, influence and reverse undesirable trends while accelerating the positive.

Cash flow is the cash received, spent and available in a business. It is arguably the single most important financial statistic to determine the financial progress and health of the business. The most realistic historic cash flow for a business is the comprehensive summary found in cash-flow statements appearing in audited financial reports. However, two other inadequate measures of cash flow, EBIT and EBITDA, have come into usage. EBIT is earnings before interest and taxes and EBITDA is earnings before interest, taxes, depreciation and amortization. Multiples of EBIT or EBITDA are most commonly used by investors to establish price ranges considered fair, or at least those they are willing to pay. They are also applied as rough estimates of cash flow with often misleading results, because they do not reflect cash items such as working capital changes, capital expenditures, asset sales, dividends and debt repayment.

Due diligence should provide an understanding of past cash flow for use as a basis combined with projected income, business programs and conditions to develop forecasts of future cash flow. If the business has its own cash-flow history and projections they should be reviewed. However, an investor should only rely on his own forecast. Cash-flow forecasts have greater value and importance than income projections that are only one aspect of cash flow. A business may be showing profits on its financial statements while being unable to pay its bills because of inadequate cash flow. The reverse may be true with a business experiencing healthy positive cash flow, but reporting losses. Neither condition can continue indefinitely. Short-term cash-flow projections should be on a month-by-month basis, since many businesses experience extreme variations of available cash during a year. Cash flow for an entire year may appear excellent, but closer inspection could reveal months with the business relying on loans.

The financial statements serve as a secondary checklist. For each line item on the statements, the investor must understand the terminology and the specific composition of each account. Accounting statements are extremely diverse in format, definitions of terminology and content of accounts. How business transactions are recorded and the flow in and out of accounts is vital information for comprehension of the statements. Accounting terminology is not precisely defined like the laws of nature, nor is there a universal chart of accounts that precisely states each account's contents.

Auditors give opinions on financial statements "as a whole" rather than on each individual account, partially in recognition of accounting's imprecision. An all too common due diligence mistake is to assume the definitions for accounting terminology of the business being studied are similar to the investor's. Another mistake is to forget that the financial statements only purport to describe the financial condition on a specific day in the past and that changes begin immediately thereafter.

The notes to the financial statements provide critical information clarifying, supplementing and augmenting the numerical portion of the financial statements. The notes can cover any subjects accountants consider important and are carefully crafted with precise language to disclose and summarize facts. While the austere notes may meet disclosure requirements, they are at best a starting point for a due diligence investigator. An exceptionally voluminous set of notes to a financial statement is a warning for an investor to proceed with caution.

All extraordinary income and expenses must be identified because they distort financial statements, trends, ratios and forecasts. Non-operating extraordinary and non-recurring income result from the sale of assets, refinancing, insurance proceeds, litigation settlements and other unusual transactions outside the normal course of business. These may or may not be identified separately in financial statements. Managements intent on improving the appearance of financial statements may shift all or part of non-operating extraordinary income to operating income. Operating extraordinary income results from unusually large and highly profitable orders of the business's products or services for which there is little chance of repetition. The orders may be windfalls but are recorded as operating income and gross profit-making identification is difficult.

Historical financial data are of importance to understand the business, but emphasis must be placed on future income that will be at best an intelligent guess. Financial forecasts should reflect anticipated extraordinary operating and non-operating income as well as regular operating income. Income deterioration from portions of the business that will decline or be terminated because of market conditions, contract expirations or probable management decisions usually can be predicted with adequate investigations. A prudent investor cannot ignore any income stream affected by events that might occur.

Investors should identify all unusual expenses and evaluate management's decisions to classify any as extraordinary or non-recurring. Managements may improperly classify expenses as extraordinary in an effort to improve the business's appearance. Expenses charged or reserved for restructuring or discontinued operations is one of the most fertile areas for discretionary excesses designed to assure future income. The concept of "recast" financials used to lure investors involves the deletion of selected prior expenses by rationalizing that they were extraordinary and implying they will never occur again. Remarkable feats of imagination are often displayed in recast financials.

Examples of expenses properly classified as non-recurring are losses from natural disasters, fires or unusual accidents, large and unique litigation expenses and losses from discontinued businesses or product lines. Examples of dubious expenses claimed as extraordinary would be cost overruns, misquoted jobs, excessive sales or administrative expenses, litigation costs and technological failures. Unusual but predictable future expenses may be associated with events such as litigation settlements, recalls of products, major maintenance and repairs, relocations, restructuring, facility shutdowns, sales of overvalued assets, write-off of intangibles, cost overruns on large contracts and purchase or construction of new facilities.

For purposes of financial analysis and to discern trends of both discontinued and new product lines, divisions or businesses should be identified along with the dates they impacted financial statements. Included should be those products started that have already failed. Some of the most spectacular and acrimonious losses have resulted from failed ventures that management quickly recognized as a mistake and took action to cut losses.

Nearly all acquisitions and introductions of products or services are supported by business plans or studies that include forecasts of costs, revenues and profits. The original rationale for the introduction and a comparison of plans to actual results is helpful in evaluating both new products and management's judgment and ability. Questions of why new products or services for which there is an obvious demand (usually evidenced by competitive activity) have not been introduced are also appropriate. The answers may disclose previously unknown weaknesses.

Capital expenditures are a critical element of past cash flow and cash-flow forecasts. But funds spent in prior years and planned for the current year are only a partial indication of future requirements. Historical data may include expenditures not to be repeated for decades and will not indicate future expenditures to replace outmoded facilities or for expansion plans. Historical data do constitute a starting point from which to estimate future requirements and a means to guard against unrealistic forecasts. Comparisons of actual expenditures to planned amounts constitutes a test of how realistic management's capital expenditure budgets have been.

OWNER AND MANAGEMENT ISSUES

There are a series of questions relating to those in control and the decisions they can make. During due diligence the investor should confirm that he is negotiating with the proper parties. Who controls the business and who can make binding commitments are paramount issues not to be ignored. Investors have wasted large amounts of time and money contacting the wrong parties or assuming the individuals they were meeting could deliver. Often an immense chasm in views and objectives exists between owners and/or individuals able to make binding decisions and those who purport to represent the owners or claim they can influence the outcome. Feuding owners or boards of directors further complicate matters. Managements with little ownership, minority shareholders and inexperienced or unscrupulous intermediaries all should be suspect until proven reliable. Widely dispersed ownership necessitates a search for the individual or co-alition that can deliver on its commitments.

Business deals requiring due diligence are all too commonly fertile ground for litigation. The proliferation of attorneys and the tendency to file lawsuits, almost as a business strategy, add another risk and emphasize the importance of knowing with whom one is dealing. There are individuals who have the experience, willingness and resources to sue whenever they perceive an opportunity for financial gain. A record of many outstanding suits or one or more suits in which they were successful portends an ap-petite for additional suits. Any investor eyeing a business in which the key shareholders or executives have a record and/or propensity for litigation should assume a high probability exists that he may be the next victim. Regardless of how persuasively past lawsuits are explained and how charm-ing the plaintiff, an investor should be wary, construct defenses or walk away.

Prior activity involving efforts to sell the business, bring in investors or secure significant financing may influence present negotiations. The expe-rience tends to make owners and managers more sophisticated and realistic. Price expectations may be tempered by prior negotiations. However, past casual (often oral) offers that were not pursued or accepted or proposals received in failed negotiations may now be viewed as firm offers and the current minimum price. Differences of opinions among selling shareholders may become more clearly defined and either sharpened or reconciled. Ob-ligations to provide warranties and representations are now known, and many selling shareholders are better informed about the business than be-fore.

If the business has been actively on the market for sale, a potential buyer should learn for how long and why it has not sold. How many active competing investors are involved? Who is handling the negotiations and sale? Is this business worth becoming involved in competitive bidding in which the price may be too high? What has changed in the condition of the business or the views of the sellers that could result in a different out-come?

Due diligence should provide confirmation of why the business is for sale and/or why it needs new cash. An investor cannot be satisfied until con-vinced of the true and complete reasons for the transaction. Legitimate fears are always present that a concealed reason will adversely affect current or future prospects for the business. A possibility often exists of multiple motives in which several individuals reached the same conclusion but for very different reasons. As an example, a business may be for sale because a major shareholder needs cash for estate problems, the business needs additional cash to grow or the hired CEO wants to cash-out his options. Whatever the reasons, they should be verified during due diligence.

Management may have knowingly created or unwillingly agreed to barriers to the deal. Takeover defenses can be as simple as a major shareholder or group of shareholders refusing to sell under any conditions, the existence of buy-sell agreements, loan covenants or "poison pill" provisions, any of which can be difficult to overcome. Takeover barriers usually are designed to protect the perceived interests of controlling owners, entrenched management or creditors rather than the business, minority shareholders, employees or customers. In early discussions an investor should determine the presence of any barriers and assess the difficulty and cost of their removal or circumvention. They can be deal killers.

The departure of key employees can devastate a business. In industries such as securities and real estate, the problem of "big producers" departing one firm and taking customers to a competitor or starting a new firm is ever present and well publicized but the possibility is prevalent in nearly all industries. Personal relationships with customers constitute one of the most important assets of a business that are automatically taken by departing employees. In addition to customers, resigning executives may have a "following" of able junior executives. Engineering personnel and scientists may take not only subordinates but critical technology.

The entrance of a new owner or major investor may incite key employees to consider their alternatives. The loss of an important executive is serious, but if enough employees or customers depart with him it can be a calamity. So many businesses have experienced severe damage of this sort that an investor should in all cases assess its probability and devise means to prevent or mitigate its occurrence. The earlier in the due diligence process the risk is identified and assessed, the easier it will be to take measures to retain key employees.

To encourage investors and attempt to justify a high price, management may take steps producing short-term positive effects upon the financial statements. Usually these moves cannot be sustained permanently and are detrimental over the long term. Among the more common schemes are accelerating income, reduction in normal maintenance and repair expenditures, reduction in necessary capital expenditures, salary freezes or reductions, bonus plan revisions, revisions of benefit plans, sales of assets and termination of employees. Programs to improve appearances are likely to be initiated without publicity or explanation and result in vigorous employee opposition and dissatisfaction. While some programs can be justified as good business practices long overdue, those that cannot be sustained or are detrimental to the business should be viewed for what they are—efforts to deceive an investor. Once an investor senses the existence of any programs to improve appearances, all aspects of the program must be identified and quantified and long-term damage evaluated.

More serious is the discovery of gross improprieties such as illegal activities, deceitful accounting, dishonesty and rapacious management practices. An investor should assume that the presence of one such incident indicates there is a high probability of more, and ask himself, "Why get involved?"

Investors often have predetermined investment criteria designed to limit their investments to those with desirable characteristics. While the criteria can be anything an investor believes important, characteristics frequently mentioned are type of business, size, location, industry, technology level, profitability, management talent and continuity, management investment and acceptable financial ratios. Whatever their criteria, investors at this stage should decide before spending further time and money on a due diligence study whether the available data indicates the investment meets their criteria and if not, are they prepared to ignore their standards.

In nearly all deals, the investor enters with the expectation the business can improve and steps will be taken to ensure improvement. If the investor's plans include management or capital additions or a merger of operations, then the investment may be predicated upon achieving significant expense reductions. These may be financial, such as lower interest rates, taking discounts, or realizing better prices by eliminating indirect vendor financing. Other major savings may be anticipated by consolidating facilities, operations and marketing and making long-delayed, difficult decisions. If the investment concept involves expense reductions, the due diligence program should include identification of the expense reductions and quantifying each.

CHAPTER 7

Capital Structure and Ownership

A basic part of any due diligence program is to determine how the business is legally and financially structured and who owns each unit. An investor must know what he is buying, whom he is buying it from and who makes the key decisions. This should be confirmed for each legal entity under consideration, including subsidiaries, joint ventures, partnerships and other business entities. The legal structures may be simple and uncomplicated or complex with multiple classes of securities and debt instruments, each of which has its own rights and obligations. Ownership may be obvious or intricate, difficult to determine and in some cases mysterious.

There are two appropriate, revealing follow-up questions relative to structure and ownership issues: why and/or how. Insight can be gained by probing to learn the factors, rationale or chance events that led to current conditions. For example, why is this a corporation rather than a limited partnership? Why are 20 million common shares of stock authorized and only 1 million issued? Why were preferential rights granted to the share-holders? How many shares were acquired for the employee stock owner-ship plan (ESOP) and why not more or less? By asking such "how" or "why" follow-up questions, the investigator will pursue information in greater depth.

Questions on the legal structure, ownership and control should come early in the due diligence process, since serious issues may emerge requiring resolutions before a deal can proceed. A buy-sell agreement may emerge. A major shareholder may not be committed to the deal. Conversion rights could exist that make the transaction impractical. Dissidents may oppose any transaction supported by the majority. There are endless possible own-ership and control problems.

For every business, documents describing the legal structure should exist and must be located and reviewed. Usually, this will be the charter and bylaws for a corporation, while partnerships will have partnership agreements. Proprietorships have little or no documentation beyond what is necessary for tax purposes. Divisions and product lines are not legal entities in themselves but are parts of a business and are owned by some type of parent organization. In transactions involving divisions or product lines it is necessary to know the parent's legal structure to discern where decisions are made. The capital structure can be extremely varied, but nearly all corporations have common stock. If the business is audited, the annual report will state the number and type of common shares authorized, issued and held as treasury shares. Multiple classes of common stock with differing voting rights designed to concentrate control may exist. If treasury shares exist, the circumstances of their origin should be determined. Reports of the types of securities and number issued that appear in audit reports will not reflect changes since the reports were issued.

If the company's common shares are publicly traded, the price and volume history will be of intense interest. Volume is the number of shares traded in a period of time. Daily reports of price and volume should be recorded as soon as there is the slightest interest in the company. Historical and current data are available from various computer services, simplifying this task. Graphs are helpful to identify unusual activity, with average weekly and monthly trends often more enlightening than daily activity.

Most corporations have only common stock and institutional debt, but some have a whole array of securities including bonds and debentures whose terms and covenants can be bewildering. The title of any security should not be used as a guide to its nature. The underlying documents that established the security should be requested and reviewed. These will describe the security holders' rights and restrictions affecting the conduct of the business. The security documents have almost certainly been written some time ago by outside professionals and probably only a few executives, possibly none, are familiar with their contents.

The existence of any of these securities can affect the investor's entire strategy and the structure of the transaction. Control may very well rest with the holders of securities other than common stock. Under certain conditions seats on the board of directors or full control may have been ceded to holders of any type of security or debt instrument. Conversion rights may be attached to preferred stock, bonds or debentures as an inducement to investors and because the business expected eventually to exchange the fixed obligations of dividends or interest for the more variable obligations of common stock.

Private sales or gifts of unregistered securities of public or private companies may have occurred. The procedures and restrictions on ownership changes of unregistered securities are proscribed by law with legal assistance often required to consummate sales. Although these transactions may not directly involve the company, the company should be aware of their occurrence because of the necessity to change the names on the securities and revise company records. The extent of private sales and the prices paid will give an investor insight into the value some shareholders have attached to their shares and may reveal programs to accumulate shares. Litigation can easily result if someone with confidential knowledge of an investor's intentions unfairly buys shares in private transactions from shareholders who have no such knowledge.

In the early stages of negotiations it is only necessary to know the large shareholders or owners, but eventually a complete, current list must be obtained. Management may be reluctant to provide the list in hostile situations or before convinced the deal will transpire. If there are securities outstanding other than common shares, the key holders should be identified and complete lists requested. They may be a totally different group from the holders of the common shares and have investment objectives and views that diverge drastically. The extent to which holders of these securities can influence or even control the deal needs to be evaluated and a strategy developed.

Early identification of securities held by trusts, estates and institutions is helpful, since their sale will be approved and controlled by individuals who have fiduciary responsibilities. They may be trust officers, executors, fund managers or foundation board members, all of whom are concerned to protect themselves. They may demand evidence that an offer is proper, and before releasing the securities, require formal fairness opinions or other evidence of the fairness of the proposed transaction. If there are hard-to-find or unknown shareholders, plans should be made to find, bypass or structure the transaction to accommodate their absence.

Most businesses have policies relative to the amounts paid in dividends. These may range from informal and unwritten policies to the precisely written and frequently publicized. A closely controlled company may have only a practice of reviewing accumulated profits and paying those in control what they need and/or want. The other extremes are a public company that has a policy of no dividends and none planned or one in which dividends have always been paid and are increased regularly. The dividend history and outlook is particularly important to an investor in negotiating the transaction. Current holders of securities who have been paid dividends or interest will compare amounts received with income under a new proposal. They will expect the new proposal to be superior.

A business that has had or is having severe financial problems may be unable or may refuse to pay interest on debt and/or forego dividends. The consequences may be known immediately or may be difficult to determine. Unpaid interest usually remains a legal obligation until paid or renegotiated. Unpaid dividends remain an obligation if the securities have cumulative provisions. A business has defaulted on its debt or security agreements when it fails to comply with any of the covenants proscribed in the agreements or their amendments, not just repayment schedules. The covenants can cover almost any subject the originators of the agreement believed necessary to comfort the lender or securities investor. Examples are: collateral, liquidation rights, maintenance of the certain financial ratios, minimum current assets and prohibitions on changes of control. Covenants may restrict control of the business to the existing management, prevent the sale of new shares or sale of shares by individual shareholders. They may also allow security holders, upon default, to elect members to the board or take control of the business.

The due diligence tasks are to identify covenants and defaults and evaluate the consequences, including actions creditors or security holders have taken or threatened. Are they aggressive in pursuing their rights or docile, patient and sympathetic to the business's problems? What is required to cure the default or void onerous restrictions?

OWNERS' RIGHTS

In closely held private businesses, it is not uncommon to have an agreement with all or some of the shareholders or partners to repurchase their interests in the event of termination of employment, retirement or death. The price to be paid is usually based upon a predetermined formula, although it is nearly impossible to construct a formula that all parties will consider fair at time of repurchase. Closely held businesses often have buy-back agreements for the major shareholder financed by key man insurance policies. Partnerships and employee-owned professional service businesses have such arrangements, created with the intent of maintaining control of the company by repurchasing shares of departing employees and then making the shares available for purchase by new employees. Over a period of time, and particularly if the company grows and prospers, repurchase obligations may become impossible to fulfill and younger employees may not have the money or desire to purchase shares.

Repurchase obligations have been granted for other reasons in both public and private companies. They may be part of a compensation program for senior executives or a recruitment inducement. Prior owners of an acquired company may have accepted stock with a minimum price guaranteed. Often the guaranteed minimum price buy-back obligation is granted with the expectation that the market price will rise and the buy-back right will not be exercised.

Preferential rights and "buy-sell" agreements are rights of existing shareholders to first purchase the shares of other shareholders or new securities of the company before any outsider or third party can acquire the shares. The right to purchase new securities is a safeguard against dilution of ownership. In private companies the business may have an obligation to repurchase shares either before they are offered to shareholders or in the event no shareholder desires to purchase the shares.

For an investor, the existence of repurchase, buy-sell or preferential rights agreements may create a major roadblock and the agreements must be voided to permit the transaction. Due diligence investigators, upon confirming their existence, should seek copies of the documents and begin a search for remedies.

Stock repurchase programs are ones in which a company buys its own stock either on the open market or privately. Objectives may vary substantially but may include: accumulation of shares to be used in acquisition programs; backup for executive compensation programs and investing surplus earnings to enhance the shares' value. In closely held companies the controlling shareholders may arrange for the company to buy back shares of minority holders to increase their own percent of ownership. Any repurchase of stock in a private transaction that is not priced at a fair market value is an invitation to litigation. An investor must ascertain the reasons for any recent repurchases and verify the price rationale.

Any change in the number of shares authorized, issued or in treasury stock represents activity of which the investor should be aware. Changes may indicate repurchase or resale activity, major revisions in company policies, new financing, preparation for new programs or efforts to provide generous benefits to employees, friends or shareholders. In any due diligence investigation, whether in public or private companies, determination of the reasons for each change is essential.

Employee stock ownership plans—ESOPs—require intense due diligence. Established and regulated by federal law, they are conceived to promote employee ownership. The assumption was that ownership would better distribute capitalism's bounty and make more loyal and dedicated employees. However, concern for employee welfare is rarely the primary reason companies establish an ESOP. There are many problems associated with ESOPs, such as improper valuation of the stock, lack of liquidity of the shares received, cost of repurchasing shares and lack of voting rights by employees while the stock is in the trust. The most troublesome problems for an investor center around valuation of the shares.

Shares held by ESOPs of public companies are valued at market but shares of private companies must be valued periodically by a business appraiser. Business appraisals are highly subjective and it is common to find extraordinarily high values that benefit, at least initially, those who control the business and who sold the original block of stock to set up the plan, and those who employed the appraiser. Shareholders frequently come to believe the theoretical business appraisals that become guidelines for the price they expect to receive in a sale of the entire business. The investor should request a copy of the last appraisal conducted. If it has an inflated conclusion, it may create a serious impediment to realistic negotiations and efforts will have to be made to discredit the appraisal. If realistic, it can provide valuable information to the investor and price guidelines for the negotiations.

OTHER FACTORS INFLUENCING OWNERS

It would be a rare business in which all shareholders and employees were fully satisfied with management's policies or the business's performance. The dissenters' views may be valid or result from ignorance of all the facts, desire for political power, concerns over self interests or a myriad of other factors. Serious open or near-open controversy is an indication of low morale. The due diligence task is to sort out normal grousing from debilitating conflict and controversy.

The immediate concern is whether the dissenters hinder, prevent, make much more costly or unattractive the contemplated transaction. The investor must decide if the problems associated with the controversies are so severe that he does not want to become involved. Or, will the investment in itself resolve the conflicts (management or dissenters will be out) or can the investor settle the conflicts over time and bring harmony and teamwork to the business?

Dissention often surfaces at shareholder meetings that range from no meeting in some closely held private companies to elaborate, theatrical productions in public companies. They may be uneventful or arenas for rancorous controversy and suspenseful drama. Planning for the annual meetings may be non-existent or be in tedious detail for all contingencies and with every participant's words and actions in a prepared script. The CEO may view the annual meeting as no more than a legally required nuisance or the most stressful event of the year. Whatever occurred at previous meetings will provide insight into the company. Minutes are important to review but discussions with participants are more enlightening. Internal controversies, the interest or lack of interest by shareholders, management's attitude toward shareholders and data, plans, explanations and excuses developed by management may be revealed.

The strategy and pricing by an investor will have to take into account the original costs for the potential sellers. The maximum price an investor can pay will be heavily influenced by his expectations for the business when it is under his control. The sellers will have in their minds what they originally paid and their alternatives. For many sellers, the cost of their investment is the most important factor. In most cases, original cost constitutes the tax basis for the seller. Amounts received over the tax base will be taxed as a capital gain and amounts received under the tax base will be a capital loss. Sellers tend to look carefully at what will remain after taxes are paid. An investor is naive if he believes a seller's perceptions and tax problems are exclusively the seller's. These factors often determine if there will be a deal at all.

Public companies or companies about to go public with their shares may employ specialists internally and/or hire outside financial public relations firms to both keep the public and investment community apprised of the company's achievements and rationalize its shortcomings. More cynical observers refer to such programs as "hyping the stock." The extent and effectiveness of a financial PR program can vary widely from largely ineffective to having a major impact. A financial PR program's existence should alert an investor to evaluate its purposes and effectiveness and determine if the PR people could be enlisted by management to rebuff the outside investor or assist in smoothing the way.

Unless the business has only a few shareholders, some means, either formal or informal, will exist to keep the shareholders informed. This may center around annual reports, shareholders' meetings, quarterly reports or other information that management provides. Shareholders want to know how their investments are faring; if not kept informed, they will be calling individually for answers. Public companies may provide periodic presentations and submit to grillings by security analysts. Security analysts are not always respected by management for their ability and perceptiveness but they are very much respected for their ability to write reports that impact the business's share price. The system of shareholders' communications in all aspects needs to be understood by an investor, since this system may be used in assisting or thwarting any transaction contemplated. It may also be a candidate for expense reduction, as is financial PR.

Due diligence must include a history and understanding of any stock option plans. Often the individuals who can decide or influence whether the proposed transaction occurs or who can determine the future success of the business hold stock options. If a stock option plan exists, the investor must study the plan and its outstanding options. How these shares will be treated under the contemplated transaction can be a major cost item for the investor and a matter of intense interest for the options' holders. Generous treatment of the outstanding options may be essential to gain support for the deal.

Another group whose members can control the deal is the board of directors. If a corporation is to be sold, merged or debt incurred, the board of directors will be involved and its support essential. Due diligence must confirm who the board members are and examine their backgrounds, compensation and role. The better understood their influence, motivation and reasons for being on the board, the better chance an investor has to receive their approval. Board members normally are elected by the stockholders for a specific term. Staggered voting occurs when the terms of all directors do not expire simultaneously. If the proposed transaction is at all controversial, the duration of opposing directors' terms and what it takes to vote them out may be critical information. How and why members were selected for the board, including who initiated their nomination, is information helpful in assessing their independence.

Frequency of meetings often indicates the involvement and strength of the board in overseeing the affairs of the business and its possible role in major transactions. Some boards never meet, some only when necessary and others regularly in addition to special meetings. In many closely held corporations, board meetings, if held at all, tend to be more social events to confirm what already has been decided. Public companies tend to have regular board meetings, but this is hardly universal.

For some the status of being a director would be adequate compensation, but most receive remuneration. An investor must weigh the price of compensation and benefits to each director as well as possible expense reductions if they are eliminated. Directors in closely held companies may receive little or no compensation, but in some instances overly large compensation and benefits are paid to major shareholder directors and even their relatives. In public companies director compensation can range from token to extraordinarily generous amounts. While there is some correlation between size of a company and director remuneration, there are such extreme variations that an investor should make no assumptions and secure the actual amounts. An obvious concern is whether the potential loss of the compensation could influence a director's judgment in supporting or opposing the proposed transaction. The direct compensation, fringe benefits and status may be very dear to a director and offsetting or continuing compensation and titles may be necessary.

The extent of the board's participation in the business's affairs indicates its interest and involvement in the proposed transaction. However, the role in actually discussing, evaluating and making decisions can vary widely from nonexistent to total control. In a company dominated by a strong shareholder and/or CEO, board members may be passive, have little actual knowledge of the business and care less. They are along for the ride. For inside (employee) directors, the directorship is an adjunct to their regular jobs in which they are subordinate to the CEO. However, the board may play a very independent and active role in forcing policy and management changes. For most companies, the actual role of the board of directors is unknown except to the participants.

Larger and more active boards appoint committees to review and make recommendations in specific areas of business. The audit committee works with outside auditors and is concerned about internal controls. The compensation committee recommends salaries for executives and compensation plans, including stock option and retirement programs. If any committees exist, the investor will want to secure copies of any of their formal reports and recommendations. These may prove to be confidential and difficult to procure. Members of the board appointed to head committees are often the stronger, more active and influential members.

Lawsuits have proliferated against boards for their actions or mere participation and the exposure is so ominous that few nominees will participate without protection from personal liability. This protection is usually in the form of insurance and indemnity agreements provided by the company. The magnitude of the insurance coverage, strength of the insurance carrier and financial capability of the company determine the actual amount of protection. The probability of litigation increases if the board is split into factions, engaged in/or the subject of a controversial acquisition or the company has severe financial problems. The amount of personal liability protection board members have can influence their willingness to support or resist a controversial proposal. As part of the transition, decisions are required as to what directors' insurance, if any, will be continued after an acquisition.

It's essential for a new owner to take total control of a corporation's subsidiaries. Subsidiaries must have boards of directors, and while frequently without actual authority or responsibility, they do have the same legal responsibilities and liabilities as do the directors of independent corporations. However, in corporations that advocate decentralized management control, the subsidiary boards may be given considerable authority and encouraged to act as an independent board. These board members are usually employees and too much independence may be perilous to their careers.

Whenever there are business units less than fully owned by the business being considered for investment, complete information on the other owners is important. They may be valuable assets and opportunities for greatly expanded business relationships. Or they may be passive investors with little interest in the business and possibly willing to sell their ownership position. They also may be difficult partners of low reputation and any association would be troublesome. A new investor will automatically acquire a business relationship with whomever they may be.

The rights of the other shareholders or partners will be determined by the percent of their ownership position, any agreements that may have been negotiated and applicable statutes and regulations protecting their rights. If the other shareholders own a majority, then the new investor should be concerned with his rights and liabilities as a minority holder. The nature of the relationship with other owners requires particular attention. Is it one of cooperation, passivity, hostility or embarrassment?

CHAPTER 8

Management

Management built the business, operates the business today, and will manage the business in the future. These simple truths should be foremost in the mind of any investor. Due diligence activity relative to management consists primarily of identification of executives and professionals in positions of substantial responsibility, determining their total compensation and associated expenses and, most importantly, evaluating their competence and potential. Current and anticipated vacancies must also be identified.

Management is usually viewed as a group or team, but any study will focus on individual members and team vacancies. The future role for each member of the current team will require decisions after review of their responsibilities, estimates of potential and, not to be overlooked, the individual's wishes. No due diligence should be considered complete or adequate without personal interviews.

Identification of key management members is a critical first step, but not always a simple one. Officers may not be key employees and key employees may not be officers, because job titles can be misleading. Some companies have both a chairman of the board and a president with either one CEO and the other's job poorly defined. Some businesses have few officers, while in others, such as financial institutions, there may be a large number. Key employees who are not officers, such as managers of important divisions, may have greater responsibility than all officers other than the president. There may be executives with officers' titles who are not formally elected officers, such as division presidents. Compensation may not always indicate importance to the business, since shareholdings, age, former positions and relationships influence compensation. Formal job descriptions cannot be relied upon to learn the true nature of an executive's job. The diversity is so great among businesses that all factors must be considered to sort out the management team.

When determining and evaluating officers' and key employees' compensation and perquisites, assume nothing and don't be surprised by anything. Past compensation history is important, but far more important are present levels and future compensation commitments. A good place to start is with employment agreements, if they exist, although these are often incomplete or out-of-date. Board of director's minutes may contain records of approved compensation plans. Proxy statements should contain helpful information. Accounting and payroll records can confirm cash payments. Incentive plans, stock options and deferred compensation plans further complicate the task. Retirement and generous severance pay benefits can represent large financial commitments that may or may not be funded. Direct questioning of the key employees may be the only way to learn the total package.

An investor must know precisely the outstanding compensation commitments, to decide if they are acceptable. Excessive compensation may be rationalized as part of the price in acquisition-pricing calculations. However, compensation may be so large and inconsistent with the investor's thinking that a deal is impossible. All continuing compensation must be included in the investor's pro forma projections.

The total cost of an executive may surprise everyone, including the executive. There is a tendency to view an executive's cost only in terms of salary and bonus while other expenses are ignored. Accounting systems (often with the blessing of the executives) may contribute to this blurring or concealment of costs by not isolating all costs associated with an executive. Travel and entertainment expenses, secretarial services, bonuses and benefits, chauffeurs and administrative assistants are all added expenses. Total costs permit savings calculations if the position is eliminated or the executive replaced by a less expensive person.

Executive vacancies and turnover or lack of such are informative. Rare openings and few management changes may indicate a stable, well-functioning team or ossification protected by excessive security. Management changes may reflect failed performance or simple replacement of a retiring executive. Changes may result from conflicts within the organization, reorganizations to accommodate growth or downsizing, policy revisions and new business directions. Open positions may have been of short duration and easily filled or of such demanding specifications that compromises were necessary. An investor will gain insight into the management by reviewing the past job vacancies, why they occurred and why the individual chosen to fill a position was selected. Was it ability, nepotism or just convenience? Regardless of the past, current and projected management vacancies are most important to the investor.

Filling executive vacancies through internal promotions is desirable but not always practical. In larger businesses, this is easier to accomplish because of formalized programs for identifying and grooming successors from larger pools of executives. Small businesses cannot afford a stable of promotable individuals and must resort to hiring. Since businesses are so dependent upon management, an investor must evaluate his options to fill vacancies. Obviously, if there is depth in management and employees promotable to fill key positions, an investor's risk is minimal. Without depth or identified available outside prospects, the risk is much greater.

The chief executive officer may be a controversial executive with doubtful tenure or of such stature that he is the principal asset. Regardless, the CEO's opinion of the performance and potential of subordinates will be of value in assessing management and recommending promotions. The CEO knows their strengths and idiosyncrasies and has observed their ability to work as part of the management team. His opinions may not always be accurate but they certainly should not be ignored. The investor should guard against overly grand evaluations when the CEO is promoting the transaction. For such CEOs, everyone is a star.

Nepotism is the employment of relatives or close friends. Some businesses employ no relatives and have formal policies prohibiting their employment. Others have an abundance of relatives, particularly in closely held companies. There are questions that need to be addressed if relatives are employed. Are these employees productive and compensated consistently with wages paid others? Were they employed only because they were relatives? Are they resented by other employees? Are they voting shareholders? Are they united or split with independent views? An investor must consider what happens to the relatives if the transaction is completed. Will they leave en masse, seriously damaging the business? Will it be possible to terminate unproductive and/or over-compensated relatives without losing the remainder? The existence of a large number of relatives, or relatives in key executive positions, should cause any investor ample reason to review his plans. The risks may be too great.

Another risk is in the form of executives who could destroy the business if they left on a hostile basis with a determination to settle old scores. They could become active competitors, hire away key employees and take key clients or customers. Hostile former employees can display a devastating vengeance against which it is difficult to defend. Employment agreements are of some value and under certain circumstances, depending upon the state, legal action may be possible. The investor should recognize the possibility of his actions creating such a monster. A hostile executive may already exist but the investor should do all he can to avoid creating his own.

Many businesses are so dependent upon one individual that if the key employee became inactive for any reason, the business would be severely damaged or possibly have to be liquidated. The smaller the business, the greater the possibility of this condition. However, larger businesses are at risk whenever the CEO is a dominant executive with weak subordinates and no successors. It can also occur when an engineer or scientist has all the key technology in his head. An executive's importance may be exaggerated or a belief may exist that anyone can be replaced, but these thoughts are perilous to an investor. But there are defenses. Key man life insurance, which is available and relatively inexpensive, would help the investor recover his investment in the event of death or disability. Employment agreements can lock in a critical executive for a period of time by providing both an incentive to stay and penalties for leaving. One of the soundest defenses is to groom a backup, if the business can afford the individual. Reorganization, to make the business less dependent upon one individual, is another alternative worth consideration.

QUESTIONABLE EXPENSES

Employees at all levels who are employed part-time may be paid fairly and their expenses fully justified. However, there may be officers, wives of officers, relatives, retired employees, disabled employees, employees on lengthy termination pay plans, children of major shareholders and officers "working" their way through college, children of major customers and cronies of executives paid on a part-time basis. Some may fully earn their compensation but others constitute an unnecessary expense and/or technique for taking income from the business as a pretax expense.

Employees on government payrolls because of political influence who perform little or no work or never show up are called "payrollers." Private industry has its share of "payrollers" thanks to the power of controlling shareholders or key executives. These may be relatives, cronies or professionals who occasionally assist key executives in their personal affairs. However, inactive individuals may be on the payroll for more valid reasons. Terminated employees may be receiving substantial separation pay paid on a regular basis rather than by lump sum. Employees no longer active or beneficiaries of deceased employees may receive pay under employment contracts. Professionals may receive fees for past services paid monthly rather than by lump sum. If companies have been acquired, part of the consideration may have been consulting or employment contracts in which it was understood the employee would not actually work. The investor's task is to identify inactive individuals receiving compensation and determine which represent unnecessary expense, when the expense is scheduled to end and which can be terminated.

Concurrent with a search for phantom employees should be checking for excess compensation. Excessive compensation is difficult to define but, like pornography, you know it when you see it. The most common form of excess compensation is the amount paid to owner/managers in closely held businesses to avoid the double taxation associated with dividends. Excessive compensation, in the opinion of most investors, occurs when someone

is paid substantially in excess of what it would cost to employ a replacement. The nature of commitments to continue the level of compensation,
renegotiate the pay or even to terminate the individual should all be evaluated.

Officers and key employees may devote large amounts of time to non-
business activities. Any recreational activity can become obsessive, such as
golf or hunting, and non-profit organizations and charitable groups always
need talented individuals to serve on their boards. Executives may devote
excessive time to personal investments and directorships. The investor
should determine how unrelated activity affects both an executive's and the
business's performance. Has it been a costly luxury for the business, has it
had no effect, or even been beneficial? If the contemplated transaction is
completed, can the business tolerate the expense and diversion of time?
Would the activity be an embarrassment to the business if it became widely
known? Whatever the outside activity, the executive will probably be reluctant to give it up and has rationalized it as desirable for the business or
part of his compensation package.

Conflicts of interest are not always detrimental to the business or illegal,
but they are suspect and must be identified. A business all or partly owned
by shareholders, officers or employees who sell products or services to the
business being studied is the most common conflict. The relationship may
be totally open with all transactions on an "arm's length" basis, or highly
secretive and totally non-competitive. The more secretive it is, the more
suspicious it is. Property sales and leases either to or from the business can
be sources of conflict. Co-investments in which the business financed another business in which insiders have invested may represent serious conflicts.

Conflicts of interest are not confined to senior executives. The person
charged with selling scrap may have his brother-in-law in the scrap business
or the office manager may buy forms from a printing company in which
he has an interest. All such conflicts must be evaluated. Some may prove
to be highly desirable and should be retained while others cancelled with
the beneficial effect included in pro forma forecasts. Some may not adversely affect the business but yet have to be terminated to avoid the appearance of impropriety. Some, if threatened with cancellation or exposure,
could kill the deal.

Executive perquisites, or "perks," may be standard benefits of limited
interest in the form of insurance, automobiles or the occasional combination of business trips with vacations. However, there is a nearly endless list
of perks management may provide itself that are out of the ordinary. Excessive perks are costly and become the subject of IRS claims and/or used
as fodder in shareholder controversies and lawsuits. Household expenses,
airplanes for personal use, frequent trips to golf tournaments and other
sporting events, boats, executive dining rooms, family automobiles, extra

apartments or other residences, legal, medical and financial services, loans and the financing of personal hobbies or interests are all perks subject to criticism. Hunting and fishing camps, lodges, ski lodges and airplanes may have value to a business but also become coveted perks. Entertaining of customers at recreational facilities is a proven means of securing business, and customers come to expect annual invitations in exchange for their business. However, some facilities are used exclusively by senior executives or nearly exclusively with only a few token customers or business acquaintances invited to justify the facility cost as a tax deductible business expense.

The use of private aircraft by executives should be studied to determine business need and hours flown for personal use. This may prove difficult because of problems associated with separating business from personal travel. Complicating the study will be executives' love of private airplanes and potential IRS interest. In any event, the costs and benefits of private aircraft are complex problems.

All perks should be identified, their costs estimated and benefits to the business measured, if possible. As part of the due diligence, losses to the business if the perks are modified or discontinued must also be considered. An investor may find certain perks unnecessary or even offensive, but should assess potential damage to the business before cancellation. Of course, some investors will look forward to taking over the perks for themselves.

In closely held businesses it is extremely common for bonuses to be paid to shareholder executives instead of dividends, to avoid the tax on business profits. What is a reasonable bonus and what is a device for avoidance of corporate tax is not easy to define or establish. A murky line lies between the two, complicated by IRS regulations on excess compensation. The investor must decide future policy with regard to bonuses to negotiate the investment. A calculation to estimate the difference between amounts paid shareholder executives and what would have been paid to non-shareholders performing the same roles should be used in calculating true earnings.

Reorganization of the management structures is in response to perceived problems, either existing or anticipated. They usually are touted by those responsible as great improvements and may very well be. However, it is well to remember the writings attributed to Petronious in 210 B.C. "We trained hard, but it seemed that every time we were beginning to form up into teams we would be reorganized. I was to learn late in life that we tend to meet any new situation by reorganizing, and a wonderful method it can be for creating the illusion of progress while producing confusion, inefficiency, and demoralization."

Due diligence should disclose the problems and reasons for any reorganization. Were the problems delayed, aggravated or solved? Who were the winners and losers? Are the losers still about and resisting? Major reorganizations can be traumatic for a business and no investor should be satisfied until the impact is assessed. Don't forget, those who originated the reorganization are the survivors who may be reluctant to describe shortcomings. If reorganizations are in progress or contemplated, identify the causative problems. Equally important, learn management's philosophy or principles to determine if they are compatible.

The reputation of management in a business should be evaluated separately from that of the business. The business may enjoy an excellent reputation independent from management or the reverse may be true. However, the longer management has been in office, the more identical will be the reputations. Queries to employees may be helpful but customers, suppliers and competitors are most revealing. A search of newspapers and trade magazines can be enlightening.

From the investor's viewpoint the question is, to what degree do reputations benefit, damage or have no effect? The reputation of management and the business, whether fair, unfair, deserving or inaccurate, can affect its success. It is what customers and clients believe to be true that influences their decisions, not what is true. An investor is buying the existing reputations and the task is to preserve and enhance the desirable and take measures to correct the unsatisfactory.

CHAPTER 9

Products and Services

Comprehensive due diligence requires gauging the importance of products and services to the business. Public perceptions and initial impressions often deviate from reality because many businesses are best known for activity representing only a small fraction of their total business. Extensive promotion of new products thought to have great potential catches the public eye but today may have minimal revenues or serious quality problems. A business may have a famous name, but the products or services that brought the name into prominence may have long since been replaced. Use of trade names and private label manufacturing contributes to misconceptions. Actual amounts and proportions of sales revenues and operating profits for each product line within a business may prove to be a real surprise. Product line operating income is rarely in direct proportion to sales revenues.

What constitutes a product line or category of service will be defined by the business, its organizational structure and its accounting system. The more detailed the breakdown by product segment, the more valuable the information to an investor. However, the existing accounting system that tends to track the organizational structure will largely determine the product breakdown possible. In many businesses this is sales revenue without calculation of separate operating profits. At some point the cost of calculating profits for each small segment of a business, plus the uncertainty caused by the subjective nature of overhead allocations, discourages detailed accounting. The result can be highly profitable or very unprofitable product lines or product line segments concealed in a broad financial report.

An investor will likely have to accept whatever product or service breakdowns are contained in the financial statement. However, additional product information may exist in accountants' work papers or reports utilized internally by management. Special studies of product line profitability may have been conducted and copies of the studies should be requested. The investor, by one means or another, must learn the business's true nature and the financial performance of each segment. He may be forced to construct his own profitability studies.

Remaining market life and growth potential are of critical importance in evaluation of products and services. Unfortunately, estimates of both are always subjective but essential for forecasts. All one has to do is look about to confirm that virtually no products have either definite market lives or unlimited growth potential. Taste and technology cause constant changes. Another problem in estimates is that a product may have the same use that it did 50 years ago, yet is today vastly different. Automobiles are an obvious example. What was the market life or growth potential of a Model-T Ford?

The investor should be particularly concerned with short market lives of products resulting from fads or fashion. Will it be possible to recover the investment with the existing products or services? Is there time to accomplish redesigns or add new technology before sales decline? When will the growth in sales cease? The ability of the business in such markets to quickly design and develop new products is of paramount importance. The past record should be insightful to the investor.

Technological obsolescence is not limited to the invention of a product that obsoletes all existing products such as regularly occurs in the electronics industry. It can include the advent of low-cost manufacturing processes, new materials or even innovative low-cost distribution, any of which could destroy a competitor. An investor's concern is whether technological innovations introduced either by the business under study or a competitor obsoletes existing products or services. If such threats exist, can the business effectively respond?

There are marketing and strategic reasons to discontinue products or services, but low or nonexistent profitability is the most common. Most managements are well aware of the product lines or services that are candidates to be phased out. They usually have been under study and the decision may already have been made. The investor may have different views from management on what should be discontinued and the effect upon financial projections.

Businesses engaged in leasing are of necessity involved in eventually selling the products leased. Sales may be to lessees or to anyone willing, as is the case in the rental car business. "Involuntary conversions" are required purchases of leased assets by a customer who damaged or destroyed the asset, usually through his own negligence. Involuntary conversions of well-depreciated assets may constitute windfall level profits, since the customer is usually charged replacement cost. Asset sales should be segregated from other revenues and income to properly understand the business. The sale of assets can easily become a major part of the business and in some businesses more important than the leasing itself. Asset sales may also be erratic and distort monthly financial reports, and thus complicate due diligence evaluation.

Due diligence demands careful investigation of all after-market sales in the form of parts, upgrades, service, enhancement and expendables. They easily may be the most important segments of a business. For most businesses, spare or replacement parts sales and service are extremely profitable, often commanding higher gross profits than the original product. The parts and service business not only can be profitable but essential for the original sale because few customers would buy if service was unavailable. The investor must fully understand the role of the parts and service business. What percent of revenues and profits do they contribute? Are sales increasing or decreasing? Have competitors entered into the business? Could the business be expanded? The investor may find one of the easiest ways to increase profits is to aggressively expand the parts and service business.

Expendables are products used only once or a very few times, such as hoses and filters in medical devices, vacuum cleaner trash bags and coffee filters. For some manufacturers, more income is realized from expendables than the original equipment and the challenge is to design equipment to retain the expendables after market and exclude competitors. For expendable manufacturers, the problem exists of creating, finding or maintaining a distribution system capable of servicing widely dispersed customers.

Products or services scheduled to be introduced should be at an advanced stage of planning or development to be credible. Managements usually have more ideas for new products or services than actual programs under way to bring them to market by a specific date. While dreams of possible new products or services are interesting and may have potential, what counts are the products and services for which planning and development is actually in progress.

Placing a value on products or services that have not reached the market is one of the more vexing problems in due diligence. Management's conviction of a product's value, augmented by originator or inventor enthusiasm, has to be balanced with the hard statistics showing that most new products fail. In an attempt to value a new product or service, the first step is to determine the probability of it actually being introduced. As a generality, the more remote the scheduled introduction date, the greater the probability it will not happen. All factors that may delay its introduction should be reviewed. A second step is to review studies and financial projections describing the market and potential. A third is for the investor to secure the opinions of knowledgeable individuals in his own organizations and, if necessary, of outside experts.

Due diligence should define and quantify continuing obligations of the business incurred through issuance of guarantees and warranties. Performance guarantees or warranties are provided to customers both to define the nature of the guarantee and to place specific limits on the guarantee. The terms "guarantee" and "warranty" are both used to indicate assurances and remedies relative to performance and quality. They essentially have identical meanings in this context. Guarantees are not limited to tangible products for parts and labor but may cover software systems, process specifications, level of workmen's performance, machine performance and any other characteristics important to a customer.

Written guarantees attempt to define the limit of the seller's obligation to perform and correct problems by describing (usually in written forms) precisely the nature of the guarantee. Businesses strive to limit their guarantees to that described in their written guarantees. Customer relations considerations may make it necessary to correct problems not covered by guarantees, if the customer is to be retained. Unusual or outrageous failures may result in litigation, regardless of the limiting language in a guarantee or warranty.

Service is the repair, maintenance or adjustment of products owned or leased by customers. Service may be all expense resulting from warranty obligations, or a profitable segment charging for service outside of warranty and for service of products manufactured by others. Service is an essential part of most manufacturing or distribution businesses and may be performed by employees or subcontracted. Additional broad questions should be whether service supports the marketing effort, what is its cost, is it profitable, how organized is it and can it be improved?

When quality products are sold, warranty costs and exposure is negligible, but they become extremely significant when repeated failures occur within a specified period of time following purchase or lease. For some businesses warranty costs are so low they are not even recorded as a separate expense on the financial statements. For others the cost is continual but at manageable levels and is recorded, making it possible to identify trends. To evaluate warranty expense and claims, the causes must be identified. Do they result from an expected and normal level of failures? Are they excessive and well above expectations? What corrective measures have been taken to reduce failures and claims? Is the warranty unreasonably generous and in excess of that provided by competitors? Are claims concentrated in one segment of the product line or in all? Are there many claims or a few for very large amounts? The answers to these questions should assist an investor in identifying the problems.

Claims paid and reported on financial statements only record history, while an investor's real concerns are known and unknown future costs. Will warranty costs remain constant and only fluctuate with sales revenues? Are there significant problems emerging that indicate an upsurge of expensive warranty claims? Suspected but difficult to quantify exposure can complicate the negotiations of the contemplated investment.

If warranty costs are fairly predictable over an entire year but erratic month to month, or an increase in exposure is likely, the business may establish a reserve on the financial statements to cover the expense. If there was a major product failure, a large, immediate reserve would be appropriate. The difficult question for the investor is whether reserves are adequate to cover probable costs. Start by requesting information on how reserves were calculated.

Seasonal factors have an enormous impact upon production and sales and must be recognized during the due diligence study. Monthly or any partial-year interim financial statements of seasonal companies are of limited value other than to compare with prior years. Some may only show profits a few months of the year. Fiscal year-end statements best indicate the business's overall profitability, but the balance sheets may be misleading. Depending upon the point in the seasonal cycle where the fiscal year ended, cash could be in excess with inventory and receivables at a low point or the reverse true. Seasonal businesses can be highly profitable, but an investor must understand that seasonal factors affect all aspects of the business and force management to focus on planning for the seasonal booms and mitigating losses off-season.

Many businesses' right to operate as a business are dependent upon government licenses and permits. Some may be readily attained but others only with great difficulty. The types of licenses and permits are endless and are issued at the federal, state, county and municipal level as well as by a multitude of agencies and regulatory bodies created at various levels of government. An investor must identify all licenses and permits required, determine if all are in effect and if any required have expired. The problem of renewal or securing new permits must also be assessed. In all cases the actual written permit should be reviewed, since it may be a conditional approval with severe limitations. The qualifications and conditions may be so complex and voluminous that expert assistance will be required to interpret the full meaning. Present relations with regulatory agencies is an indication of the difficulty to be experienced with renewals.

CHAPTER 10

R&D and Technology

Research and development (R&D) is defined by the U.S. Internal Revenue Service as:

research and development arising from laboratory or experimental procedures. It includes the cost of developing, or improving a product, a formula, an invention, a plant process, an experimental or pilot model, or something similar. It also includes the cost of any research or experimental work carried on for you by someone else (such as research institute, foundation, engineering company or similar contractor).

However, the terms R&D, research, development and design may have working definitions that vary from business to business and with the IRS. An understanding of how management defines the terms will avoid confusion during the due diligence study.

To evaluate the R&D effort, the historical and forecast costs should be equated with results, both actual and anticipated. "Results" are commercially profitable products or services. Projected costs to complete R&D projects in progress and the quantity and quality of proposals for new R&D projects should be part of the study. Evaluation may be difficult and require a team of technical, marketing and financial people to ask pertinent questions and comprehend the responses. R&D, by its very nature, represents the hopes and commitments of individuals and the business with the stakes very high. Since success or failure of R&D projects can easily influence careers, it is understandable that overly optimistic comments may abound from those involved.

Identify early the accounts in the financial statements recording R&D expenses. From these, both the amounts being spent and the subsidiary, division or other type profit or cost center in which R&D is conducted should be apparent. However, in small businesses and subsidiaries or divisions of large corporations, R&D expense may be buried in other accounts. Small businesses may not be concerned with precise accounting and subsidiaries or divisions may not want the parent aware of the R&D, for fear of disapproval. Early identification of costs, wherever they may be, will aid in keeping discussions realistic with members of management.

Most businesses actively engaged in R&D have budgets and written plans describing the overall R&D effort, specific R&D projects and stated objectives or goals. Prior years and current plans will be helpful in measuring success and evaluating the overall direction of the program. If the business does not have a formal plan but conducts R&D, the reasons for not having a plan should be explored while securing an oral description of whatever R&D is in progress.

A list of new or improved products, services or processes that resulted from the R&D program during the past three years should be requested. A comparison of R&D expenses to accomplishments and anticipated potential profits will give an investor some indication of the R&D program's contribution. Long-term potential for new products is never certain, but initial market acceptance is an indication.

The expense of current R&D programs is justified by the expectation of new or improved products, services or processes. Past glories and successes are an indication of competence, but neither guarantees the success of current projects nor justifies their cost. A list of the individual R&D projects or programs, along with their cost-estimated completion date and forecast revenues, should be compiled and the economic rationale evaluated. Comparisons are also possible with an investor's R&D program for consistency of objectives, synergy and possible duplication. If the new products or services replace existing products, a review of the program and cost to phase out the obsolete is appropriate.

When most R&D projects are initiated, a timetable is established with milestones for completion of certain phases as well as for the entire project. Other departments, such as manufacturing and marketing, plan their activities to coincide with the R&D timetable. Future products may be announced before all R&D is complete, to alert potential customers and dissuade them from buying from competitors. Early announcements are also used to influence security analysts and investors, but if schedules are not met the business's credibility, reputation and stock value suffer. A comparison of original scheduled completion dates for new products or services will provide insight into the R&D program's ability to meet future schedules. Any R&D project behind schedule is behind because something went wrong, and the investor should learn the causes, which may include mismanagement, technology more difficult than anticipated, unexpected or insurmountable problems or the fact that the original schedule was never realistic.

Along with dollars spent, the number of professional employees and the level of their education is important. The number of employees holding Ph.D.s tends to indicate a high level of original research or "state-of-the-art" activities. Professional and technical employees and scientists can be some of the business's most valuable assets missing from the balance sheet, and an asset that investors should be careful to preserve.

Commercial benefits of an R&D program may be in the form of royalties received by licensing its technology. The specific terms for the use of the technology and the amounts to be paid are found in licensing agreements that are usually lengthy, detailed and contain obligations for both parties. The investor should review the agreements and confirm the amount of licensing income, how long it will continue and whether it is expected to increase or decrease. If significant amounts are involved, the investor may want to contact licensees for their views and estimates of the level of future payments.

A business may enter into licensing agreements to gain access to the technology of others. Licensing technology is a means of avoiding R&D expense and securing technology not readily attainable by other means. The licensee's attitude toward a licensing agreement can vary from enthusiastic acceptance to resentment from the start, with studies to circumvent or "design around" the patent under way. All licensing agreements and their importance require evaluation.

Licenses in which the business may be either licensee or licensor may be essential to the business's success. As a licensor, the license revenues may account for a significant portion of income. As a licensee, the business may not be able to operate competitively without the technology. For these dependent businesses, a detailed study of the license documents and questions relative to the relationship between the parties to the license is essential. Is the relationship cordial and working effectively? Do both parties have the financial strength to continue in business? Do both parties enjoy material benefits from the license? Would either party be better off if the license was terminated? Since licenses eventually expire or have termination provisions, consideration should be given to when and what happens upon termination. Will it be catastrophic or immaterial?

Patents may be among the most valuable assets of a business. A business may own a large number of patents with only a handful of value and the remainder either expired or not commercial successes. One patent in a list of 100 can be more valuable than the other 99, and technical experts may be necessary to identify the valuable one. Particular attention should be given to the expiration date of important patents and the effect upon the business. Expiring patents can change the character of an industry.

A business may have exclusive use of a patent but not full ownership and royalty obligations, due to a variety of circumstances. The owner of the business may be the inventor and may have licensed his own business.

The business may have purchased or licensed rights to the patent from the inventor. The business may have a generous policy of rewarding employee inventors with royalty payments. As part of a prior acquisition, a portion of the price may have been structured as royalty payments. Whatever the reason, the documents granting the royalties should be reviewed and the investor made aware of the extent of the obligation.

Many businesses have had unhappy experiences with inventors as a result of agreements to develop and/or commercialize their inventions and pay royalties. The convictions of inventors of the viability and potential of their inventions may exceed reality. Inventors' claims that a business failed to properly develop the technology or vigorously market the invention are common. Whenever such disputes exist, an investor should be extremely wary. The disputes tend to end in litigation where the case becomes one of an individual inventor exploited by a rapacious business. Outrageous damages are normally claimed.

Certain R&D results cannot be commercialized without prior approval of a government agency. The most well-known is the Food and Drug Administration's (FDA) role in approving pharmaceuticals and medical devices, but many other agencies are involved in approving products and services. Approvals by government agencies may be difficult to secure and very slow to be issued. The business's prior experience in securing agency approvals is an indication of how realistic are management's predicted approval dates. Financial projections of the business based upon an expected date of government approval should be viewed with skepticism.

U.S. government departments and agencies are the largest buyers of research from a variety of institutions, including for-profit businesses. Whenever government-funded research is present, there are certain basic due diligence issues and questions. How dependent is the business upon the government funds? When do the contracts expire or grants run out? Who receives patent rights? Is the research of real value and likely to be continued? Has it progressed to the commercialization phase? What is the relationship with the government agency providing funds? The critical answers an investor is seeking are the magnitude of the funding, probability of its continuance and prospects for future funding. Major investments based on anticipated but uncommitted government research funding are definitely of a high-risk nature.

R&D programs and trade secrets may represent assets of great value to be protected by security measures. The business's written and unwritten policies and practices relative to security should be reviewed, along with an estimate of the probability and potential damage to the business if security were breached. Security requirements coupled with management's fears may be so severe that only late in the investment process will the investor be provided with full information.

Trade secrets include not only R&D but customer lists, marketing data and manufacturing processes or systems, and all are subject to theft. Theft most commonly occurs when terminated employees take information to a competitor or start their own businesses rather than by industrial espionage involving professional spies. There is a limited market for trade secrets and, either for ethical reasons or fear of apprehension, most established businesses will not become involved. The amount of theft of trade secrets in the industry is an indication of whether the business being studied either has or may have a problem.

Accusations of theft of important trade secrets constitutes a grave situation. A recipient of trade secrets may cause great damage through their use but also may be subject to litigation to prevent their use, and forced to pay heavy monetary damages. Since thefts of trade secrets are such a serious matter, the existence of an accusation should cause an investor to be extremely wary. Until the matter is completely resolved, an investor may find it prudent to delay his final decision. Fortunately, these controversies are usually quickly resolved because the parties are well aware of the repercussions.

CHAPTER 11

Real Estate and Facilities

There are four general categories of real estate due diligence subjects: description and location, environmental, financial issues relative to costs and values and operational involving adequacy and continued availability. Unfortunately, opportunities for erroneous, misleading or withheld information, often totally unintentional, regularly occur to confuse or mislead an investor. Book values may have little relationship to true market value, which may in turn have little correlation with appraised values, whether tax, contemporary or anecdotal estimates. Known or unknown title defects may exist. Old photographs or descriptions may describe younger days rather than present conditions. Facilities may be underutilized, creating unwanted expenses, or be inefficiently crowded, necessitating a costly relocation or expansion. Additionally, leases may expire, forcing an unwanted move, or long-term leases may be a burden or of debatable value.

A visit to each facility and review of ownership or lease documents is highly desirable. Visits confirm prior information, provide information on maintenance upkeep, general condition of facilities, housekeeping, safety, type of neighborhood, appearance of employees and level of utilization. Leases, deeds, title insurance, contracts for leasehold improvements and other documents relating to real estate must be located and reviewed for defects and unusual provisions, and to verify basic information.

One business's real estate activity may be static with few past changes and none anticipated. But for others, there are constant requirements to sell existing and/or lease or build new space. Due diligence should not only identify the activity but evaluate the causes or need for each sale or new facility. The causes may reveal or confirm information about the business previously unknown or only suspected. The importance of any real estate for sale is a function of the size of the sale in relation to the business's size. The length of time the property has been for sale and the asking price should indicate its value. Property on the market for a long period is either overpriced or has very limited use. Activity, or lack of it, is a general indication of the probable value that may eventually be received.

New facilities represent a long-term commitment, either in the form of a lease or investment of funds of the business. An investor's primary concern is whether the commitment is consistent with his purposes and strategic plans. The investor may have existing facilities that could be utilized. Will merger of operations eliminate the need for new facilities? Could the financing be better arranged by the investor?

If new facilities are under construction, a commitment has been made. Management became convinced new construction was the correct business decision and the best alternative. Decisions to build facilities are usually made after substantial study and review, and copies of the studies should be requested. The method of financing almost certainly has been decided, leaving the investor in the position of having to accept the facility or decide not to invest.

A vacant or partially utilized facility not only is an asset producing no return on investment, but a drain on assets because of taxes, maintenance, utilities, insurance and security. Why is the facility shut down or under-utilized? Are there plans to dispose of the facility or bring it to a level of profitable utilization? What is the facility's annual expense? Can the real estate be sold? If sale is possible and planned, the anticipated price should be included in the investor's cash-flow forecasts. Closing dates and prices are often unpredictable, so conservative estimates are more responsible.

A common practice in closely held businesses is for the owner, his family or the major shareholders to own a facility and lease it to the business. Such arrangements are usually for tax or estate planning purposes and not in themselves improper. In public companies, the practice is improper if terms of the lease are not disclosed to all shareholders. The documentation of the leases often tends to be minimal and infrequently reviewed, since "arm's length" negotiations never occurred, and contains terms having little relationship to competitive market values. A comparison of competitive market rates to actual rents paid should be made with the difference added or subtracted from past income of the business to learn the true income. For income projections, decisions are required on the terms of future leases or whether the property will be acquired as part of the investment.

Be cynical and cautious with all appraisals. Appraisals to the liking of sellers are readily volunteered but those contrary to a seller's position tend to be withheld or forgotten. Appraisals are subjective exercises resulting only in opinions. While they help estimate value, they must be interpreted and never considered final. Their conclusions are only meaningful when the underlying assumptions are understood, and different assumptions can result in very different conclusions. The assumptions or appraisal basis may be for a going business, slow liquidation, auction sale, replacement value, discounted projected income or some other theory of valuation. The basis may have been selected to aid in producing a desired result. The conclusion of an appraisal may not be as valuable as the descriptive information contained within the appraisal. An appraisal, regardless of its conclusions, should contain a precise description of the real estate valued.

CHAPTER 12

Markets, Competition and Customers

Due diligence must define markets, competition and customers. They are typical of many nebulous and imprecise terms brandished about in business that create confusion and misunderstanding. The "market" for a specific business may be proscribed by geographical, pricing, service or other limiting factors. "Competitors" include not only today's competition but those who could enter the market in the future. Pricing changes, influenced by transportation costs or other forms of overhead, could generate new competitors. Investors also must determine how many "customers" are one-time, not repeat, buyers and decide whether potential customers, those with a need but no financial resources, should be defined in the market.

Gauging the size of a business's potential market should not be hard. Management will have some facts, estimates, opinions and possibly even detailed information. Trade publications are an excellent source of data for only the cost of a subscription, and various government agencies, security analysts, industry associations, utilities, chambers of commerce, Yellow Pages, economic development agencies and private research groups can produce market studies. Many of the publications and studies will identify both competitors and customers, and the quantity of such reports available usually makes it unnecessary to commission expensive market studies. Exactly who the market's customers are can be ascertained by reviewing customer lists and identifying individuals and businesses similar to those being served. For some businesses it is possible to identify all existing and potential customers and accurately determine the total market. Census and demographic data will be helpful in identifying trends and market size. It's absolutely essential for investors to understand markets, both their size and their customers, to understand a business. Without such information an investor cannot evaluate the present marketing scheme or estimate the business's potential.

Market share has become a key statistic in measuring a business against its competitors. Rises and falls in market share constitute specific data as to how well the business is performing and this information is readily available from trade associations and publications that publish sales and market share data with merciless regularity. For some industries, particularly those selling services, market share is indirectly presented by listing and ranking each by revenues, value of contracts or number of professional employees. In markets with a small number of competitors, each competitor probably knows the other's sales revenue, making estimates of market share simple.

Market share is important but it is only one of many factors and no guarantee of future success. While some markets remain relatively stable, most are either growing or declining. Technology, demographics, fashion, taste, costs, attitudes and product saturation all can cause upward or downward trends affecting the overall market. A primary concern for the investor is whether present market trends portend the future. Future markets are more important than today's because they are the source of income and return on investment. Recognition by management of market trends and the adequacy of the business's response is a subject for evaluation. New markets may be viewed as any in which the business presently does not sell its products or services; technological advance may enable the business to compete in these markets. Redesigns may make a product attractive to older or younger customers. Identification of logical new markets and plans to enter the markets should be of great interest to the investor. How realistic and well-developed the plans are requires careful study, along with what is entailed in implementing the plans.

Demographic trends are those affecting human populations such as age, population, growth or decline, location, density, marriage, birth rates and mortality. These trends can have a profound long-term effect upon many markets but are of particular importance to businesses selling direct to consumers. If such trends exist, then their magnitude, timing and impact upon the business should be studied. Census data, data from state and local government agencies, chambers of commerce, industrial development commissions and utilities may all be available and so negate the need for expensive surveys.

Geographical markets served can be anything from a small local area, as would be the case with a business located in an office building selling only to tenants, to the world, where a multinational company sells nearly everywhere. However, defining geographical markets requires some effort, since marketing areas actually served may not correlate with those claimed. For example, management may argue its market area is the southeastern United States. However, closer inspection reveals 80 percent of the sales are concentrated in Florida, 10 percent in Georgia, 5 percent in Alabama and 5 percent in the balance of states. The last 5 percent trickles in with little or no sales effort. To claim the southeastern states as the market is true but also misleading, since the bulk of the sales is concentrated in a small area. Customers are rarely distributed equally in any area. Due diligence includes identifying geographical markets being served and the potential to expand elsewhere. Precise questions to locate areas of current activity and why other promising areas are not served should be pursued.

In every industry there are trends affecting each business and its competitors. Some trends are very broad and fundamental, such as the consolidation of an industry. Others are less obvious but just as important, such as the conversion to new materials or manufacturing processes that enhance quality or reduce costs. An investor should determine the industry trends and the business's response. Is the business a leader, follower or oblivious of the trends? Is it benefiting from the trends or being adversely affected? If the trends continue, how will the business fare? How do the trends affect the overall value of the business?

Competition exists in essentially two forms. One is the competitor with comparable products or services, while the other offers alternatives. Due diligence evaluation of competition must include both categories. Direct competitors are relatively easy to identify but objective comparisons can be difficult. The combination of emotional views arising from daily battles with competition and the tendency to draw broad general conclusions from anecdotal evidence often lead to unrealistic views. Salespeople who lost orders or have not secured orders from an account serviced by a competitor augment erroneous views to rationalize their failures. As a consequence of these and other factors, an investor should not rely on one source to identify and evaluate competition.

After identifying competitors, the investor should determine their market share, the advantages and disadvantages each one holds, and evaluate their significance. Any comparison of marketing approach, products and services with competitors should be conducted by comparing specific traits or characteristics. It would be a rare situation if a competitor was better or worse in every aspect. It usually is meaningless to conclude one product or service to be superior or inferior to another unless the preponderance of individual characteristics is better or worse. However, in some cases, one characteristic may be so superior and desirable or totally undesirable that other traits are of minimal importance. Comparisons should be made on the critical characteristics of any product or service: costs, price, quality, performance, reliability, appearance and service.

A comparison of marketing programs and the entire system of distribution are part of the due diligence competitor evaluation. Distribution includes warehousing and the method of selling the products or services. All distribution costs are an expense of the business, whether they are direct or indirect, as is the case with price reductions to independent marketers. Individual businesses within an industry tend to evolve toward comparable systems of distribution because they have proven most efficient. Whenever one business has a totally different approach, it should be viewed with some caution until proven otherwise. An objective of the investor should be to learn if an alternate distribution system is advantageously being utilized by competitors.

The due diligence task is to identify present and potential customers, evaluate the probability of active customers continuing and then determine new markets. Customer lists and sales reports are helpful, but receivable records are the most reliable source of customer data. A concentration of sales with one large customer or a very small number entails far greater risk than when no customer accounts for more than a few percent of total sales revenue. Whenever sales are concentrated, the investor must become concerned with the probability of sales continuing at the same level to these major customers. Management's opinions are insufficient and direct interviews with the critical customers are necessary to learn the state of current relations and determine if involvement of the investor would affect relations.

Capturing new customers is primarily the task of the marketing. Retaining customers is everyone's job. Failure to land significant new customers should create doubt about the competency of the marketing effort. Customers may be lost for reasons unrelated to the business's product, such as bankruptcy or acquisition by a competitor. However, customers can be lost because of failures of the business, quality, service, noncompetitive pricing and so on. Identifying exactly why existing customers were lost and new ones not acquired may be difficult if it involves admission of management errors, shortcomings or failures. Whatever programs exist to both secure new customers and better serve existing customers should be requested and reviewed.

No due diligence would be complete without learning how customers view the business. Their views are of great importance because they influence the future of the business and can identify correctable shortcomings. Senior management and employees will have some understanding of customers' views but may be unwilling to comment if reports are negative. Interviews with a sample of customers and the largest of customers can be invaluable for the investor. Meetings with former, disgruntled customers can be particularly helpful, and can be a first step in winning them back.

CHAPTER 13

Marketing

"Marketing" is a term used to describe a broad range of activities associated with the sale of a business's products and services. Sales planning and strategy, pricing, staffing, distribution, financing and advertising are all major functions that fall under the general category of marketing. A financial review of marketing in which marketing or selling expense is solely equated to results in the form of sales would be inadequate. However, an overall review of marketing activity without equating cost to results would be equally foolish.

Understanding and evaluating a marketing program is both an objective and subjective task in which all factors need to be considered to produce a balanced judgment. Since marketing is an activity for which there may be more than one approach, differences of opinion are common and they complicate evaluations. It is easy to be enthusiastic or critical of what has or has not been accomplished, but no one knows with certainty what sales might have resulted with a different approach.

The level of marketing expense is a fundamental management decision. Whether the program is adequately, under- or overfunded are questions managements continually ponder and are basic to due diligence. There are other important questions: If the business sold more, could it finance, produce and deliver more? How can marketing be improved? Is the present program adequate or merely a good foundation upon which to build?

A business must establish a system for customers or clients to obtain information and enter into contracts or place orders. This may be as simple as a customer talking with a sole proprietor or as complex as an international sales program involving multiple methods of distribution and hundreds of individuals. The investor should learn how the selling of the business's products or services is accomplished. Is it a proven and effective method? Is management satisfied with the approach or are changes contemplated? Does the selling approach respond to market changes?

International businesses that do not have overseas subsidiaries tend to establish foreign sales representatives, commission agents, joint ventures and other types of local sales representation. All are entered into with high hopes and remain in effect unless terminated, or they expire regardless of success or failure. A review of actual sales volume helps identify the more successful marketers but not the inactive. The investor should know the countries in which sales are being made and the amounts, and should identify the local agents or representatives. Particular attention regarding exclusive territories and termination provisions should be given to agreements that established the relationships. Knowledge of where sales are being made today is also knowledge of where sales are not being made, and it may possibly point to opportunities.

Comprehensive marketing plans are often written for the total business and each major segment, but the absence of a written plan does not mean that a well-understood plan and program is not in effect. Marketing plans are usually based on a marketing philosophy. Without an underlying philosophy, whether written or unwritten, it is unlikely the plan will be totally coherent. The investor should evaluate marketing plans for effectiveness and compatibility with other businesses he controls.

Changes in marketing plans and strategy are made to correct problems and improve the existing system. They could range from converting to direct sales from manufacturer's representatives or stocking distributors to changing advertising agencies or consolidating regions and territories. Whenever changes have occurred, the investor should learn the causes and the results. An absence of change in a marketing organization with declining sales or market share is a matter for serious concern.

If the marketing arm is of any size, an organizational chart showing all personnel involved, the reporting relationships and, preferably, job descriptions, will be helpful. If the investor plans to reorganize, expand, reduce or merge the marketing organization, knowledge of the existing personnel, their job duties and compensation is a first step.

Salespeople meeting directly with customers may be one of the most important assets not reflected on the balance sheet. For many businesses, retaining and recruiting salespeople is of paramount importance. Expansion plans may be limited by the availability of frontline salespeople, and retaining existing levels of revenue may be difficult with high turnover.

The method of compensating salespeople should be examined for cost and effectiveness. Are they motivated believers in the system or are they demoralized? Sales compensation tends to be revised periodically because dissatisfaction frequently exists, either on the part of the management, the salespeople or both. High personnel turnover and poor sales performance are warning signs that the compensation system needs review.

Many businesses have calculations or estimates of the volume of sales a salesperson must produce to justify the cost. Separately, management may have set minimum acceptable levels of sales volume per salesperson that may not necessarily be a function of cost. For many industries, trade associations compile data that indicates average performance. Whatever data are available should be collected, and from this, preliminary opinions can be drawn on the organization's effectiveness as well as who are the important sales producers and who should be replaced.

If customer financing is provided either directly or by third parties, the investor should study the entire system carefully. Is financing profitable in its own right? Who assumes the credit risk? What is the recourse exposure? How is financing organized and approved? What is the source and cost of money used in financing? Customer financing can be extremely beneficial to the business but it is not without risk. It also can mask large liabilities missing from the balance sheet.

Leasing is another method of financing. It's a means of controlling access to technology, and is appropriate for customers who have limited or intermittent need. What eventually happens to leased products varies from business to business and is a major area for due diligence study. If leased on a lease-purchase basis, the customer may acquire ownership, but if not, the business eventually must make disposition. For some, the sale of previously leased products is an active and lucrative part of the business.

If leasing occurs, the investors should learn its purpose, its success, its source of funds, the advantages, disadvantages and alternatives. In all cases, the accounting for leased products requires careful study. The cost of products manufactured for lease and income recognized on leased products is not always a simple matter and has been an area of opportunity for financial improprieties.

Many business's marketing rights and very existence depend upon agreements such as franchises, distributorships or sales representation agreements. Virtually all give the grantor the right to terminate the agreement under certain conditions and usually expire after a period of time, unless renewed. Many automatically terminate in the event of a change in ownership, unless the new ownership is approved. Whenever these marketing agreements exist, the first step is their review. If the marketing agreement has any importance to the business, the investor should make his investment contingent upon the marketing agreement being continued.

Suppliers may provide financing to their distributors, agents, dealers or retailers. By doing so they can create an enforced loyalty or dependency. Financing can be in the form of direct loans, guarantees, extended terms for purchases, leases of facilities or equipment or any combination of these or others. A symbiotic relationship exists between a supplier and the independent marketers that can be nurtured through financing. However, these investments also can turn sour. The investor must determine the extent of financing provided to independent marketers. What is the probability of recovery of the investments? Does financing lock in the marketer as intended or trap the supplier into remaining with an unsatisfactory marketer just to protect the investment? How is this financing recorded on the balance sheet? If guarantees rather than direct loans are provided, how are these recorded and what is the exposure?

Independent marketers may either by contract or practice have the right to return unsold merchandise and so create a material unrecorded liability. Distributorship agreements often contain provisions that should the grantor terminate the distributorship agreement, they will buy back the distributor's inventory. In addition, either written or unwritten agreements may exist providing that slow-moving inventory may be returned. Most troublesome are situations in which manufacturers or importers guarantee to accept return of any unsold goods regardless of the reasons. The circumstances under which merchandise can be returned, the record of returns and the potential outstanding exposure require study. Are there unwritten promises? Close attention should be given to how returned merchandise is recorded on the financial statements. If products are moving slowly for the marketers, demands to return merchandise may occur, regardless of any contractual obligations.

As part of the selling process, those involved develop close personal relationships with customers that result in loyalty, more often to an individual than the business. In addition, salespeople have access to customer lists and confidential information that make it possible for them to take customers with them if they join a competitor or start a competing business. For any investor the potential loss of employees with a "following" constitutes such a serious risk that an effort should be made to both identify employees capable of taking important customers and determine the probability of their doing so. If past employees have taken customers with them, the probability is high that attempts will occur in the future. The defenses may combine both legal threats and a special effort to ensure that critical employees remain with the business.

___ **CHAPTER 14** ___

Pricing

Due diligence objectives are to analyze all factors affecting pricing, the existence of improprieties and hidden liabilities and, most important, to gather sufficient information to decide if pricing is maximizing profits. Pricing directly affects profitability, so pricing improvements may be one of the quickest ways to increase profits.

An investor should understand the pricing philosophy, the method of setting prices and the factors influencing prices. Pricing improprieties and errors are an unpleasant reality that occurs with sufficient frequency that their possible existence cannot be ignored. For each product or service line, pricing should be reviewed separately, because variations can occur regardless of broad corporate policies. Formal pricing policies may clearly set forth the overall pricing philosophy used in setting prices. Such policies tend to be guidelines from which deviations are not permitted without the approval of a senior executive. If written policies exist, copies should be requested. While policies typically are unwritten, they usually are understood within the business. Whether written or unwritten, the pricing approach and policies are as basic information as the business's name and address.

Regardless of pricing philosophy, policies and management statements, it is important to understand and verify precisely how prices are established. There may be large variations between policy and reality. Understanding the nuances can be achieved by obtaining current price lists, recently accepted quotations, or prices marked on merchandise, and then questioning in detail how the prices originated. Were they a fixed percent over cost or based on competition? What was believed to be the most a customer would pay? Were prices simply pulled out of the air? After determining how actual prices are established, a comparison can be made between prices received and those on price lists or quotations.

At some level in the business someone has the final word on day-to-day pricing. The CEO ultimately is responsible but may not be involved except for policy decisions and very large orders or contracts. Pricing decisions tend to be delegated within a business, and some give limited pricing discretion to frontline sales personnel. Since pricing so directly affects profits, who actually makes the decisions is a matter of interest for the investor. It's possible much of the business's potential profits are lost because of unnecessary price levels or concessions.

While many factors influence prices, at least a portion of the price is normally influenced by the cost of goods or services sold. Unfortunately, some businesses have such inadequate accounting systems that true costs are unknown or at best only vaguely known. In distribution and retailing businesses, costs are relatively simple in that goods are purchased and re-sold without value added. However, in manufacturing and service businesses the determination of cost and proper allocation of overhead becomes more complex and often misleading.

Pricing below costs that include full standard overhead allocations may be necessary and yet prove profitable if volume is adequate. Complaints that competitors are "selling below our cost" may actually be valid complaints about the cost system. The investor, to understand pricing, needs to understand the composition of cost of sales as it appears on the financial statement and the internal cost system used as a basis for setting normal prices and minimum acceptable prices. The quality of the cost system directly affects the viability of pricing.

"Underpricing" is pricing less than what most customers are willing or expect to pay and results in a loss of profits. "Overpricing" is pricing in excess of competitive alternatives and results in a loss of business. The optimum level of pricing is not always apparent or easy to determine and it changes with market conditions. Possible indications of under- or over-pricing and lack of aggressive pricing would be prices not revised in more than a year, significant decline or increase in the percentage of quotations accepted and ignoring competitor prices or lack of intelligence regarding competitor prices. An investor should try to determine if an opportunity exists to raise prices or increase volume and overall profits by reducing prices.

Manufacturers may attempt to control retailers' prices for their products. Agreements calling for set prices or minimum prices may violate government regulations. However, indirect, subtle and not so subtle methods may be employed to force retailers to maintain prices specified by the manufacturer. These include providing suggested retail prices and cutting off or restricting supplies if prices are not maintained. Withholding advertising or cooperative advertising revenue is another device to force compliance. Verbal persuasion coupled with implied threats are not uncommon. If an investor finds the business makes any effort to enforce retail price levels for its products, careful investigation is in order. There has been minimal enforcement of applicable laws, but this may change.

Estimating is the activity of systematically accumulating the projected total cost of labor and material that will be required in a future project. To this direct cost is added an amount for overhead and profit with the resulting price submitted to a customer as a proposal or bid. The ability of a business to know its costs and prepare competitive bids is critical to its success, and the importance of competent estimating should be recognized.

The most effective way to evaluate an estimating department is to compare past cost estimates on jobs received with actual performance. How close were the estimated costs to the actual? Another test is the tenure and experience of those involved in estimating. Frequent turnover or new key employees can be a warning sign that the business will have difficulty in making valid estimates.

CHAPTER 15

Advertising and Public Relations

Except for businesses with substantial advertising and PR expenditures, most investors limit their due diligence efforts on these activities. Deal-killing problems and perils are improbable, but knowledge of the functions will be useful in planning a transition if acquisition occurs. Since the functions are not precisely defined and do overlap, it is usually wise to study both simultaneously.

Wide variances exist between industries and businesses within industries in the extent and use of advertising and public relations. For smaller businesses, expenditures are minimal, but as businesses grow or try to grow, advertising and public relations become more prevalent. In medium-sized businesses, both advertising and public relations often are combined. In larger businesses, advertising and public relations tend to eventually separate into independent functions.

Advertising is primarily concerned with promoting the sale of products and services, preparing literature, brochures, advertisements and buying media time or space, while PR seeks publicity through news releases, lobbying and events. PR is more concerned with promoting the overall image of the business, government relations, its securities and often its key executives. Public relations informs the public of what the business wants the public to know and tries to cast in the best light whatever it wishes the public did not know.

Budgets for the current year and actual expenditures for the last fiscal year indicate the extent of the advertising and PR programs and may identify projects and programs. Information on specific activities and programs can then be requested for evaluation. Any measures that the business may have of its advertising effectiveness should also be requested. A list of employees and their specific functions will clarify responsibilities.

If the advertising program is of any size, an agency normally will be employed. Evaluation of advertising agencies may be puzzling, and results difficult to measure because of budget constraints, client whims and preferences and other factors beyond the agency's control or influence. Investors looking to consolidate marketing operations are likely to conclude that one advertising agency will suffice and require objective information to select the best.

Businesses spend large sums to create and maintain a public awareness of their trade names, trade marks and logos. Since they are extremely valuable assets, an investor should verify that all are properly registered. Unless acquired in a prior acquisition, these intangible assets usually have no value on the balance sheet, but value can be assigned if the investment is an acquisition of assets for an amount in excess of book value.

PUBLIC RELATIONS

The role, costs and functions of public relations (PR) can be extremely varied but may include writing and distributing press releases; announcing significant news regarding the business; organizing events; arranging interviews of key executives; writing speeches, articles and even books for executives; maintaining contacts with government agencies; arranging meetings with security analysts; writing annual reports and advising management on how to announce good news for maximum effect and how to minimize damage when adversity occurs.

PR has been known to be involved in "the dirty work," activities the business prefers to keep quiet and, in some cases, highly improper or illegal activities. The stated purpose of most PR is to enhance or preserve the business's image with the expectation that increased demand for the business's products, services and securities will result. However, PR is frequently engaged in programs of aggrandizement of the CEO and lobbying government officials. It can become a broad mantle for tasks that do not fit others' regular job activities.

PR firms may be retained on a continuous or an as-needed basis to perform all the functions of in-house PR departments. The larger agencies usually have superbly skilled personnel. If a firm or individual is retained for PR, then the purpose, assignment, cost and results should be evaluated. Why and how the firm was selected should be questioned. Is a senior executive in the PR firm an advisor and confidant to the CEO? If the investor is not entirely welcome, will the outside PR firm become an adversary?

Publicity in the news media, including trade publications, helps mold the overall reputation of the business. Information brought to the public's attention, such as favorable financial results, new products, expansion activities and awards, can be desirable. On the other hand, securities violations, lawsuits, layoffs, plant closings and management failures or indiscretions damage the reputation. An investor invests in the entire business, including its reputation, which can be an asset or a liability. A review of prior publicity can identify company activities, including those management would prefer to forget. The level of prior publicity may confirm skills in securing favorable publicity or the difficulty in suppressing bad news.

CHAPTER 16

Manufacturing

Due diligence should produce a complete knowledge of manufacturing facilities, equipment, systems, operations, financial results, the work force and, particularly, management. Competent management cannot be underestimated because in its absence the most competitive manufacturing facilities will flounder.

Manufacturing management is primarily judged by how efficiently and profitably plants operate and whether customers receive quality products on a timely basis. Corporate explanations of opportunities, problems, shortcomings, corrective measures in progress and improvement or expansion programs should be considered during personal interviews.

Manufacturing management has the responsibility to profitably produce quality merchandise on a schedule acceptable to customers. Starting with a review of production schedules, the due diligence task is to determine whether that responsibility is being met. Overproduction creates excess inventory and prematurely draws down order backlogs, which forces reductions in future schedules. Premature shipment of orders and/or the building of excess inventory are common techniques to temporarily maintain or increase profits during a period when investors are being sought. When schedules are not met, customer dissatisfaction becomes a problem and business may be lost.

Most manufacturing operations are broken down as separate profit centers with financial statements reporting income, expenses and usually balance sheets. While studying these statements, pay attention to any arbitrary allocation of overhead expenses and the absence of expenses that should be charged to derive a profit comparable to a pretax profit. Supplemental reports created by the accounting department, manufacturing management or their staff are almost certain to exist and should be requested. These may detail production levels, unit output, costs, efficiencies, variances, safety or any other statistic management believes important.

Managements have strong opinions regarding the adequacy and value of their machinery and equipment, but an investor's personnel or outside experts may be necessary for objective opinions. Appraisals may be required to establish collateral values and to allocate purchase price.

In assessing the machinery and processes, there are several basic questions:

- Can demand be met with present equipment?
- Is the machinery producing quality products?
- Would cost savings justify the purchase of new machinery?

Older machinery often is adequate for existing production levels and new machinery and production lines might not be justified. However, one or more competitors may have such an advantage in manufacturing that major expenditures would be required to remain competitive. If the target business has the advantage, how long will it last?

Capital expenditures indicate management's commitment to maintaining, updating and modernizing their plants. A comparison of annual expenditures for new machinery to amounts budgeted and depreciation charged is helpful. Historical capital expenditures tend to indicate levels realistically required in the future. While precise forecasts of future capital expenditures based on specific items or categories are best, an investor should be wary of projections below historical levels. Delaying capital expenditures is one way to temporarily improve cash flow and brighten financial statements to impress investors. Delays may also indicate cash shortages that are preventing normal capital expenditures.

Expensive machinery should be examined to see if it is designed for a specific application or is "off-the-shelf," mass-produced machinery. Special machines are limited in application and, while expensive to build and purchase, cannot be readily sold and receive little value as collateral. "Off-the-shelf" machine tools are easily valued and have excellent collateral value because of the active machinery market. In addition to the collateral problem, special machines are not built until ordered and construction may take months. If rapid expansion of production is planned, lead times for special machines must be factored into the planning.

Manufacturing organizations should be judged on the basis of results. Since there is no one best organizational structure, those evaluating corporate structures should not assume structures with which they are familiar are the norm, or that structures conforming to organization theories would be superior. Any variety of structure can work well, depending upon the type of business, its history, management preferences and the availability of able personnel. If changes have recently been made in the organizational structure, the causes and results should also be reviewed. For most investors, an understanding of the manufacturing structure will be adequate initial information.

Customer demands, competition, litigation and regulations have increased the quality requirements. The investor should question whether management emphasizes and stresses quality. Who is responsible for quality control and at what level in the organization does this person report? Are there established quality control procedures and a written manual? Does management have quality control goals or objectives? Is the rate of rejected products or scrap declining? Is the rate of defective products shipped to customers declining? What are warranty costs? Are receivables disputed because of defects? An investor should be extremely cautious about investing in any business with severe quality problems.

Since transportation costs constitute a significant expense for most businesses, unless carefully controlled they can make the difference between profit or loss. Unfortunately, many businesses are unaware of all their transportation costs and make little effort to control them. As a result, the investor should determine if transportation costs are a major expense and what controls exist. If there are controls, is someone responsible for managing these costs and does the business have any advantages or disadvantages when compared to competitors?

Subcontracting labor, parts or products may be surrounded by controversy. Certain questions, often without easy answers, are appropriate to evaluate the wisdom of subcontracting: Can opportunities for additional subcontracting be identified and would they be less costly than continuing the work in-house? Were overhead costs and gain or loss of overhead absorption calculated in subcontracting decisions? Since labor often resents subcontracting because of the loss of jobs, has the target business encountered any labor relations disputes over subcontracting? How reliable are the subcontractors? Has subcontracting created friction with the community, or received adverse national publicity? An investor should identify and review present subcontracting and consider possible opportunities. The original rationale or cost advantages may no longer exist. Does the investor control other businesses that could perform the subcontracting?

Relocation of a manufacturing plant or product line is a major undertaking because moves are costly, disruptive and often engender unanticipated expenses and problems. They are seldom undertaken without study and planning and are expected to solve existing or foreseeable problems. The investor should review studies justifying relocations and determine if the desired results were achieved. Has the move been completed within amounts budgeted? Is production at forecasted levels? Some relocations are so disruptive it takes years for the business to recover. If relocation of manufacturing operations is in the planning stage, a review of the project should be conducted. A decision to proceed or cancel the project may be one of the first confronting an investor.

The ability to increase production levels with and without significant capital expenditures should be evaluated, along with the lowest possible level to which production can be decreased and remain profitable. Break-even calculations are helpful for each manufacturing operation and the business as a whole. Maximum and minimum levels of production can be projected, but seldom with precision, because of the variety or "mix" of the products with differing gross profits. Labor content also can greatly affect estimates. However, rough estimates adequate for evaluation and planning should be possible. Records of past levels of production and the results can be used to verify estimates.

Management's opinions on the ability to increase or decrease production and break-even levels are probably the best that are readily available. Management has the experience associated with varying production levels and should be well aware of the break-even point. Whatever plans or hopes the investor may have for the business are likely to affect production levels and management's views should not be ignored.

CHAPTER 17

Purchasing

Purchasing decisions spur broad due diligence questions. Is the function well managed with adequate controls? Does it have the authority and status to be effective? Does it contribute to business success with aggressive buying and by providing a source of intelligence for the entire business? Or is it simply a neglected arm and possibly a center of conflict of interest and corruption? The importance and stature of purchasing may be evident in the existence of procedural controls and the placement of purchasing executives at senior levels. Regardless of its status, purchasing should be closely reviewed during due diligence, as every dollar saved in purchasing becomes a dollar of pretax income.

The role and impact of purchasing may be large and not limited to selection and evaluation of suppliers, negotiations, placing and expediting orders. It can be a conduit of information to the organization on what is available from suppliers. It also can identify supply alternatives and be a valuable source of intelligence on competitors, industry trends and practices. Purchasing establishes controls so orders are precisely written and entered into the financial reporting system. Purchasing monitors and, when necessary, pressures suppliers to meet delivery dates and grant price concessions.

Purchasing does have a dark side because of the opportunities and temptations for personal enrichment. Few employees are entrusted with the business's money like those in purchasing and no other function has the breadth of opportunity for dishonesty. It ranges from the secretary buying personal items from the petty cash fund, to a clerk typing fictitious invoices, to the CEO receiving kickbacks. Entertainment, gifts, kickbacks, conflicts of interest and fictitious purchases can and do happen. Due diligence investigators should be alert to any indication of misplaced trust.

The status of purchasing in an organization is reflected in the degree of control the individual or department has over purchasing. Maximum control occurs when all final purchasing decisions and purchase orders are issued by purchasing executives. A middle level of control exists when others make final purchasing decisions, with or without the advice and concurrence of purchasing executives, with the purchase orders issued by the purchasing department. The least control exists when numerous non-purchasing executives make purchase commitments with or without formal purchase orders. Most well-managed businesses with substantial purchasing activity recognize the value of tight controls. An investor needs to understand how purchasing decisions are made, what are the existing policies and controls and which individuals are involved.

In a business with limited purchasing activities, only one part-time person may be involved, but as business expands, purchasing tends to grow into major departments headed by experienced professionals and staffed with buyers and senior buyers. To whom the top purchasing executive reports is an indication of both his status and the purchasing function. Status is important for control because of a tendency for non-purchasing executives to make independent purchasing decisions and bypass the purchasing department. Salespersons often find ways to bypass the purchasing department and deal with executives believed to be more easily persuaded. A strong and well-controlled purchasing function should comfort an investor. The opposite can be viewed with concern but also as an almost certain opportunity for rapid, profitable improvements.

The percentage of the sales dollar represented by the cost of purchased goods and services is an important statistic in due diligence. The greater the percentage, the more important purchasing becomes. If an aggressive professional purchasing organization exists, it is unlikely that further reductions of any magnitude in the purchased component of cost of sales can be expected. But a poorly run purchasing organization with weak buying power because of volume limitations or a tight cash position might indicate that a significant opportunity exists to reduce costs.

At the same time, a high purchase component with the cost passed on to the customer with minimal profits may contribute to accurate but unintentionally misleading financial statements. Pass-through costs tend to inflate revenues and reduce gross profit percentages. While the purchased portion may be virtually risk-free and any markup nearly all profit, the impact on the financial statements needs to be understood before conclusions are drawn.

A list of the suppliers and amounts spent with each will show where and how the business is spending its money. An investor must know the suppliers' identity to evaluate both their reliability and the possibility of expanding the relationships as well as to consider alternative vendors. Long-term contracts with suppliers are relatively common. Some involve commitments to purchase a set quantity, others a minimum quantity and some only set a price at which the buyer can buy on an "as needed" basis. There are endless variations in the terms of such contracts. When long-term supply contracts are signed, both parties believe it to be advantageous, but conditions can change and a supply contract may become a burden. Price declines, obligations to purchase unneeded goods or services, and loss of flexibility to consider other alternatives all can and do happen. The investor should review all supply contracts and their value to the business. If of no benefit, when do they expire and what obligations exist?

A sole-source-of-supply situation exists when a business buys from only one supplier. This source might be the only one producing the item or the only supplier capable of providing the necessary quantity and quality. Since a sole source supplier has no competitors and can price accordingly, dependence on such a source is a costly risk to avoid. The inherent risk may be so great that a buyer may assist a second source to become active. An investor should be alert to any sole source suppliers and assess the associated risks. How seriously would the business be affected if the supplier was lost for any reason? What steps are being taken to find a second source or develop alternatives?

Special supplier relationships tend to lock in the use of a particular supplier. Results can and do vary from those beneficial to the business to those that primarily benefit individuals. Suppliers in which management or shareholders have a financial interest may provide competitive products or services but they will always be suspect. Such relationships are usually sensed by competitors, who then refuse to bid or supply high quotations, knowing they have no chance. Under these conditions, competitive prices are not known.

Other special relationships exist when a supplier's executives have such close personal friendships with senior executives that other suppliers are not considered. If competitors seek the business, the friendly supplier usually receives a "last look" to equal or exceed the competitor's price. Of course, in some cases suppliers become locked in simply because they provide excellent products and services. They are so effective that no competitor is able to beat them. An investor should be concerned with flexibility to choose suppliers, to ensure that products or services are purchased competitively. Special relationships limit flexibility that may not benefit the business.

Vendor financing can be provided by a variety of direct and indirect methods. This may be as simple as granting longer than the customary time to pay or dating programs, floor plans and other more complex formalized schemes. Delayed payment plans usually do not appear on a business's financial statements other than as payables.

Generous payment terms have a cost passed on to the buyer in the form of higher prices. Due diligence must question the cost and determine whether a lower cost with less favorable terms would be wiser. Vendor financing can be some of the most expensive, with the buyer better off to pay promptly with other borrowed funds. Could its presence prevent the business from considering other vendors with superior products or more attractive prices? Could the vendor create a serious financial problem by terminating the financing and demand immediate payment? How dependent is the business upon vendor financing?

Employees involved in purchasing are frequently offered gifts and entertainment by suppliers in hopes of securing additional orders, while businesses usually want purchasing decisions to be as objective as possible and their employees free from improper influence. Where to draw the line between allowable and improper gifts is often difficult and subject to internal debate, since policies also affect those writing policies. Some businesses prohibit even the smallest of items, including business lunches, while others place a dollar value on what may be accepted. Some leave it to the recipient's discretion and a few have no policy. An enforced policy placing limits on gifts, whether written or unwritten, recognizes the problem will always exist despite the business' desires to maintain a high level of integrity in its procurement activities. The absence of a policy may indicate the purchasing function is badly in need of controls.

A basic control is the issuance of numbered purchase orders to make actual purchase commitments. An enforced policy within a business that no negotiations are consummated until a purchase order is issued or no purchase commitments are final until a purchase order is issued gives control to the purchasing department and prevents buying outside the department. Purchase orders are contracts containing precise information describing the items being purchased, quantity, price, delivery date and other sale terms. Some terms may be in fine print and on the back of the purchase order but still are legally enforceable. Formal purchase orders make it possible to compare what was received to what was ordered. A disciplined system of issuing purchase orders is a good indication that purchasing has controls and buying is restricted. Absence of a purchase order system, coupled with many non-purchasing employees making purchase commitments, should cause concern for an investor.

Other controls in the purchasing function probably exist and require review. They may require the approval of one or more senior executives for purchases above a set dollar amount, for large quantities, for changes in suppliers, to modify existing products specifications or to enter into long-term supply contracts. In some cases only the CEO can approve purchases. The policy on approvals and identification of the individuals with authority to commit the business will further indicate the degree of existing controls. Absence of such policies would be a matter of concern for any investor.

Still, too much control can be a danger signal. An executive who tightly controls purchasing may be honest and loyal to the business, with the business buying on a most prudent basis. A less honorable executive who jealously guards his purchasing prerogatives may not be buying well and enjoying benefits other than those paid by the business. When excessive control, little or no review procedures, and secrecy or an unwillingness to discuss the purchasing function prevail, an investor should be very suspicious.

Those conducting the due diligence investigation should question whether any improper acts have occurred or are suspected in the purchasing function. Improprieties can range from kickbacks, excessive gifts, entertainment, conflicts of interest and major violations of the business's policies and procedures. If such has occurred, the investor will want to learn the circumstances and what steps have been taken to prevent future occurrences. There is no perfect system to eliminate all improprieties, but enforced controls and policies should go a long way toward doing so.

CHAPTER 18

Human Resources

A thorough knowledge of employees, employee costs, employee relations and commitments to current and former employees is an essential part of any due diligence program. This chapter on human resources is devoted to employee issues except for compensation and benefits, which are discussed in Chapter 19.

An investor should know the total number of employees as well as the number in each category and at each location. This information provides another measure of the size and importance of each segment of the business. Careful attention should be given to defining the employment relationship for all individuals providing regular services to the business, including those on a contractual basis. Seasonal factors must also be considered when applicable.

The number of job openings, the length of time each has been open and the circumstances creating the vacancies and any recruiting problems should be reviewed. It might be that no one is available to fill the positions, that compensation is too low, working conditions unsatisfactory, the job specifications unreasonably high, or the business is ineffective at recruiting. Basic questions for an investor are whether a shortage of employees at any level is adversely affecting the business and what corrective measures are possible. If personnel are not available locally, could they be recruited from other areas? Is subcontracting a partial solution? If the condition does not improve, must relocation be considered? Is the shortage temporary or has it been a chronic problem? Is it possible to quantify how seriously the business has been hurt by the shortages?

Management vacancies and the recruiting and selection methods deserve special attention. The philosophy and attitude of the board of directors and CEO may be reflected in the selection procedures. Some select managers almost exclusively from within the organization and build depth to create a pool of promotable employees. Others hire from the outside, either because they prefer "new blood" or don't believe in-house candidates are qualified. If executive search firms or psychologists are used, their effectiveness and cost should be studied. Since additional openings may occur as a result of the investment, the possibility of selecting from within and/or using existing capabilities to recruit should be known.

As businesses and employment grow, personnel policies, benefits and rules become formalized into written documents. These personnel manuals and brochures describe a portion of the employment relationship and copies should be requested. Documents may be accurate and current or dated and inconsistent with actual practices. All such documents should be reviewed both for content and to determine if they could constitute an employment agreement or create other legal obligations. In numerous cases employers have inadvertently created employment agreements with the issuance of brochures. Review of policies becomes particularly important if work forces are to be merged.

Agreements not to compete and confidential information agreements may be combined or separate instruments. Their purpose is to prohibit an employee during or following employment from working for a competitor and/or disclosing confidential information. These agreements can be enforceable contracts that, while invaluable in protecting the business's interest, are frequently the subject of litigation. The outcome of the litigation may be uncertain but the threat of a costly lawsuit may be sufficient to deter a former employee. The investor should have an attorney knowledgeable in the field review existing agreements and obtain an opinion as to their validity. Verification should be made of the number of key employee agreements actually signed, since some employees may have avoided signing or their agreements might have disappeared. If any litigation has been threatened or occurred regarding these agreements, full details of the circumstances and outcome should be requested. Actual events and court rulings are enlightening as to the level of protection the business enjoys.

Automobiles and airplanes may be essential for employees to carry out their jobs but their use and availability are matters of status and direct economic benefit if personal use is permitted. Which employees are provided an automobile or the use of aircraft usually are designated in policies, written or unwritten. Since so much status and expense is associated with automobiles and aircraft, the investor should identify the policies and users. Are the perks the result of job requirements, status or supplemental compensation? Does the business own or lease the automobiles or are employees given an allowance with which to purchase and operate an automobile? Which employees are entitled to fly on business-owned aircraft? Are cost savings possible without serious morale problems by reducing the number of automobiles and aircraft?

Safety in a business encompasses all activities designed to prevent accidents, recording of accidents and care for the injured. Accident statistics should be requested and the nature of safety programs and their effectiveness should be reviewed. Experience with OSHA inspection and accident investigations should be studied. The importance management imparts to safety and the calibre of the individual responsible are key due diligence topics. The observations that safety is good business are true. The costs of accidents are such that a business with a bad safety record will eventually be forced to improve or go out of business. A very bad record is ample cause for the investor to reconsider the investment.

Workmen's compensation expenses resulting from employee injuries may be in the form of insurance premiums or self-insurance. If self-insured, the business directly pays expenses of the injured but usually carries insurance to cover catastrophic injuries. Verification of the existence of the catastrophic insurance is essential. Each state has its own laws governing workmen's compensation and there are wide coverage variations among states. An investor should evaluate the state laws, possible revisions of the laws, administrative practices, the business's accident rate, past costs, this year's costs and costs anticipated next year.

Occupational health problems are those of an insidious nature that usually develop over time. They range from silicosis and black lung disease to cancers from exposure to carcinogens or radiation. Industries, based only on anecdotal evidence, are often suspected and accused of creating occupational health hazards. If the industry has or is suspected of creating occupational health problems, the investor should assume the business being studied is likely to be involved. The cost of occupational health claims can be staggering and the business can expect no mercy from plaintiff attorneys. If there is any evidence of debilitating occupational health problems, the investor should study the potential exposure and assume the worst.

UNIONS

The competence of management to negotiate with unions and foster satisfactory labor relations that permit the business to thrive is as important in the due diligence evaluation as is the nature and militancy of the unions. Labor relations are extremely varied, with some employers who accept unions as just another condition and fact of doing business, and others who elect to resist with a vengeance bordering on war. Managements usually freely volunteer their opinions of unions, which will give a partial indication of the status of labor relations in the business.

An investor's primary concerns are the status of labor relations and whether there are any festering problems with adverse effects upon the business. Is the business forced to pay significantly higher wage rates and more costly benefits than non-union competitors? Has the business been hit with work stoppages and strikes? Is management forced to spend dis-

proportionate time on labor relations? How many of the serious labor relations problems are caused by management errors or policies? Does
management have the experienced personnel to negotiate with union lead-
ers and fairly administer agreed contracts?

Managements usually know if they anticipate difficulty in negotiating the
next union contracts. Major conflict definitely can be expected if management plans to rescind benefits in existing contracts. If a major labor dispute
is in progress or anticipated, most investors will prefer to wait until matters
are settled. An investor should check the expiration dates of the union
contracts to learn when possible walkouts could occur.

CHAPTER 19

Employee Compensation and Benefits

Employee compensation and benefits, for most businesses, constitute a substantial expense that is burdensome but not crushing. However, for some the costs are so great they cannot remain viable without change. In others, unless wages and benefits are increased to attract and hold employees, the business cannot grow or survive. Due diligence should review actual compensation and benefits and causative factors such as competition, affordability, government regulations, customs, employee demands, levels necessary to recruit and retain employees and industry standards. Knowledge of these key factors is particularly important if the investment results in a merger necessitating the integration of operations and work forces.

Care should be given to understand and evaluate both current and future costs, because present benefits and commitments for future benefits may not be reflected in financial statements. The lack of disclosure and understanding of future benefit costs is one of the most important areas for due diligence investigation. While reviewing the financial implications, investigators should be alert for compliance with federal and state laws and regulations governing benefit plans.

If retirement plans exist, what are their costs and the method and adequacy of funding? What current contributions are required under the plans and are these being made on a timely basis? There is a strong trend away from defined benefit pension plans, but thousands exist with large liabilities. "Unfunded past service liability" is the amount not paid into a fund actuarially adequate to pay for promised future benefits. The unfunded past service liability can be of such magnitude that a business's ability to ever fund the benefits may be in question. Investigate to learn if these liabilities are fully disclosed in the financial statements and whether practical measures can be taken to fund or reduce the liability. A secondary investor concern is the impact on employee relations of benefits provided under the plans or their absence. What pressures exist to increase benefits or establish a new plan?

Relentless annual increases in medical costs have caused corresponding large increases in health insurance premiums. The cost of insurance is now at a level where it is a significant expense for nearly all employers and has achieved an out-of-reach level for some. The cost of benefits promised to laid-off and retired employees has become a serious problem for many businesses. Efforts to reduce medical benefits or costs are usually met with strong resistance and litigation. The investor should learn the cost to the business and employees of all programs and the nature of benefits provided. Can the business afford the present programs? What rights has the business retained to change, revise or reduce benefits? Does the business have the right to insist that employees or retirees pay a larger share of the cost? Have health insurance costs for both employees and retirees been fully factored into the investor's financial projections?

The most common supplemental compensation plans are profit-sharing, bonus, incentive, deferred compensation, stock option, stock bonus, stock saving, stock purchase and 401K plans. A search for such plans should be conducted and copies of the documentation establishing them requested. A series of questions relatively standard for all plans can be used to study them. Who are the participants? What benefits have been paid and what has been the total cost? What are the future commitments? How are expenses and future liabilities recorded on the financial statements? Is the documentation correct and have necessary approvals been received in accordance with governmental regulations? How are accumulated funds invested? What was the reason for establishing the plan and has the desired result been achieved?

The terms of employment contracts vary widely but usually cover compensation, job responsibilities, and provisions for termination, non-competition and confidentiality. Their enforceability is dependent upon how well they are drafted, state laws and the attitude of local judges. More often than not, an employment agreement provides only a starting point in negotiations if either party elects to terminate. Regardless, they do have value and standing and cannot be ignored. An investor should determine whether existing agreements will benefit or hinder his objectives. An investor may want new or additional employment agreements as comfort that key employees will remain.

Severance pay is compensation to a terminated employee with the amounts payable usually influenced by the employee's wage level, length of service and reason for termination. The business's written policies and practices as well as employment agreements must be reviewed to estimate the liability. In many countries, the government establishes the terms and amounts of separation pay with amounts so large that significant changes in the business are discouraged. This potential liability probably will not appear on financial statements but must be considered in any reorganization plans. Because some separation pay plans are interpreted as contracts, a change of ownership may trigger separation pay benefits even though employees do not actually lose their jobs. If the investor is planning reductions or consolidation of operations, separation pay costs must be included in financial projections.

Along with reviewing the level of vacations and sick leave benefits, an investor should determine if days not taken in one year can be taken in future years and whether unused days are paid when the employee terminates. This practice has permitted employees to build huge nest eggs, worked contrary to the purpose of vacations and sick leave and created large, unrecorded employer liabilities. If accumulation has been permitted, the records should be reviewed and verified to calculate the liability and avoid controversy with employees.

Vacations and sick pay are based on length of service and considered to be earned in the year prior to the year taken; the cost should be accrued in the year earned. This is not always done, particularly in smaller businesses. If an investor is buying the assets and selected liabilities of the business, a problem in the negotiations will be who pays the current vacation benefits for employees hired by the investor.

Businesses often have a general policy regarding employee compensation that may be written or unwritten, but nevertheless followed. The policy may be to pay superior compensation to employ and retain superior employees, pay substandard rates and expect high turnover, or simply pay rates comparable to those paid in the area. Wage surveys are usually available from industry associations, chambers of commerce and trade groups or can be conducted. The investor's primary concerns are whether the compensation philosophy makes good business sense and if management's and the investor's approach are compatible.

Wage and benefit cost differentials between the business and some or all competitors become significant when the cost of the product or service sold is affected to a material degree. Benefit costs have become so large that cost comparisons must include both wages and benefits. Since a competitor with a significant labor cost advantage can underprice his competition, the investor's concern is whether a serious competitive advantage or disadvantage exists. What will be the short- and long-term impact upon the business? Unfortunately, locating accurate labor costs of competitors may be difficult, unless some third party is gathering information for the entire industry.

CHAPTER 20

Corporate Culture

Business deals all too frequently fail because differences in corporate cultures prevent the parties from understanding, accepting, reconciling or compromising. Unfortunately, cultural clashes are usually less a barrier to completing a deal than to success after the deal closes, because investors tend to minimize or ignore differences during due diligence.

Cultural factors may exist because of chance but more likely because individuals in power are convinced they are the right thing for the business. The factors become deeply ingrained and difficult to modify. Naive beliefs that cultural differences are interesting but insignificant or can easily be changed have caused many investors to regret the day of their involvement. Cultural clashes are most severe when a business is acquired with a very different culture from the investor, who promptly attempts to revise practices to conform with his convictions or methods. However, if cultural practices have been clearly detrimental to the business, such as oppressive management styles, dishonest or rapacious marketing, excessive political activity and discriminatory employee selection practices, their elimination may have a liberation effect highly beneficial to the business.

Business culture is composed of numerous factors, both obvious and subtle, that have varying degrees of importance. Importance is partially a function of how long a practice has been in existence and if entrenched, fully accepted and expected to continue. Practices and conditions are far more significant when carried to extremes, as would be an authoritarian structure where all decisions are made by the CEO, or a work force that is nearly all one religion or race. Common components of business culture are level of centralization of authority; relative independence of business units; management approach to employee relations including paternalism, fads, compensation and dress codes; community involvement and charitable contributions; political activity and beliefs and imbalances or concentrations of employees of one religion, race or nationality.

An investor's objective should be to determine the presence of significant cultural differences and decide if they can be accepted while recognizing that the cost of immediate change may be severe. To do so the investor should not hesitate to ask whatever questions he wishes nor be restrained by matters believed sensitive. In a perfect world such factors as race, religion and political beliefs would not matter, but the investor is investing in a less-than-perfect business and world. In measuring cultural factors, it is the deviation from the investor's philosophy of management and policies that is most important, but deviation from industry, community or theoretical ideal practices must also be considered.

Whenever a business's policies and practices substantially deviate from those considered customary, most people familiar with the business are well aware of the practices. They are not secret and the business becomes known for the practices. Whatever they may be, they exist because either those who control the business believe they are excellent or they fear adverse repercussions if changes are attempted.

Examples of those more frequently encountered help illustrate extreme policies and practices.

An inordinate degree of centralized authoritarian management that reduces lower-level managers to functionaries without authority or initiative is an extreme, as opposed to the other extreme of a business excessively decentralized with each manager touted as an entrepreneur resulting in no direction or control. Employee compensation limited to wages only for hours worked, with a total absence of benefits except those reluctantly provided because of legal requirements by a management without the slightest compassion for its employees, is considered extreme. Paternalism on a grand scale can include highly unusual benefits such as vacation trips, paid time off for many personal reasons, surprise bonuses, housing and cradle-to-grave security. Severe discipline and programs of peer pressure to force ever-higher levels of performance and production encouraging constant, justifiable worry over preserving one's job are far too common. Highly "democratic" work environments, with employees setting their own hours and work pace, are considered to be more interesting experiments than proven successful concepts. Whenever extremes exist in the business culture, the investor should learn their origin and prevalence, and evaluate the necessity for change and the cost.

In studying the racial and ethnic composition of the work force, the business should be viewed as a whole and by segment such as subsidiaries, divisions or even departments or facility. Racial and ethnic imbalances can be a source of friction and litigation. When a business or any unit of a business is predominately of one race, members of other races may be prevented or discouraged from working there or forced from it, resulting in bitter, irrational and difficult-to-control conflicts. Resolution of the conflicts through elimination of the imbalance may be impractical except with a very long-term program. The investor's concern is primarily whether and to what extent any racial or ethnic imbalance affects the business. Is productivity reduced, enhanced or unaffected? Have conflicts disrupted the business? Are tensions increasing that could erupt into serious conflicts? Have any conflicts resulted in legal action? If a dispute develops with an employee, is there such cohesiveness within his racial or ethnic group that there is a dispute with all?

If the management and the work force are predominately of one religion, this may merely reflect the composition of the community and be of no significance. However, there may be a serious problem if management's religious beliefs are so strong that active membership in the religion is a criterion for employment and promotions, religious activities are conducted during or after business hours, religious statues and icons adorn the facilities, the business makes contributions to religious institutions and proselytizing of non-member employees is prevalent. If any of these practices exist, it is because individuals are sincerely convinced they are in the best interest of the business and employees and the practices will be extremely difficult, if not impossible, to modify. Employees and customers offended by religious practices are considered by the believers to be unworthy and wrongheaded. If an investor finds that zealous adherents to a religion control the business, he should accept the fact or forget the investment, because change will be difficult. Of course, if the investor holds similar religious beliefs it will not be a problem.

Every business is besieged with requests for donations and contributions of cash, products, services and the time of employees. Requests for worthy causes always far exceed the financial capability of any business, making some method of evaluating and selecting beneficiaries of donations essential. There is also an abundance of unworthy causes and outright frauds and scams that must be screened out. Contribution budgets tell much about the philosophy of management. The budget's size tends to indicate management's beliefs regarding social responsibility, although sincere beliefs are tempered by available resources of the business. The contributions and the beneficiaries indicate management's, or in some cases their wives', areas of interest. These interests are better revealed by the relative size of a contribution in comparison to others than just size alone. Charitable contributions may or may not involve large sums but they often are sacred to an executive or shareholder and the dependent charity.

Contributions by business to support political causes, parties and candidates is widespread and a fact of business life. For some contributors, the quid pro quo is simply supporting their version of good government but for others it's the expectation of contracts for goods and services or legislation favorable to the business. The two most common benefits of contributions are privilege and access. Privilege is invitation to political and government functions controlled by the officeholder and access is an open door to the officeholder, affording the contributor an opportunity to express his views.

Businesses are restricted by state and federal laws in making political contributions, but the laws are often circumvented or ignored. Limits on the amount of individual contributions have been accommodated by candidates establishing numerous separate organizations, each of which can receive the maximum amounts. Executives make contributions that are reimbursed with bonuses, padded expense accounts or other means. Purchases of tickets to fund-raising events are treated as entertainment expense. Payments in kind in which the business provides travel, donates rent of a facility or buys meals is common. "Soft money" contributions are permitted in which money is donated to a political party for use in "get out the vote" campaigns and other so-called non-partisan political activity. Contributions to political action committees (PACs) is highly controversial but thousands of PACs exist. It is safe to assume that if there is a desire and perceived need to contribute, executives will find a way.

An investor should have multiple concerns. How much money is being given? Is the amount adequate or too low to accomplish whatever is the purpose? What risks are associated with non-compliance of election laws? What happens if contributions are not made? What happens if the beneficiary of the contribution loses? Is the investor in sympathy with the purpose of the contribution. A prudent investor will view political contributions as high-risk investments.

Many businesses have developed and distributed formal codes of conduct to inform employees that unethical practices will not be tolerated. A legal defense is a policy stating that if offenses occur they are the activity of renegade employees rather than the company. Policy statements may constitute sincere expressions of management's philosophy or simply be a facade behind which business continues as usual. They may cover a wide range of subjects such as price-fixing, kickbacks, excessive commissions, bribes and a variety of non-discrimination matters. The investor will want to know the purpose of the policy, why the formal policy was issued and whether there is actual compliance. In some cases the policy originated after scandals the management would prefer to forget.

Executives persist in seeking a Holy Grail of management that will motivate and inspire employees to new levels of productivity, eliminate human relations conflicts and communication failures, improve quality, cut costs and solve most other problems that others have resolved with common sense, proven techniques, hard work and intelligence. Consequently, managements often accept faddish concepts that appear to have some merit but all too often have transitory beneficial effects, if any. What may have value to one business may fail when applied to others. The concepts are usually promoted by consultants who sell the programs for substantial fees by pointing to alleged success stories. For the investor, concern should exist that management has placed an excessive reliance upon fads to solve problems. Usually, CEOs sold on a fad are initially convinced of the fad's value and will vigorously defend it until disillusioned. A serious conflict of management style and philosophy may occur if the investor has doubts about the fad or believes it to be nonsense.

CHAPTER 21

Legal

Most due diligence issues could conceivably be categorized under the heading "legal" because they directly relate to the compliance or non-compliance with laws. Of particular concern to any investor is whether the business is involved in litigation, and whether as a defendant or as a plaintiff. Similarly, an investor will need to know if the business is under investigation by any governmental agency, if it is subject to fines or penalties, or whether it has been prohibited by the government, by court order, or by agreement, from engaging in any activities. In addition, the investor will want to probe whether the business's operations meet all legal and regulatory requirements.

An investor does not want to invest in a company that, shortly after closing, will be fined millions of dollars by a government agency, such as OSHA, or subject to a large jury verdict. In fashioning legal questions, the investor will find helpful the assistance of an attorney to ensure that all aspects of the business's operations are adequately investigated. As with other due diligence questions, legal questions should be coordinated with the representations and warranties in the transaction document. In addition, although these questions may be termed "legal" in nature, the investor's financial and operational people, as well as his lawyers, should carefully review the results.

At the heart of the legal due diligence is a review of pending or prospective litigation. The investor will want to review any lawsuits involving the business. Not only might the business be liable for the underlying claim, but even if the claim is without merit, the business will incur litigation costs. The lawsuits or claims may also indicate a foreboding trend in the business or its industry. The investor should, at a minimum, request the name of the case; the court where the suit is filed; a description of the general nature of the case; the amount sought; the status of the case; and the likely outcome in the opinion of the attorneys handling it. The due diligence should also be broad enough to cover not only pending lawsuits but disputes that could proceed to legal action. By using the word "anticipate" in questioning, the investor will have a better chance of catching disputes that at this point appear minor but which could evolve into major litigation.

Also important is the "flip-side" of litigation: Are there any claims or lawsuits by the business against other parties? A claim may involve any number of matters, including one that the party has breached a contract (such as to provide goods or services or to pay for goods or services); an infringement of a patent or trademark; tortious interference with a contract the business has with another party; a former key employee is in breach of a covenant not to compete or is divulging confidential information; or an employee or agent of the business has somehow wronged the business. Although a matter is at the dispute stage and has not yet ripened into a claim by the business, it may involve the potential loss of a valuable asset and should be reviewed. The investor will need to know all the details to form a judgment on the probable outcome and decide if litigation is worth the cost.

In disclosing litigation to the investor, the management may try to describe it in the best possible light. It may also, either intentionally or inadvertently, fail to disclose issues that the investor may deem important. By obtaining copies of the actual pleadings and other important documents, the investor can see firsthand the essential facts of the case. The investor will also be better able to determine the status of the case and judge the possible outcome. Depending upon how far the case has advanced, there may be a voluminous amount of court documents and correspondence. The investor's attorneys should review the disclosed documents to determine how the case is proceeding and what other documents should be requested. Of particular importance would be the parties' pleadings, motions in the case, any orders by the court and depositions and interrogatories of key witnesses.

Because most litigation is eventually settled, it is important to obtain copies of all settlement agreements. A settlement may require the business to do certain things or it may prohibit the business from engaging in certain activities and have a significant impact on the operations of the business. The investor also should obtain drafts of any proposed settlement agreements, because the business may have claimed it was vigorously contesting a particular litigation matter but was actually entertaining or entering into settlement negotiations on terms the investor may not find favorable.

One of the best places to obtain an objective summary of pending litigation is from copies of the letters sent by the business's attorney to the business's independent public accountant for purposes of the audit of the business (the so-called "audit response letters"). A letter of audit inquiry to the business's lawyer is the auditor's primary means of corroborating information furnished by the business, in its financial statements, concerning litigation, claims and assessments. The auditor will generally request that the attorney disclose all material "loss contingencies." A loss contingency is defined in the Statement of Financial Accounting Standards No. 5 as "an existing condition, situation or set of circumstances involving uncertainty as to the possible loss to an enterprise that will ultimately be resolved when one or more events occur or fail to occur."

The standard of what is material will generally be agreed upon by the business and its auditor and will be set forth in the attorney's letter. In the letter, the attorney will provide information as to the nature of the claim, the progress to date, and the position taken by the business. Under the American Bar Association's Statement of Policy Regarding Lawyers' Responses to Auditors' Request for Information (ABA Statement), Paragraph No. 5, a lawyer should furnish information to the auditor only if the business has determined that it is probable that a possible claim will be asserted, that there is a reasonable possibility that the outcome will be unfavorable, and that the resulting liability would be material to the financial condition of the business. However, under the ABA Statement, the lawyer should provide an evaluation of the outcome of the case only in those cases where it appears to the lawyer that an unfavorable outcome is either probable or remote. Further, the attorney should provide an estimate of potential losses only if the probability of inaccuracy is slight. With all these standards in mind, the investor should be able to obtain an objective summary of pending litigation.

Knowledge of any past, current or anticipated litigation against any officers or directors may be extremely significant to verify the personal integrity of the officers and directors of the business. Even when claims are defensible, if the officers and directors of the business are tied up in personal litigation, they may not be able to devote a sufficient amount of time and attention to the proper operation of the business. Also, if the officers, directors, or controlling shareholders of the business have been convicted in the past five years of any felony or misdemeanor involving the sale of securities, or any felony involving fraud or deceit, the business may be restricted under state and federal securities regulations in trying to raise capital.

Reviewing legal expenses is another means of confirming the amount of litigation and identifying the attorneys representing the business. Although the business may be able to cast its present litigation in a favorable light, it will not be able to mask the amount of expenses it has incurred in defending or pursuing the litigation. By looking at the costs of defending a claim, the investor will be able to determine how damaging a particular claim really may be. An investor will want to see how much money the business has spent pursuing a claim to determine whether it is worth the costs. Legal expenses will highlight areas of the business's operations that require significant and continuous legal attention or that may be in jeopardy.

Reserves reported on financial statements reveal potential losses by litigation and indicate how concerned management is about a particular claim and what results it expects. Reserves further highlight areas of the business's operations that may involve significant legal attention. It is important for the investor to know whether the business has reserved proper amounts for potential losses. Litigation reserves have been a convenient means to manipulate income by intentionally under- or overstating the amount reserved.

If a business's shareholders think an officer or director has breached his or her fiduciary duty to the business by such acts as misappropriating funds or not using care in managing the business, they may bring a shareholder derivative suit. In a derivative action, the shareholder or shareholders sue on behalf of and for the benefit of the business. It is important for the investor to know of any shareholder derivative suits and if there is any basis for a claim that the directors or officers have acted inappropriately or have not acted in the best interest of the shareholders. If the shareholders' claim is successful, the corporation will be required to reimburse them for litigation expenses incurred in the lawsuit. Because shareholder derivative suits are often hotly contested, the expenses may be significant. Any lawsuit will likely divert the attention of the officers and directors away from the proper management of the business.

If the business is involved in manufacturing, licensing, selling or renting products, a chief concern to the investor will be the possibility of any claims or suits based upon the products being defective. The investor will want to know what type of warranties exist, the claims' history and amount spent annually on warranty claims. It is also extremely important for the investor to know if there are any pending claims against the business for personal injury or for property damages based upon a defective product and the claims history for any such lawsuits. The type of insurance the business maintains to cover such claims and its adequacy should be reviewed simultaneously.

Questioning the Consumer Product Safety Commission or other governmental agencies relative to investigations or inquiries about products sold by the business is another means to determine if the business has sold defective products. It is also important to learn if governmental agencies have made investigations about similar products manufactured by other entities and why this business is or is not different.

The investor needs to know if anyone is infringing on the business's proprietary rights such as patents, trademarks, copyrights and licenses or permits to use any of the foregoing. Investors should also ask whether the business's patents, trademarks or copyrights are registered and if the business licenses any of its rights to third parties or whether it licenses rights from third parties. For example, does the business have an exclusive license to use a particular patent? What procedures does the business have to detect whether third parties are infringing on the business's rights? The investor also needs to know if the business is infringing on the proprietary rights of others.

There are both civil and criminal issues relating to benefits either being given by the business (usually by an employee of the business) or being received by the business or its employees. First of all, if such benefits are being given or received, they may be illegal and may subject the business to criminal or civil fines or penalties. For instance, a business may be subject to criminal liability under the Foreign Corrupt Practices Act if it pays anything of value to influence the decisions of foreign officials. The Robinson-Patman Act and various state "commercial bribery" laws prohibit the payment of commissions to another unless that party actually renders services for the payment. These statutes are designed to stop commercial bribery, such as an officer of a company receiving a kickback without the knowledge of the company. In addition to being illegal, the investor needs to know whether, if the benefit is stopped, the business might be adversely affected. For example, the business may have lucrative contracts dependent upon someone receiving money "under the table" and if revealed, the other party would be inclined to fire its employee and terminate the contracts.

Price-fixing generally involves agreements either among competitors or persons in the chain of distribution, such as wholesalers and retailers, to fix product prices. Price-fixing done to either raise, depress, or stabilize prices is generally anti-competitive and illegal under federal and state antitrust laws.

The term "market splitting" refers to other types of anti-competitive schemes in which businesses with a substantial market share of an industry agree to drive out lesser competitors. "Kickbacks" and "payoffs" refer to activities that may be illegal either under the Robinson-Patman Act or under state commercial bribery laws. If the business is in the health care industry and is a provider to persons receiving Medicare, it is prohibited from providing kickbacks to persons who are in a position to refer Medicare patients.

It is important for the investor to know if the business has engaged or been suspected of any of these schemes and if it has been investigated by the Federal Trade Commission, any state attorney general's office, or any other governmental entity.

Although a business may not admit to price-fixing, bid-rigging, and the like, if it is in an industry where such activities are commonplace, it is probably difficult for the business not to engage in such acts. Starting with this industry information, the investor should ask how the business competes and survives without engaging in these activities. The responses may be so revealing the investor will decide not to invest.

CHAPTER 22

Information Systems

Most information obtained during a due diligence review of a business's information systems will be utilized after the investment is completed rather than to decide whether to invest. This will be particularly true if integration of the business's and the investor's systems is contemplated.

Knowledge of the present state of the systems is essential to decide what further additions or improvements are needed and economically justified. However, there are a few broad questions that could affect the investment decision. Are the systems compatible with the investor's? Can the software licenses be readily transferred to a new owner? Are the present systems inadequate or obsolete and in need of large capital expenditures? Specific questions regarding the nature, effectiveness, costs of systems, compatibility of systems, proper licensing and future programs should help answer the broad questions for an investor.

Information systems include communications of all types. While computer technology changes at a rapid rate, the entire field of communications is changing equally fast. Whatever is the state of the art in both technologies, all agree today's technology will soon be obsolete and therefore will complicate any due diligence evaluation.

The first step is to find out what hardware and software is used, what systems they support and what information is provided. An inventory of all systems, records and reports provided through the use of computers and associated electronic equipment will indicate the end product. A second inventory of all hardware, computers, peripherals and software will indicate the type of equipment and software used to provide the systems and reports in the first inventory. The inventories should indicate which systems are being revised or scheduled to be replaced and if any hardware is considered to be surplus either now or in the near future. With these inventories the investor will have an overview from which to determine opportunities for further automation and the degree of compatibility with his systems.

Software developed in-house or when the source code is purchased from others is owned by the business, but most software developed by others is not sold but licensed. The license agreements are designed to protect the developer from others copying the software and to restrict its use by the licensee. The licenses are usually nontransferable and technically cannot be transferred without developer approval during sales of assets, or in some cases, if control of the business changes hands. In practice, licensing agreements are usually ignored for inexpensive, off-the-shelf software except when flagrantly large numbers of copies are made or when software limited to one computer is networked to a large number. However, the software for large systems may contain licensing provisions that could require an investor, in the event of a change of control, to seek approval for continued use. An investor must review the licenses for all software in use to verify that there are no violations of the licensing agreements. Violations can result in confiscation of the software and the computers on which it was used.

Numerous factors can enter into the decision to buy or lease computers, but use of capital, service responsibility and availability of leasing are primary issues. If computers have been leased, the leases should be reviewed. For an investor, the main concerns with leases are costs, length of lease obligations and cancellation charges if the lease is cancelled prior to expiration. Managements often regret signing long-term leases because technology and a business's requirements change rapidly. Investors looking to integrate systems or upgrade may find leases to be serious roadblocks. Owned computers present less of a problem but they do have a remaining book value that has to be considered in any plans that would result in their abandonment or sale.

Software not developed and owned by the business is licensed or leased. Some software is a combination in that the basic system has been licensed but modifications were made to meet the requirements of the business. Software costs may be expensed or capitalized, depending on the circumstances. Proprietary software may have been very costly to develop, with all costs expensed, thus creating a substantial intangible value not appearing on the balance sheet. If the expenses were capitalized, the reflected asset may be of real value or worthless. The investor needs to know what he is buying, what are the future obligations and how it has been recorded on the financial statements.

Companies providing components or complete information systems often offer lease options. While leasing often can be attractive to both the lessor and buyer, leases lock in the users for a substantial period of time during which they may find the system to be inadequate or that better alternatives exist. Lessors are well aware of these potential problems and write as onerous cancellation clauses as possible into the leases for their protection. Investors wanting to replace a leased system will have to weigh the advantages against the costs of cancellation.

It is difficult to have a coordinated information program to best serve the business unless someone is charged with that responsibility. The larger the business, the greater the coordination problem and need. The role may be filled by a line executive with direct responsibility for personnel involved in operating hardware, developing software and installing and maintaining systems. It also can be a staff position with some authority given to approve purchases and licensing of hardware and software. The senior person should be interviewed during due diligence. He almost certainly will know more about the status of the systems, problems and prospects than anyone. His stature and status in the business will be an indication of the importance given to information systems.

Dependency upon electronic information systems increases the risk of severe business disruption, or possibly termination, if for any reason the systems are destroyed. Fires and floods are the most probable risks, but terrorism, social protests and violence by disgruntled employees can occur. Consequently, most have developed backup procedures and methods to store duplicate data in secure locations. Since the potential to irreparably damage or bankrupt a business exists if information systems are destroyed, an investor needs to be confident that duplicate data exist and realistic disaster recovery plans are in place.

Security requirements are not limited to the physical protection of the systems. Methods to prevent unauthorized use of data, falsification of data, improper use of hardware and transmission or interception of unauthorized or improper messages are some of the more common security concerns. Infections by software viruses are possible and recognized as a potential problem, but their actual incidence is far less than the publicity indicates. Information systems can be vehicles for very sophisticated theft and fraud in finance and accounting that is extremely difficult to detect.

The history of any security breaches should be reviewed by an investor along with identification of whatever security systems or procedures are in place. Are security concerns and risks taken seriously? Is this a business with systems that would be an attractive target? Who is responsible for security?

CHAPTER 23

Budgeting and Planning

Planning consists of studies, recommendations and decisions as to what products, services and industries the business should be in and what direction it should take. Planning involves establishing an overall philosophy, plan and objectives for the business, while in budgeting, pro forma financial statements are created to forecast, monitor and control existing business units. The financial statements normally reflect anticipated revenues, expense levels and approved capital expenditures. Most budgets have monthly financial statements for the first year and then quarterly or longer periods for future years.

In large corporations, planning and budgeting tend to be segregated into two distinct functions. In medium-size businesses, planning and budgeting often merge, with the CEO or CFO assuming more of the planning function with budgeting folded into the responsibility of the controller or some other financial executive. In small businesses, neither function may formally exist, with planning remaining in the head (or dreams) of an owner consumed with day-to-day operations, and budgeting considered unnecessary.

A primary due diligence target should be copies of existing budgets and plans. No documents other than financial statements will be more informative. A comparison of prior years to actual results will provide insight into management's competence, failures, successes and changes in direction. The latest budgets and plans will indicate current thinking and management's views of the prospects for the business. There is little uniformity among businesses and great variation exists in both format and content of plans and budgets. Both become molded to the needs of a business and the preferences or whims of those in charge. They tend to increase in size and scope each year as executives not only see areas to improve and new subjects to cover, but learn from prior failures or overlooked problem areas.

Most plans and budgets are revised annually, at which time their review and approval is a major management activity usually presided over by the CEO, who finds the event an opportunity to closely review performance and express his opinions. The timing of an investor's request for plans and budgets will influence what he receives. The worst time is just prior to the review process for the ensuing year, and the best time is immediately following the review process when the plans and budgets are finalized. Regardless of the time, the investor should seek whatever is available, because no reports will better indicate how management sees the business and its future.

If planning is a separate function from budgeting, then an understanding of the role of each is required. How long each has existed and what management expects should be determined. Planning is a function that tends to be less stable than budgeting, for which there is a perceived need as long as the business continues. Planning is looked at by many as a desirable but costly luxury that can be dispensed with in business downturns. The instability is somewhat enhanced by planning executives who believe the experience to be excellent but only a stepping-stone to more senior positions.

Most businesses have highly formalized policies and procedures governing the planning and budgeting programs. Budgeting in particular requires specific plans in a given format to be prepared by a designated date. Participants in the review and approval procedures have defined roles and responsibilities, depending on whether they are staff personnel or line executives. For an investor, the degree of formalization of the programs, the years that planning and budgeting have been in effect and the experience and sophistication of those involved all indicate the seriousness with which management views the activity and its importance. The importance given to the programs will be reflected in the quality of the plans and budgets produced. The products of well-managed programs will be of much greater value and validity than those written in a perfunctory or careless manner and which tend to be forgotten or disregarded shortly after approval.

Underlying every plan or budget is a philosophy or attitude that influenced its preparation. In practice, there may be more than one philosophy when the stated official philosophy is ignored because the preparers perceive something outside the official policy is wanted or tolerated. The official stated position of most CEOs is that all plans and budgets are to be prepared on a realistic basis and should be attainable, barring unforeseen events or conditions. However, realism usually appears after years of experience during which the participants realize the CEO will not tolerate unrealistic plans and budgets. It also takes a while for managers to learn how to prepare meaningful budgets.

Conservative budgets are produced by managers who want a budget they are certain to attain. They reason an easy way to avoid criticism is to have a budget they can beat. Easy budgets make them appear as heroes and affect their compensation either directly or indirectly, because businesses often tie incentive bonuses to actual performance compared to a budget.

Optimistic plans and budgets are prepared by those who believe such plans are what senior managers want or because they believe rosy forecasts will preserve their jobs. If that is not the case, it may buy them time to look for a job. Senior managers may only want good news or believe it better to have very difficult goals that may not be achieved rather than easy objectives. Some executives of public companies use an old trick of confiding optimistic internal budget projections to security analysts in hopes they will write a favorable report.

The investor's best guide to the underlying philosophies used in preparation is to request copies of old plans and budgets and compare them to actual results. If most budgets are being exceeded by higher revenues and lower forecast expenses, one can assume a very conservative approach is at play. If few budgets are being met because revenues are consistently lower than budgeted and expenses higher, one can assume this is not an accident. Identifying the philosophy at work will help determine the degree of reliance that can be placed on the latest projections. Regardless, an investor should always remember that failure to follow or meet a plan or budget may indicate the plan is defective rather than that management is making inappropriate decisions.

For some businesses, planning and budgeting are given great importance and considered to be an indispensable management tool. Others look at them as more of a necessary nuisance and annual drill to be conducted and largely ignored afterwards. The investor should understand how planning and budgeting are currently viewed to gain insight into the reliability of existing plans and budgets. This information will also indicate how compatible the views of the investor are with the business's management. An investor with very strong convictions relative to the value of well-prepared plans and budgets could have a difficult time educating an inexperienced or indifferent management.

Some businesses establish plans and budgets annually and don't revise them until the next year. Others have systems where the budgets are reviewed periodically (typically quarterly) and revised to reflect current conditions and unexpected events. There are valid arguments for both approaches. Annual budgets can become meaningless and useless during the course of a year if the original budget was poorly crafted or there were major unexpected changes in the business. However, frequent budget revisions tend to negate the primary purposes of planning and operating the business to achieve predetermined objectives. The investor should be wary of frequently revised budgets. While they may provide a more current picture of operations and the near-term outlook, they also obscure how well the business is performing compared to the original projections.

CHAPTER 24

Insurance and Bonding

Professional assistance is usually necessary to adequately evaluate a business's insurance and bonding coverage. For most investors, the professional will be the insurance broker providing their existing insurance, but other consultants free of conflicts of interest can be employed. It is a relatively simple matter to gather the policies, secure premium and other related information, but to fully understand the policies' terms, coverage and common risks not covered is another matter. Most businessmen have a general knowledge of the policies and costs but very limited information on specific terms, at least until a disputed claim occurs.

Evaluation of the adequacy of any insurance coverage is no longer complete with just a study comparing probable risks to the terms of the contracts. The practices of the carriers and their financial capability to pay must also be considered. Carriers are private companies and, as in any industry, there are a few who are disreputable, engage in sharp practice and have limited or no financial ability to pay losses. Even some of the larger, better-known carriers have experienced substantial losses from poor investments, underwriting or both. The well-publicized financial problems of Lloyds of London, the large number of carriers that have failed, and the shortcomings of regulatory agencies should be a warning, in every due diligence evaluation, that review of the contracts is not enough. There are several companies involved in rating insurance and bonding companies that can be a quick reference and starting point. If the business has a significant outstanding but unpaid claim, carrier evaluation will take on immediate importance.

All insurance in effect is described in a contract between the carrier and the insured, and one should assume that if there is no contract or policy, there is no insurance. An exception would be new insurance in which coverage was orally agreed to take effect at a certain time with the understanding the full policy would soon follow. However, in these new coverage exceptions, the written policy should quickly follow and be available for inspection. Businesses commonly have a number of different insurance policies and plans, thus making it convenient for those conducting due diligence to create a summary of the various plans. From the summary an overview is possible as well as another means of identifying any gaps in the coverage.

The investor's primary concerns are the adequacy of coverage and possible excess coverage for the type business. Is the business at risk by not having proper insurance coverage? While what is proper and adequate insurance for any business is a judgment call, in most cases the range of opinion will be relatively small. Cost of the insurance is nearly as important for an investor, since substantial savings may be possible through consolidation with plans the investor has at other businesses, or by seeking competitive bids when the present policies expire.

In acquisitions of businesses in which only selected assets and liabilities (asset deals) are acquired, but not the corporation, insurance presents a special problem, since in that case the legal entity is not acquired. Insurance coverage will have to be transferred and if not possible or desirable, new coverage purchased. This may be a relatively easy or a serious problem that could delay the entire deal.

All policies are for a set period of time with renewal often at the carrier's option. Even when the insured has an option to renew, the carrier can set a high premium to discourage renewal. Insurance carriers are in business to make money and when, in their view, an industry or business has or is expected to have a poor loss experience, premiums must be increased or the insurance discontinued. Premium increases or cancellations of insurance can present a difficult problem for a business because most other carriers will have a similar view of the risks. The possibility of major premium increases that will adversely affect profitability, or exposure to loss that could exist if risks were not insured should concern an investor.

Insurance purchased on a retrospective basis is so structured that if the insured has good experience with few losses, a portion of the premium paid will be refunded. Heavy losses can result in no refunds and premium increases when the policies are to be renewed. A retrospective basis provides a financial incentive for the business to install programs to reduce or eliminate conditions that could cause claims. Premium refunds can be of a magnitude that they substantially distort income in the month received. They also reflect the business's loss experience in prior years rather than the present year, which may be very different. The investor's interest is in whether there is a history of premium refunds and the amounts usually received. Refunds are also an indication of loss prevention programs conducted by the business. Regardless of past history, refunds cannot be depended upon in future years.

Policies are not renewed or are cancelled because of unacceptable or anticipated losses, because they are unprofitable or the level of risk in the industry as a whole is too high, or because the carrier has problems unrelated to the business being studied. If any policies have been cancelled, the investor should find out why. A cancelled policy can mean higher premiums with a new carrier, unsafe and/ or unsound practices on the part of the business, or can create an uninsured business or one with inadequate coverage.

Major losses can be either one or more very large losses, such as a fire, fatalities or litigation with a huge adverse award, or a large number of smaller claims that add up to a total far in excess of premiums paid. Carriers may not readily pay large claims, and disputes between the insured and the carriers are common. For most businessmen, there always seems to be an abundance of terms that spur arguments. Even when there are no exclusions or limitations that would disqualify the claim, there can still be much to argue over concerning the extent of damages and actual losses. An investor should evaluate the impact of major losses upon the business and its insurance program. Are there unpaid claims in dispute over the validity or the amount? What are the likely outcome and amounts to be recovered? What amounts, yet to be received, have been recorded on the financial records?

In a broad sense, whenever a business does not have coverage for a specific risk, it is self-insured. However, self-insurance is usually thought of as a program in which a business makes the conscious decision to set up its own program and not use an outside carrier. The self-insurance program involves either paying into a self-administered fund to cover claims or simply reserving on the financial statements a certain amount each month or quarter. Most businesses that self-insure purchase catastrophe or umbrella policies that cover losses that individually or in total exceed specified amounts. Whenever self-insurance exists, investors must question how the reserves are set and recorded on financial statements. They also need to know if reserves are excessive and depressing income, what the loss experience has been and whether employees are intimidated to not file workmen's compensation claims. If a business is self-insured, the investor should learn the underlying rationale for that as well as what level of losses catastrophic insurance covers. Considering all factors, is self-insurance appropriate for this business?

In certain industries, most commonly construction, bid and performance bonds are required. Bid bonds are usually of lesser amounts and are provided at the time a bid or proposal is made, to guarantee that if the job is awarded, the contractor will accept it. Performance bonds guarantee that a job awarded will be completed. Bonding companies carefully evaluate businesses on the basis of their financial strength, past record and ability to perform before issuing bonds, since they much prefer collecting bonding fees to paying claims.

An investor must evaluate a business's record in securing bonds and its current bonding limits. Bonding ability can govern the growth of a business and be a competitive advantage over weaker competitors or a disadvantage if the business cannot bid jobs because of an inability to secure bonds. Any change in control of the business can influence bonding capability. If financial strength is added and management retained or enhanced, bonding limits may be increased, but if there is increased debt or a new, unproven management, bonding capability may disappear.

Bonding of employees is a form of insurance that pays claims to offset losses caused by dishonest acts. Claims may be filed by the employer for their losses or for losses of customers or others caused by improper acts. Bonding may be a requirement of the customer, a decision by the employer who considers it a prudent business move, or primarily a marketing ploy to secure the customer's confidence. Many bonding contracts contain restrictions that limit claim payments to those cases in which criminal charges are filed. Claims may be an indication of the existence of a serious theft problem. The investor needs to identify dishonest incidents where both claims were filed and not filed.

Key man life insurance is coverage on the life of key executives or major shareholders with benefits payable to the business. The benefits may compensate the business for the loss of the executive's services and tide over the business until a replacement is located. Proceeds may be used to pay creditors or investors, but most commonly they are used to buy back the shares of the deceased shareholder. Private companies do not have a ready market for their shares and this is a common technique for creating liquidity. Key man insurance policies may accumulate a substantial cash value against which the business can borrow funds on an attractive basis. The investor's main interest is what to do with the insurance, because the reasons for it often disappear with a change of control. The insurance can either be transferred to the insured key individual as part of the price to be paid or simply surrendered for cash value.

CHAPTER 25

Environmental Issues

A public awareness of environmental hazards has resulted in broad, complex legislation, vigorous enforcement, endless litigation and horror stories in which investors found themselves owners of environmental liabilities that often exceeded their original investment. Today, few investments involving real estate or manufacturing are completed without an extensive review of environmental risks and negotiations to establish responsibility for remedial costs of any hazards that may exist—known or unknown. While no statistics are available, anecdotal evidence indicates that more deals upon which preliminary agreements were reached were eventually terminated over environmental issues than any other. An even larger category are failed deals that never reached the preliminary agreement stage because investors learned of environmental problems.

Due diligence of environmental issues is difficult because of their complexity, nebulous and untested legislation, unreasonable and ill-considered regulations, conflicting and changing regulations, changing technology, difficulty in securing estimates of the cost of remedial measures, difficulty of proving what does not exist and the large number of individuals and firms who have entered the environmental field claiming to be experts with superior solutions.

When environmental issues arise, expert opinions may be necessary to evaluate the risks. Environmental engineers evaluate the nature and extent of the problem. An attorney specializing in environmental law may be needed. Direct meetings with regulatory agencies may be advisable. All of these activities can become time-consuming, expensive and often discouraging because of the difficulty of securing precise answers, and differing opinions from the experts. The investor must constantly be alert to conflicts of interest in which those evaluating an environmental risk and recommending solutions may also be involved, either directly or indirectly, in the recommended remedial activity.

For each location there may be several files or a central file containing copies of all documents and permits relative to environmental matters. An objective of due diligence should be review of all information in the files. However, information not in the file can be most troublesome, as would be the case if an environmental hazard was concealed.

The questions and subjects to be explored in the checklist (see the Appendix) are detailed, and some overlap. However, the stakes are so high with environmental issues that an investor cannot be in a position of not knowing because he failed to ask a precise question. See Chapter 4 for a discussion of legal issues and consequences relative to the environments.

Once an environmental problem is suspected or known to exist by any government agency, a paper trail begins and the condition is unlikely to be ignored. Initial documents may be notices, correspondence or applications for permits that eventually may lead to voluminous studies, reports, audits and civil or even criminal charges. The Environmental Protection Agency is the federal agency created and charged under the Environment Protection Act with the responsibility of administering the Act. However, states, counties and municipalities also have agencies created to monitor the environment and enforce regulations. Sorting out which agency has primary responsibility in a given situation can be perplexing, and receiving approval for proposed remedial action may prove frustrating. An investor must identify all environmental hazards and their status vis-à-vis all regulatory agencies. What will be the cost of remedial activity? What is the position of the regulatory agency? Are solutions known or still being sought? If proposed solutions are disputed, what can the business expect to accomplish?

Government actions, anticipation of demands from governments or investors, or simply an awareness of environmental hazards may cause businesses to conduct studies to evaluate the suspected hazards. The studies should indicate if suspected hazards do indeed exist and provide the basis for deciding upon appropriate remedial action. Environmental studies are classified as phases 1, 2 and 3, with phase 1 the preliminary survey. Whatever studies exist, an investor will want to review each in detail. They can identify problem areas that may or may not be known to government agencies. Why the studies were conducted and the competence of those who prepared them are a necessary part of the investor's review.

Environmental hazards, problems and issues have such enormous potential to impair the financial health of a business that specific questions should be asked about each parcel of real estate, mobile equipment and operations of the business, during due diligence. Systematic questioning not only reduces the chances of an undesirable condition remaining undisclosed but may cause a business to recognize hazards of which they were unaware. It is not uncommon for management to be oblivious of environmental problems and the further senior managers are removed from operations, the greater will be the chance they are poorly informed. The most effective due diligence will be at the location securing data from those who best know the operations. Once a hazardous condition is found to exist, further studies, laboratory tests and professional opinions will likely be necessary for evaluation.

Legislation and regulations governing the environment are frequently reviewed, amended, revised and changed in recognition of new problems, revaluation of old and improved technology. The practice of legislation stating broad principles and delegating the writing of specific regulations to administrative agencies contributes to the uncertainty. Nearly all legislation regarding the environment is controversial and serious proposals to change existing or create new are generally well publicized. Detailed regulations from administrative agencies are usually preceded by public notices and hearings. The result is those affected should know what may be coming. They will not know exactly until the legislation passes or the formal regulations are issued, but they will have a good idea of what is probable. The investor should be able to learn from management if changes are possible that could affect the business either adversely or favorably. If management is not forthcoming, professional advisors should easily be able to offer insight. When changes could have a very serious impact on the business, consultations with elected officials and the government agencies involved would be appropriate.

Permits are issued by governmental agencies to allow and control the use and disposal of hazardous or toxic materials and equipment. Examples are permits allowing emissions into the air but limiting the content of the emissions, discharges of effluent into streams or sewer systems and permits to use underground storage tanks. Most permits are issued for a set period of time, after which they must be renewed. Waivers are grants to exceed allowable standards, but usually for a limited period, until it is practical to correct the condition. The investor must know if all required permits are in order, since failure to have permits can result in fines and shut down operations.

The amount of money spent and amounts predicted to be spent for environmental compliance and remedial work are another indicator of the extent of problems and management's commitment, either voluntary or involuntary. Amounts spent may be segregated in the accounting system and readily available or may have to be estimated. Businesses like to publicize large expenditures on environmental matters to their shareholders and the public to emphasize their commitment and, in some instances, to gain sympathy and understanding. For the investor, past expenditures should be segregated between those that will continue and the non-recurring. Large non-recurring expenditures can distort actual earning capability of the business. Future estimated expenditures should be evaluated and incorporated into forecasts.

CHAPTER 26

Debt and Banking

"Debt" is an extraordinarily broad term that describes financial obligations that must be identified and fully understood during the due diligence study. Debt and all its conditions have variations limited only by human imagination. Timing and terms of repayment, collateral, penalties for default, guarantees and various covenants can result in debt obligations that are extremely onerous or impossible to repay and others in which the debtor can largely repay at his discretion. Due diligence of debt requires studying the details of the actual financial instruments. The tedious fine print cannot be ignored.

An initial step is to identify all indebtedness of the business. Debts may be owed to banks and other financial institutions, shareholders, officers, security holders, individuals, a government and anything or anyone who can be defined as a legal entity. Supporting each debt should be documentation describing the terms and conditions of the indebtedness. Since such documents are often revised or amended, care must be taken to have the complete and latest documentation.

An investor will find it helpful to develop a list summarizing all debt, its terms and conditions for use in evaluating the business and planning his program. At a minimum, the list should include the amount owed, name of lender, repayment schedule, rate of interest, restrictions on use of funds, borrowing base, collateral, prepayment provisions and guarantees. A summary list does not reduce the need to study the individual loan documents. For most businessmen, the detailed study will be a task for their attorneys and accountants.

Any bank or financial institution with which there has been or is a business relationship will have an opinion regarding the business and its management. The nature of the relationship and the opinion of the institution will largely determine the future relationship. If the business is not in compliance with its loan agreements and the lenders have lost confidence in the management of the business, one can assume the relationship will not be expanded. However, if loans have been paid on or ahead of schedule and the lenders believe in the management, it will be in the lender's interest to continue or expand the relationship. The investor needs to know which lending institutions will call their loans if given the opportunity and which can be counted on to continue, or even increase, their loans. If special relationships exist, usually in the form of close personal friendships, these should be identified and evaluated in light of the possible presence of the investor.

Knowledge of the bank accounts and authorized signers is essential if the investor is to take control of the business. The authorization to spend the money of the business is a fundamental element of control. A detail often overlooked in takeovers of corporations is that certified minutes of resolutions of the board of directors are required to inform a bank of those authorized to sign checks.

Lines of credit are essentially the preapproved right to borrow money up to a predetermined maximum amount for a period of time. The maximum may vary with the financial condition of the business or "borrowing base," usually consisting of current assets that serve as collateral. Lines of credit permit the borrower to draw down funds as needed and pay back with excess cash, with neither tied to a predetermined schedule. Depending upon the overall business relationship between the institution and the borrower, there may be a small fee for the standby unused portion of the line of credit. Lines of credit are short-term debt that can be terminated when the term of the line expires or covenants are broken. Lines of credit are sometimes referred to as "revolvers" because the lines commonly continue upon expiration and revolve, but if the lender is dissatisfied, he can refuse to extend the line and the borrower is financially shot dead if other sources of money are not available. Any investor will want to know the probability of each line continuing and whether it can be increased or extended. Unused lines of credit and their associated costs should also be studied, to determine if they are needed.

A business must plan to meet both short- and long-term repayment schedules. Present plans may be quite different from the original because of changed conditions. If there is no plan the investor will either have to insist on one being created or do so himself. The viability of the business is dependent upon its ability to meet its financial obligations, and success is partially dependent upon financing at as low a cost as possible, without onerous repayment terms. Any investor will be intensely interested in financing activities to be certain that they serve the business and none are inconsistent with his programs and capability.

Businesses structured with a parent company and one or more subsidiaries may have the subsidiaries borrow funds. Depending upon the financial strength of the subsidiary, policies of the lender and restrictions on up-stream payments to the parent, the lender may or may not demand the indebtedness be guaranteed by the parent company. Lenders prefer the added assurance and collateral of a parent company guarantee, while businesses prefer the flexibility retained by not granting guarantees. Parent companies also like the concept of each subsidiary having the financial independence to go broke without dragging down the parent. More often than not, parent company guarantees are necessary for borrowing and an investor must know the nature of the guarantees. If no guarantees are required, a major issue could be whether the presence of the investor will cause a need for guarantees.

Personal guarantees are guarantees by individuals, usually shareholders or key executives, that if the business fails to pay a guaranteed debt, the individual will become personally liable. Lenders often insist upon personal guarantees as a condition for making a loan to medium- or small-sized businesses, because they constitute additional collateral, lock in the individual to do his best to help the business succeed and pay off its indebtedness and provide comfort that the loan application was accurate. Individuals resist giving guarantees because they are well aware of the vicissitudes of business and, despite confidence in their business, are reluctant to jeopardize their own wealth.

Investors looking to take control of a business will have to resolve in negotiations how to treat outstanding personal guarantees. Anyone in control of a business who has guaranteed a loan will be unlikely to give up control unless the debt is retired, he is replaced by another guarantor or the investor agrees to indemnify the guarantor from any personal losses. The latter approach is often necessary when lenders refuse to surrender any collateral or release a guarantor.

Pledge collateral may have a market value far different than the amount of the outstanding loan. Excessive collateral may have been required because the lender viewed the loan as one of high risk, but usually, excessive collateral exists because the loan has been largely paid off. Since lenders are seldom willing to give up any collateral until a loan is repaid, regardless of how disproportionate, a business may find it prudent to repay a loan and free the collateral as part of a refinancing program.

Loans with little or no collateral or guarantees should also be reviewed to learn how and why they were granted under such favorable conditions. Was this simply a lender's confidence in the business and management or were some improprieties involved? An investor will want to compare the collateral value with loan value. Comparisons can provide insight into how lenders view the business and identify assets for possible use in refinancing.

Letters of credit are third-party guarantees of payments usually issued by banks. The most common usage is when a business purchases materials or equipment and secures a letter of credit from a bank with provisions that, upon satisfactory receipt of the material or services, the vendor will be paid by the purchaser or the bank. The bank may make the payment and collect from the purchaser, but however handled, the vendor is assured of payment. Banks' fees for letters of credit are partially determined by the level of risk assumed by the bank. Regardless, banks do not issue letters of credit unless they are confident they will be reimbursed for whatever obligations are assumed. Letters of credit can represent a very significant obligation of a business that may not be recorded in the financial statements. When the obligations guaranteed by the letters come due, the business must provide the cash. The extent of the outstanding obligations through letters of credit must be determined to understand cash-flow requirements.

Businesses, executives, shareholders, industries and geographical areas all can develop reputations that may influence lenders either favorably or negatively. The reputations may or may not be based on fact, but they are real and they influence lending decisions. Businesses or industries that have had difficult and declining fortunes or are involved in socially or politically controversial activities will have a more difficult time borrowing than successful and exciting businesses free from controversy. An investor who plans to borrow funds or refinance has to be concerned with the business's reputation and factors affecting the business. The reputation can constitute an advantage or conversely cause financing to be nearly impossible. The reputation problem should not be underestimated.

Vendor financing can be in the form of direct loans, favorable leases of property or equipment and, most commonly, in extended payment terms for purchases. The financing may be given to meet competition but more often to lock out competitors. A vendor supplying financing either formally or informally does so with the understanding that in exchange for the financing, all purchases possible will be from the vendor. Vendors must cover their costs and make a profit, so in one form or another the financing cost is passed on to the recipient. If vendor financing exists in any form, an investor should determine the extent and the cost. Vendor financing, while not readily visible, may be some of the most expensive, and alternatives should be explored.

There are many reasons why a business could have outstanding loans from shareholders or officers, but several are most common. Rather than contribute equity to the business, a controlling shareholder may have elected to lend the business money under the rationale that the loan could be repaid or that he would end up as a creditor if the business failed. A business short of cash may call upon its shareholders and officers for loans when credit cannot be found elsewhere. One unable to pay salaries, bonuses or dividends may persuade those owed to accept promissory notes. There are also situations in which shareholders or officers believe there is no better place to invest and are eager to do so. Loans of this type may be structured and documented as arm's length transactions, but they are always something less because the lenders either control or influence the borrower. This relationship between borrower and lender creates the opportunity to frequently disregard the original terms of the note to accommodate either party's current needs. If any loans from shareholders or executives exist, the investor must know complete details on the history, payment schedule, terms, amounts outstanding, degree of documentation and plans for repayment.

Leasing is a form of financing in which a fee is paid periodically for the use of an asset. Leases that are firm contracts and cannot be cancelled at the discretion of the lessee are usually reported on the business's financial statements and disclose the extent of the liability for future payments. Leases can contain whatever terms the parties negotiate and a business's view of a lease may range from an "undervalued asset" to a "burden from which management is seeking escape." Information on leases is critical for investors because all lease obligations are financial liabilities. The specific terms of greatest interest, other than the financial terms, are those indicating the time the lease has to run, options to renew the lease, penalties for failure to pay agreed rent, escalation clauses and rights to purchase the leased asset.

In certain investments (asset deals) where selected assets, but not the corporation, are acquired, the lease has to be transferred to the new owner, a transaction that may or may not be difficult. In all "asset deals" the lease obligations should be studied early and a strategy developed.

CHAPTER 27

Investments and Cash Management

Investments are extremely variable in their nature and require separate study. An investment may have a market value higher or lower than that recorded or its original cost. Restrictions on liquidity either by contract terms, government regulations or the market's ability to absorb the investment all can affect the value. The value of an investment may be instantly discernible, as would be the case with government securities, or extremely difficult to determine, as would be the case with unregistered securities in a private company that was losing money. Some investments have no present market value and cannot be sold, but there remains the possibility that value would return at some future date and under the right circumstances. The due diligence objectives for each investment are to determine present value, quality and liquidity.

Businesses invest surplus cash in nearly every manner imaginable. Each investment should be reviewed, along with the decisions and policies that led to the investment. The investor should understand the rationale for the policies, how they were developed, and how investments were selected. Also to be determined is who makes the investment decisions and what have been the results. Investors should review the business's plans for using the invested funds and determine whether any investments were improper or insider deals. Additionally, the investor will want to review the financial instruments and documentation to confirm each investment.

Loans to shareholders and executives are usually insider transactions for the benefit of the borrower and as such those investments need careful review early in the due diligence process. Their most common purposes are a means of extra compensation, a method of financing stock purchases, financing for personal residences or other executive perquisites. They also serve as a device for temporarily removing funds from the business without paying personal income taxes. An investor needs full information on these loans and must determine how the contemplated investment will affect their value and the possibility of repayment. The borrower may have had no plans to repay the loan. What happens to the loans may be a sensitive issue in negotiations, particularly if the borrower can influence the negotiations.

Businesses tend to have substantial swings in their cash requirements. Temporary shortages are typically accommodated by sums drawn from lines of credit while surpluses present an opportunity for short-term investments. Even for a short time, funds can produce income at little or no risk that would have been lost if the funds were not invested. Of the many available short-term investments, government securities, commercial paper and interest-bearing accounts are the most common. Short-term investments are also an opportunity for clever treasurers to demonstrate their value to the business. An aggressive cash-management system will prevent cash from accumulating uninvested. The amount of temporary funds that accumulate and the way they are invested or allowed to sit idle can be of interest to an investor, as it indicates how tightly the business manages its cash. Surplus cash not aggressively invested can represent an opportunity to increase income.

CASH MANAGEMENT

Cash management is a broad term generally referring to how well the business collects and utilizes its cash. The objectives of most cash-management programs are to meet the business's financial obligations when due but not a minute before, and to invest all surplus funds. Unfortunately, for some, cash management is a euphemism for taking advantage of suppliers and creditors by delaying payments until legal action is threatened.

Cash flow is one of the most important of all due diligence subjects. If the investor is to receive a return on his investment, it must come from cash flow or a sale of the investment whose value would be influenced by cash-flow history. Cash flow can be greatly affected by how well the business manages its cash. Limiting credit, aggressive collection of receivables and bad debts, taking discounts, paying creditors when due but not before, tight internal controls on expenditures, investment of surplus funds and renegotiating loans to secure lower interest rates all are characteristics of effective cash-management programs. An investor will want to learn how carefully the business controls its cash. If cash management is not paramount in management's mind, this may represent an additional opportunity for profit improvement.

The granting of credit and collection of receivables is an important part of cash-management activities. However, the evaluation of customers for credit worthiness can vary greatly in scope and importance. A business with customers of the Fortune 500 type is concerned primarily with when receivables will be collected rather than inability to collect. However, businesses selling to many customers must have a substantial credit and collection function unless sales are for cash or on a COD basis. The credit function, of necessity, can become a sizable operation with the authority to approve all sales and set limits on the amount of credit granted to any one customer. Most businesses could not survive without a credit function, and for many the credit manger is an unsung hero who daily prevents the business from making serious errors.

Credit departments can play a very constructive role in marketing programs by arranging payment schedules and third-party financing to make sales possible. Their role as a positive element in sales can be every bit as important as their somewhat negative role in disapproving questionable credit risks. In measuring the effectiveness of the credit function, the contribution to making sales is as important as the level of bad debts. The evaluation of customers and granting of credit is so critical for many businesses that it cannot be overlooked. The credit function is often not conspicuous, but it is somewhere in the business.

There has to be some sort of system for a credit approval program to function well. The system may be highly structured and formalized or very informal. Whatever it is, an excellent way for an investor to understand the credit function is to ask precisely how the system works. Are there written procedures? What is the flow of paperwork? How are disputes between credit and marketing employees resolved? Can one overrule the other? Is credit responsible for collection of receivables?

Any business receiving cash directly from customers must be concerned with theft and skimming. Theft in this context is usually stealing of cash by employees. Skimming is taking of cash by the owner or manager without reporting it on business or personal tax returns—a criminal offense. For most businesses theft is a problem, but for those where employees handle cash, it is a serious and continuous problem. The theft problem is hardly limited to cash, since consumer goods, food and anything that can be sold or consumed are popular targets. But cash is most attractive, tempting and often easiest to steal. Systems and controls that discourage theft and indicate when theft may be occurring are essential for cash businesses to survive. While no statistical evidence exists or is ever likely to, there is ample anecdotal evidence to indicate that in small- to medium-size businesses selling on a cash basis, skimming by the owner-operators is an all too common practice. Retail and food service businesses are notorious. Skimming makes the sale of a business very difficult because the true earnings cannot be disclosed or verified without the admission of a crime.

During due diligence of businesses selling products or services for cash, it is practical to start with the assumption that theft and skimming exist and attempt to estimate the amounts rather than assume they do not. There may very well prove to be no problem, but it is more realistic to assume there is. Past incidents of theft and their frequency will give some indication of the magnitude. The type and sophistication of controls need to be reviewed and their effectiveness evaluated. How much can be learned about skimming will depend on how candid, indiscrete and foolish the owner wants to be.

The relative value of the currency of foreign governments fluctuates as the financial markets perceive the current and future value of each country's currency. Businesses holding cash assets in the currency of another country or engaged in international transactions in which payments are received in another countries' currency must be concerned about losses in foreign exchange. Gains are as possible as losses, but unless the business is engaged in speculation in foreign currency, the objective is to avoid losses. The most common approach to minimize currency losses is through hedging in the futures market. The record of gains and losses because of currency fluctuations is a guide to assess how well the business protects itself. History, current exposure, an understanding of the relevant policies and procedures and the sophistication of the financial executives involved will indicate if this is a risk under control or an area for immediate attention.

Unrepatriated foreign profits are funds earned in a foreign business owned or controlled by the business under study. In general, foreign profits are not taxable in the United States until the funds are transferred to the United States. This is an unintended incentive to keep the funds out of the United States. Some managements view these profits as funds that can be invested in higher risk investments or used for unusual executive perks when traveling abroad. Consequently, the record of how and when foreign profits have been reinvested or spent should be of great interest during due diligence. The larger the profits of the foreign businesses, the greater will be the importance of the subject to an investor. What are the current amounts and management's plans for the funds? What has been the policy and practice on repatriation? How are the funds presently invested, or have they been spent on executive perks? Is there planning in progress to reduce the tax impact?

EMPLOYEE BENEFIT FUNDS

Businesses generate large funds as a result of employee benefit plans. Pension, profit sharing, 401K, savings and deferred compensation plans are the most common funds held in trust that must be invested. They may be placed in the custody of an institution specializing in the receipt, disbursement and investment of funds, such as a bank or insurance company. Or an independent trust may be set up to handle and administer the funds with executives and employees serving as trustees and making investment decisions. While most exercise their fiduciary duties with great care, the record is littered with those who have not. It is a mistake to assume that once money is paid into a fund the contributor has no further responsibility or concern. In certain circumstances, improper investments (particularly those that fail) can result in liability and litigation and, at a minimum, employee anger. The investment success or failure can also affect the requirement for future contributions.

Contributions by the business and employees are usually paid into a fund under the care of a trustee with responsibilities defined in a trust agreement. The trustee may or may not be responsible for investment decisions and making investments. An administrative committee may exist to set investment policy, select specific investments and resolve questions that arise in the day-to-day administration of the fund. A wide variance exists in the structures established to oversee the funds, and each has to be studied separately. In all cases, some legal entity or account must exist to receive and disburse funds. Investment policy must be established and investments made by someone. Individuals in or out of the business who are responsible for these activities should be identified and evaluated for both competence and independence.

If any money from the fund has been invested in the business or its securities, the circumstances and value of the investments need to be carefully studied. Such investments are generally frowned upon, and under some conditions are illegal. Trustees and administrators may have personal liability if the investments fail. The attitude in the United States is to discourage investing pension funds in the business, but in other countries the practice is encouraged and some are even backed by government guarantees.

The large pool of money in a fund may prove to be too much of a temptation for controlling shareholders or executives and they may arrange for the fund to make investments in which they personally benefit. Real estate and equipment loans and private placement of securities are most prevalent. While these may prove to be superior investments and are rationalized by their sponsors as a favor to the fund, they often are of a high-risk nature and are unsuccessful. If the money was readily available from conventional lenders, it probably would have been borrowed from them. Investments with conflicts of interest pose several problems. They may be improper and in some cases illegal. If they fail, the business will either directly or indirectly, through increased contributions, be required to compensate for the losses. They also give the trust an unsavory reputation and create doubts among employees as to whether they will collect their benefits.

Benefit plan contributions by the business are usually made once a year while employee contributions should be made as deducted from their compensation. Business contributions that are tax deductible expenses must be made before filing the tax return for the year in which the deduction is claimed. A business short on cash may delay its contribution as long as possible and record the liability on its year-end financial report. Since contributions can have an impact on cash flow, their timing is a due diligence subject.

CHAPTER 28

Taxes

Taxes are an unpleasant cost of doing business. They contribute nothing directly to the success of a business but indirectly make the business possible, since only the most primitive of trading could occur in the absence of government. The task during due diligence is to identify tax obligations, evaluate how well they are being met, review their impact upon competitiveness and learn the status of any disputes. Sufficient information should be gathered to determine if excessive taxes have been paid and what steps may be taken to reduce the overall tax burden without violating any laws.

Businessmen can readily gather the basic information on taxes and identify obvious problem areas and subjects for further study. However, taxes may be complex, and a professional tax expert may be required to evaluate a business's tax situation. If tax savings are a possibility, an expert usually will be required. Possibly several experts will be needed because of their tendency to specialize. An expert on U.S. federal taxes may know little of local ad valorem taxes or state taxes and their political administration, and the reverse can definitely be true. Foreign taxes require experts on a country-by-country basis and the best will most likely reside in the country involved.

The first step in the due diligence study of taxes is to identify the tax reports required. Some will be of much greater importance (such as federal returns) than others, but any of the taxing authorities has the power to take legal action against the business for failure to file required reports and pay taxes. The legal action may be slow in coming but one can assume it will eventually happen.

A summary of activity relative to each taxing authority will help to understand the effect of taxes upon the business. Identifying the actual amounts paid or due enables a rational determination of the taxes' impact upon profits and the business's competitive position. When large amounts of taxes are being paid to a particular government, alternative methods of conducting business may be possible to reduce or eliminate this tax burden.

If the business owes overdue taxes, investors must determine why. Cash-short businesses may delay tax payments and accept the penalties that in many cases are less than the business's cost of financing. Any overdue taxes should be recorded on the financial statements, regardless of the reasons.

Amounts in dispute are of particular interest and any significant amounts should be investigated. A common problem is discerning the actual amounts in dispute, because taxing authorities often overstate the amounts due. Overstated claims for taxes, coupled with the possibility of a compromise settlement, can make estimating the final liability difficult.

Failure to file tax reports on a timely basis can result in needless penalties and is evidence of mismanagement, understaffing or poor advice. Shortcomings in such a basic function is an indication that there may be other serious problems with the business's financial arms.

The IRS is empowered to conduct taxpayer audits whenever it elects to do so. An audit involves inspection of original documents supporting financial transactions and identifying transactions in which the IRS and the taxpayer have different interpretations of tax law. During an audit, and definitely at its conclusion, the agent will inform the business of errors discovered and the amounts, if any, believed owed to the IRS. The business can accept those conclusions, attempt to persuade the agent his conclusions are in error, negotiate a compromise, or appeal the decision to the IRS and eventually into the tax courts.

Open years for tax purposes are years still subject to review, audit or that have unresolved disputes. An investor will want to know how many years are closed since these years are considered safe from unknown tax liabilities. For all open years, there are possible tax liabilities for the business and those who will assume responsibility will be a subject for the investor's negotiations. Since the amounts are unknown, these can be very difficult negotiations.

Whatever adjustments have been made as a result of audits are important for the investor to understand. However, areas of the business's returns that were accepted by the auditors, despite misgivings by the management or the investor's tax professionals, may be of even greater interest. Was the actual acceptance by the auditors a result of the controversial issue being closed or an oversight that should not be expected in future audits? This is a question few would ask of the IRS.

Audits scheduled or in progress tend to create a period of uncertainty during which the investor or selling shareholders may want to delay any transaction until they are completed. The more reason either party has to be worried about an audit's results, the greater will be the anxiety and reason for delay. Most businesses attempt to comply with the tax laws and have little reason to be concerned about the outcome of an audit, but there still may be some apprehension. While audits are in progress, it is usually possible to secure preliminary findings and learn if problem areas have been found by the auditors. An investor should review adjustments made, deficiencies asserted, assessments, interest, penalties and additions as a result of the audits and decide if any are significant. Do any adjustments or claims indicate a continuing problem? Are any adjustments or claims of such magnitude that methods of conducting the business should be reconsidered?

If there are disputes or open issues with any taxing agencies, management is almost certain to be aware of their existence and should disclose the information. Disputes can be over interpretation of laws and regulations and amounts due by the taxpayer or refunds being sought. Any conflict with, or demand by, a taxing body is one neither the business nor a potential investor can ignore. The government has the funding to pursue its claims until it is satisfied or defeated in an appeals court. Under these circumstances, an investor must be concerned with any claims of a magnitude that could affect the business's financial health.

Tax refunds due or claimed or assessments of any type outstanding against the business should normally be either footnoted or recorded in the financial statements. Since the amount of refunds due or amounts owed are usually not known until agreement is reached, whatever is recorded needs to be verified. Unrealistic amounts anticipated as tax refunds and recorded as assets inflate the financial statements, while overly optimistic defenses against tax claims used to rationalize recording little or no reserve also create misleading financial statements. If tax refunds are due or claims exist against the business, an investor should review how realistic the amounts recorded are and determine when actual cash is to be received or paid. The time period between settlements and cash actually changing hands can be many months for both refunds and payments.

Net operating losses (NOLs) and tax credits are clearly important assets but only become valuable when the business is profitable. A change in control or ownership of the business can severely limit their use and tax laws discourage acquisition of a business primarily for its NOLs or tax credits. An investor seeking control of the business should consult with his tax professional to learn the limits on use of tax credits and NOLs following a change of control. In general, an investor should invest for reasons other than an expectation of utilizing NOLs and tax credits.

While taxes in some form are always a fact of business life, the laws and regulations frequently change to accommodate the government's need for revenue or to reflect changes in political philosophy and power. The agencies responsible for collection issue regulations to clarify and implement laws and the courts review and modify or affirm both laws and regulations. The result is a continually evolving and changing tax system. Fortunately, the possibilities of tax law changes are usually public knowledge and known to those who could be affected. Proposed tax revisions that could have a significant adverse effect are particularly well publicized because someone will sound the alarm. Predicting changes in tax requirements always has an element of uncertainty, but there usually is enough information to make realistic assumptions and estimate the odds for the assumptions to become fact. News reports and queries of management, tax professionals and politicians should provide adequate information for an investor to make informed judgments.

Federal taxes are similar for all businesses in the United States, but state and local taxes have extreme variations. Sales, income, property, franchise and unemployment taxes can give a business a substantial advantage, disadvantage or have little impact upon the business's competitive position. The importance of these taxes is apparent from their well-publicized role in tax concessions to retain or lure businesses. A state's relative tax position is usually well-known. Comparisons of state taxes are frequently published with business interests highly critical of those considered to be excessive and state officials pointing to any that are unusually low as a reason industry should expand or move into the state. A fair or realistic comparison between states would include the sum of all taxes rather than selecting individual ones to prove a point. Since taxes are so great an expense, the business's management should be well aware of any competitive advantages or disadvantages.

An investor should learn if there are tax advantages or severe disadvantages and attempt to quantify differentials. If advantages exist, the question of how long the favorable condition can continue must be asked. The advantage may be the result of a tax concession that is only good for a limited number of years. Since nearly all state and local governments are pressed for revenue, existing tax advantages may be threatened when the next legislature meets.

CHAPTER 29

Accounting General Questions

There are a number of subjects, questions and issues that apply to the accounting functions and systems in an overall or general way that are not specific to a particular account such as receivables or payables. Since a major part of the due diligence process consists of understanding the financial statements, background and supplemental information are essential to comprehend and verify the statements or determine the facts.

The reliability of the financial statements should be repeatedly questioned during the due diligence investigation. Few mistakes in investing are more common than to automatically assume the financial statements are accurate in all respects. There are at least three categories of financial statements: monthly or interim reports, annual reports and reports that are part of tax returns. Public companies must submit reports containing financial statements to the Securities and Exchange Commission (SEC). Interim monthly or quarterly reports are not audited except in public companies, where quarterly reports may be reviewed by auditors prior to publication. Monthly reports are the least reliable and tend to be used more for internal operating purposes than as a basis for investment decisions. Annual reports may or may not be audited and if audited still may not be adequate. Certainly, the audits conducted by the larger CPA firms have a high degree of reliability, but the plethora of litigation they have suffered does indicate some fallibility. Small CPA firms or individuals can perform excellent work but their objectivity may be tested if they become financially dependent upon individual clients.

Not all annual statements are audited. Some are "reviewed," which is less than an audit but more than a "compilation" in which the accountant only is responsible for checking the arithmetic and reading the statements. Financial statements as part of tax returns tend to have greater reliability, probably because the preparers are aware of criminal penalties for false statements. Statements prepared without footnotes and cash-flow statements or the unaudited reports of divisions or subsidiaries of large corporations have a deserved reputation for being unreliable. It is best to assume they are inaccurate and hope to be proven wrong. An investor early in his discussions and prior to commencing due diligence should ask management and/or sellers if they are prepared to warrant the accuracy of the statements and, if not, why not?

The public accounting firm retained to conduct an audit may help complete the annual financial statements, offer tax advice and prepare the tax return. CPA firms provide varied services of importance to the business. If the business's financial records are in poor condition, they may oversee creation of enough records to close the year-end books. The audit partner may become a key advisor and confidant for the CEO. Tax planning, employment services, systems consulting and installation, strategic planning and acquisition or divestment studies are all offered services. With the variety of these services, it is impossible for an investor to evaluate the reasonableness of the fees without knowing in detail the services provided. If the investor takes control of the business, he will have to decide whether to retain the public accountants. A review of the fees paid and services provided will aid in deciding the nature of services to be purchased in the future and from whom.

During an audit, auditors secure and/or develop voluminous documentation to support their conclusions. This documentation, collectively referred to as the "work papers," is invaluable for in-depth study of the financial statements. Work papers are confidential and will not be released to an investor without approval of the business under study.

Auditors express a written opinion regarding the reliability of financial statements, and opinions given without any reservations are referred to as "clean." Opinions contain reservations or qualifications when auditors find serious conditions affecting the business that cannot be reasonably quantified, or when the auditor was limited in his ability to observe or secure information. Litigation in which the outcome is unpredictable and the ultimate disposition could materially affect the financial condition of the business is an example. A large problem contract or receivable in dispute is another condition that could result in a "qualified," "except for" or "because of" opinion. Possibly the most negative opinion is a "going concern" opinion in which the auditors indicate that unless the business's operations improve and either additional financing or relief from creditors is secured, it may not be able to continue in its present form. An auditor's report may address lack of adherence to generally accepted accounting principles or omission of critical information necessary to make an informed opinion. Whatever the qualification to an opinion, it is a major subject for due diligence.

Auditors are selected by management and in corporations are approved by the board of directors. Serious differences may arise between the auditors and a business over the content of the financial statements, and that must be resolved to the satisfaction of the auditors or they will issue an opinion distasteful to the management or resign. A few businesses have a policy of automatically changing auditors after a set number of years. While some change to reduce their costs, changes often are a result of policy disputes. For any investor, a change of auditors should be a major warning and spur an investigation. An auditor resigning or being terminated can indicate most serious problems. Interviews with both management and the auditors are desirable; management's version of events should not be accepted without verification.

"Management letters" are confidential letters sent by the auditors to the chief executive officer, the audit committee of the board of directors and others in control of the business. They follow an annual audit and contain observations usually relating to problems and deficiencies in the business along with recommended solutions. The letters can range in content from a few innocuous observations to a scathing denunciation of management practices. There is no restriction on subject matter and auditors have an obligation to point out problems. Management letters are taken very seriously by the auditors, carefully crafted and reviewed within the firm before being sent. A business would be making a mistake to ignore their content. An investor should demand copies of all management letters as part of his due diligence. What they do or do not contain will be of significance to the evaluation of the business.

Financial statements, accounts and the nature of the business must be relatively consistent to discern meaningful year-to-year trends. Revenue and expense trends, financial ratios and trends in financial ratios are valuable tools for use in analyzing and evaluating a business, and many place great reliance upon these calculations. However, unless the financial reports are uniform in format along with the content of each account, the trends or ratios are of limited value and often misleading. Changes in accounting policies, acquisitions and divestitures, refinancing, extraordinary income and expenses can all create anomalies that can distort trends and ratios. Businesses can change so much that the business today may bear little resemblance to what it was five years ago. There must be consistency and sufficient detail in each of the years compared for the statements to be used to detect trends in the critical expense categories of administrative and sales expense, and cost of sales.

Managements of well-run accounting departments are continually striving to shorten the time after the close of an accounting period before financial statements are issued. The complexity and diversity of the business affect the time necessary to complete statements, but by far the greatest factors are quality of systems, competence of management and discipline. There are no precise rules, but well-managed businesses have their interim statements in five days or less and most under 15 days. Aggressive CEOs usually demand prompt statements because the information is needed to manage the business.

While many reasonable exceptions exist and there are industry variations, for due diligence purposes the following guidelines may be used:

- If interim statements are issued after more than 20 days, but before the end of the accounting period following the period reported, substantial questions are in order regarding the adequacy of the accounting systems.

- If interim statements are issued more than 30 days after the close of a period, it is reasonable to suspect the competency of personnel, the systems and the accuracy of any statements produced. Long delays in issuing statements can also be an indication that the data are being manipulated.

Internal control involves the entire spectrum of activities, systems and procedures designed to protect the integrity of the accounting records and assets of the business. An active audit committee of the board of directors indicates a desire at the top level to have strong controls and accurate, complete and timely financial statements. However, most businesses do not have an aggressive audit committee. Internal control is not just adequate documentation of transactions, multiple review of invoices and cosigners on checks. It addresses all subjects, including quality of personnel, that affect the production of financial statements. Due diligence investigators should be intensely interested in the calibre of internal controls.

A business with timely, quality financial statements, strong financial executives, no history of fraud or theft and no management conflicts of interest will almost certainly have excellent internal controls. However, if these desirable factors are not present, a vigorous search for problem areas is in order.

CHAPTER 30

Accounting Policies

A business's accounting policies and practices can have an extreme effect on the profit or loss recorded in the financial statements. In many cases a recorded profit could just as easily have been a loss with different accounting policies, or the reverse could be true. What appears to be a remarkable turnaround from losses to profitability may be due to accounting policy changes rather than brilliant management. Frequently, large one-time losses are better explained as reversions to more conservative accounting policies or a recognition of losses more properly attributed to prior years. A business's accounting policies may be precisely written and elucidated by management, but some tests are always necessary to confirm that actual practices are consistent with policies. Not all executives are willing to admit their practice is to inflate or depress income.

In the due diligence process, it is important to determine the accounting approach, policies applied and if a pattern of accounting practices is used to accomplish an objective. If any practice is discovered to either inflate or deflate income, it is highly probable a pattern of similar practices exist. An example is that a business slow to write down obsolete inventory would also be likely to delay recognition of bad debts. In very general terms, one or more of the following accounting objectives will be applicable to a business:

1. The only objective is to complete a minimal set of financial statements and tax returns adequate for internal and tax purposes. Management is more interested in cash balances than reported profit or loss.

2. Management wants comprehensive financial statements that portray the business's financial condition as accurately as possible. No efforts are made to increase or decrease reported income.

3. The objective is to increase income as much as possible. Potential income is accelerated, expenses capitalized, write-offs delayed, reserves minimized, asset lives extended and other steps of the same type are taken.

4. The objective is to avoid reporting income primarily by delaying income into the future. All possible expenses are recorded immediately, assets are rapidly depreciated or written off, prepayments are made, reserves are set on the most pessimistic basis and other similar techniques are used.

5. The objective is to reduce or delay taxes. Policies and techniques of the type described for reducing income are employed to avoid or delay taxes.

Aggressive programs to either accelerate or delay income should become apparent during the study of the financial statements. When such is the case, the objective probably pervades throughout most aspects of the accounting systems. An investor should calculate what would have been the bottom-line results if his own policies were in place.

The Generally Accepted Accounting Principles, universally referred to by the acronym GAAP, are those principles promulgated by the Financial Accounting Standards Board (FASB). FASB is an independent body of representatives of the accounting profession presently responsible for GAAP. Many of the GAAP rules were first developed by similar bodies that preceded FASB. AICPA is the acronym for American Institute of Certified Public Accountants, which is involved in setting accounting policy and audit practices. The two rule-making organizations are rarely in conflict. GAAP covers broad principles and the overall body of financial accounting knowledge, while AICPA is more concerned with specific industry issues and auditing. Another set of rules is Other Comprehensive Basis of Accounting (OCBOA), which does deviate from GAAP and is mainly used for small businesses on a cash or tax basis. During due diligence any deviations from GAAP or AICPA standards should be evaluated. Deviations are not necessarily an indication of defective financial statements but they are in many cases.

In the due diligence process it is prudent to review the major accounts to learn the policies and practices employed and estimate their effect upon the reported profit or loss of the business. The most valuable and practical standards for comparison are those utilized by an investor in his present business or those that will be used after an investment is made. An investor will normally utilize his own policies in developing forecasts that will reflect automatically the impact of policy changes.

Costing and pricing policies for inventory of LIFO (last in, first out) and FIFO (first in, first out) are well-known and do affect reported income, but it is the inventory referred to, somewhat facetiously, as FISH (first in, still here) that is the greatest source of interest and of controversy during due diligence. Old, slow-moving inventory or that which is excessive or obsolete but still retained on the records at full or near-full value inflates the balance sheet and prior income. Inventory that is nonexistent or overcounted yet on the financial statements overstates profits. Improper pricing will also give false results. Inventory of value that has been written down or off the financial records but not scrapped is a hidden asset. The business's policies and actual practices in both pricing and writing off inventory must be precisely understood.

Percent of completion accounting is applicable when large contracts for services and/or manufactured goods are received and an extended period of time will be required to complete the contracts. Construction, engineering and military contracting are examples of industries using percent of completion accounting. With this approach a portion of the total anticipated profit is recognized periodically and prior to the completion of the contract. The exact profit will not be known until the contract is completed so estimates are necessary. Even with the best of intentions, accurate estimates of the stage of completion and the amount of income to record can be extremely subjective. In the hands of a management intent on inflating or depressing income, percent of completion accounting presents an opportunity to achieve their objectives.

Reserves and allowances are charges against income recorded on the balance sheet as amounts estimated to be adequate to cover a future loss or expense. Reserves to cover uncollectable receivables, the outcome of litigation and inventory shrinkage are most common. However, reserves should be established to cover any future losses when the losses become known and are probable. This permits and requires judgment calls by management. Underreserving will inflate income and the balance sheet while overreserving will have the opposite effect.

Capitalized assets are those depreciated over a period of time. The cost of the asset for financial accounting purposes is spread over the period of depreciation. The effect of capitalizing an asset or expense is to increase current reported income and decrease future income. Treating as a current expense all possible costs to decrease income and income taxes is a common objective of profitable businesses. Capitalization has no impact on the business's cash flow other than for taxes. Accounting rules permit some discretion on the part of management as to what is capitalized and what is expensed. However, many managements greatly exceed the range that could be considered discretionary. Categories of expenses that some managements elect to capitalize are research and development, product introduction costs, facility start-up costs, acquisition costs and extensive repair and maintenance expenses that more properly could be described as new construction.

Prepayments are paying of invoices before due and advance payments apply to known future expenses or unrecorded payables. The effect of prepayments not recorded as prepayments is to reduce current income, accelerate cash disbursements and reduce income taxes in the current year. Prepayments under GAAP should be classified as other current assets.

Delays in recording payable invoices when received will temporarily inflate income and balance sheet statements. Another policy timing problem for due diligence is at what point is a payable considered paid and the cash account reduced. The practice of some businesses of printing and signing checks but holding rather than mailing them creates misleading financial statements. Investors have had the unpleasant surprise of buying a business and discovering a drawer or file full of overdue unpaid invoices that a clerk allegedly forgot.

Wholly owned subsidiaries or those 80 percent or more owned are usually consolidated into the financial statements and tax return of the parent. However, some businesses elect to keep certain subsidiaries independent both for tax and financial reporting purposes with only the net worth of the subsidiary appearing as an asset on the parent's balance sheet. Revenues and profits are not reported as part of the parent's consolidated statement, but they may be in the notes to audited statements. Reporting subsidiaries as an investment rather than consolidating their statements into the parent improves the appearance of the parent's statement when the subsidiary has poor performance and a weak balance sheet.

Income recognition and matching income to revenue allows some management judgment and has been a frequent playground for dubious, and in some cases fraudulent, financial reporting. Income matching is tying revenue and income to specific transactions while recognition refers more to the time when the income or loss will be reported on financial statements. A business with all cash receipts has revenues that are precise both in amount and time of the transaction. However, a business using the cash method of accounting can distort matching by not booking sold orders, paying expenses early, and delaying payments to a period other than the one corresponding to the revenue receipts.

However, most businesses record receivables and many have sales of some complexity and so create opportunities to increase or decrease reported income. The list of the specific practices to accelerate or delay income is endless and growing, but some of the more common examples are:

- Billing before a job or contract is complete;
- Holding open an accounting period beyond the proper cut-off time;
- Taking full profits on installment sales;
- Failing to provide for returns, rebates and minimum resale price guarantees;
- Booking extraordinary income before received, such as tax refunds, insurance rebates and litigation awards.

Common practices to delay income recognition can involve the opposite of any of the above, plus billing delays, expensing every expenditure possible and setting ultraconservative reserves for contingencies.

The policies and practices used in cost accounting can have a major impact on income and what are considered operating profits. There are a number of general cost systems but labels are not adequate for due diligence purposes. Cost-accounting systems, regardless of labels, tend to have variations to accommodate the characteristics of the business. If value is added to the product sold, as occurs in manufacturing, expenses other than direct labor and material are included in the cost of the product or cost of sales. The more expense items included in cost of sales, the higher will be the product cost. These costs also become a part of the inventory value, in effect making expenses appear as assets on the balance sheet.

During due diligence cost of sales should be analyzed to learn the nature of all expenses included and to see how the individual accounts are increased and relieved in the accounting system. How variances are recorded and relieved will be an essential part of the study. Only with the detailed study can an investor hope to understand the system.

Recording the full cost of retirement benefits and stock options can also have a major impact on the financial statements. Over the years, retirement benefit costs and liabilities have become recognized and are more fully reported in the financial statements and not ignored or limited to the footnotes. The cost of stock options is belatedly in the same evolutionary process of reporting with debate in progress over the nature of reporting required. How an individual business elects to report these costs is a critical subject for due diligence.

Restructuring is a term that came into common business use during the last half of the 1980s to describe major programs undertaken by businesses whose financial performance was considered to be inadequate and/or was burdened with debt. Restructuring usually involves a large one-time loss, renegotiation of debt, sale of major assets such as real estate, sale of subsidiaries or investments and drastic reduction in personnel. Restructurings are major programs designed to cure major problems and materially alter the character of the business. They also have become an opportunity for dubious accounting practices and a means to clean up past sins and build reserves to ensure future income. Environmental cleanup costs, overvalued inventory and intangible assets may be swept away with restructuring charges. An investor needs to understand fully the reasons for any restructuring and how the accounting affects the portions of the business under study.

CHAPTER 31

Cash

The cash account is first on the balance sheet and first in concealed characteristics. Many investors' enthusiasm for a business has been enhanced by the presence of a large cash balance only to discover later that much of the cash is gone or inaccessible. Conversely, investors have disparaged businesses because of a low or negative cash position only to belatedly learn the condition was temporary. Large cash balances can reflect a very temporary condition, bad management or failure to make short-term investments or funds the business is obligated to keep in cash form.

A balance sheet is a financial snapshot of the business that captures the cash position on a particular day. Few accounts are subject to change so rapidly and they should be viewed accordingly during due diligence. The cash account is something of a way station for cash after it is received and before it is sent to pay creditors and investors or to be invested. When reviewing cash, there are three other accounts that should be looked at simultaneously:

• Short-term investments, where surplus cash is temporarily placed;

• Receivables, from which cash is received;

• And current liabilities, where cash goes.

The amounts in these accounts have to be considered and trends identified to fully understand the overall cash account.

The business may have cash in bank accounts but all or part may be restricted and cannot be spent. Compensating balances are funds required by a bank to be left in a non-interest-bearing account as part of the price the bank charges for a loan. The effect of compensating balances is to lend less money than the face amount of the loan and charge a higher interest rate than stated. Bid and performance bonds as well as letters of credit may be issued with the provision that all or a percent of the amounts will be set aside in restricted bank accounts. These terms are usually demanded of businesses that are not financially strong. A strong investor may be able to affect savings through freeing restricted cash by refinancing debt or securing better terms for bonding or letters of credit.

Cash in currencies of smaller and Third World countries may not be readily converted into hard currencies such as the dollar. Some currencies are nearly impossible to convert or can only be converted with a severe discount. The degree of political and economic instability, as well as a country's policies of currency controls, affect the ease with which a currency can be converted. Blocked accounts are local accounts in foreign banks from which the government prohibits removal of the funds or transfers to another country, or sets other restrictions. Funds in some blocked accounts can be used for local purchases but not for export goods. An investor should value currency that cannot be converted or is located in blocked accounts to be worth less than face value. A study will have to be conducted to set a realistic value.

The cash account becomes high in some businesses when payments are received in advance of services to be performed or products produced. Periodical publishers and educational institutions, both non-profit and for-profit, are examples of businesses that receive payments in advance. Mobilization payments and "payments with receipt of order" are front-end payments, usually covering a portion of large contracts, and are designed to finance a supplier's early costs. Progress payments are made from time to time during the life of large contracts and may cover future rather than past costs. Any payments preceding the associated costs can inflate the cash account. Most investors find this type of cash flow extremely desirable but they must not forget it can quickly disappear.

The more seasonal a business, the greater the fluctuations in the cash accounts. Extremely seasonal businesses may experience huge cash surpluses for a few months of the year after which the cash flows into work in progress and inventory in anticipation of the next big season. Probably no single factor causes greater fluctuation in the cash account than seasonality. An investor must give special attention to monthly cash flow for seasonal businesses and data on the cash account are only one portion of the puzzle. Cash balances and all other current assets and current liabilities must be considered in seasonal businesses.

CHAPTER 32

Accounts and Notes Receivable

A broad study of receivables provides an insight into numerous aspects of a business. Not only is the value of this major asset quantified, but from receivables customers can be identified, the proportion of revenues coming from geographical areas or customers can be determined, knowledge of customer relations can be gained and business problems identified through the existence of disputes.

Certain critical areas of accounting (receivables, inventory, accrued liabilities and income recognition) require intense scrutiny during due diligence because of the possibility of highly discretionary management polices, controversial entries, improprieties and disputes over value. Of these, receivables are easiest to verify and evaluate. Asking the questions in the checklist, coupled with direct confirmation of individual receivables, may give an investor comfort to proceed, information to negotiate adequate guarantees or convincing evidence to forget the entire investment.

Trade receivables are amounts owed the business from the sale of products or services. Other receivables that may be included in one all-encompassing receivables account could be from the sale of patents, assets, licensing or royalty fees and other non-trade transactions. Notes receivable can be for anything but most commonly are slow-pay receivables converted into long-term notes or loans to key shareholders and executives who may or may not repay on schedule.

An overview of receivables is possible by classifying the individual receivables into categories defined by the length of time a receivable has been outstanding or unpaid. This practice is called "aging" and an important internal accounting report for most businesses compiled at least monthly is a receivables aging report. An aging report can identify the overdue amounts and individual receivables overdue but it will not identify new receivables that may become overdue. For businesses with many small receivables this is not a concern, but it can be if the business has only a few large customers. The aging reports will give an investor his best overview and aid in identifying problems, but it is only a start for the receivables analysis.

Accounts receivable aging reports should indicate "current" and "past due" accounts. "Current" for some may include only accounts within terms but for others an extended period is given and still included as current. Regardless of what internal reports state, there usually is some point at which receivables are considered past due and action becomes necessary. These actions may include refusal to sell more material or services, threats of legal action or turning the debts over to a collection agency. An investor will want to evaluate a business's aggressiveness in collecting receivables without driving off future business. There has to be a balance, since weak collection efforts cause income losses while overly aggressive efforts antagonize customers. Investors need to know how sensitive the business is to this issue and whether significant improvements are possible.

The methods of recording sales and receivables when a portion or all of the receivables are outstanding must be carefully studied. There are a number of events and circumstances where the method of recording can materially affect the business's profits or losses. Discounts, returned goods, price adjustments for defects, rebates, installment sales and consignment sales are all capable of affecting the receivable account. If any of these practices exist in the business, the investor must know precisely how well they serve their purpose and whether they are recorded. All have the potential to be very effective in the conduct of the business, but they also have a history of abuse and are a means for inflating profits.

Non-payment of a receivable may not be due to a customer's inability to pay but rather a customer's dissatisfaction with what he purchased or the amount charged. All accounts receivable, both current and past due, that may not or have not been paid because of disputes should be identified and segregated. Exactly what the disputes are, their merits and probable outcome should be determined. Not only are disputed receivables doubtful assets, but they can be a clue to major deficiencies in the operations or conduct of the business. They may reveal defective products, misrepresented services, incorrect billings, unsatisfactory maintenance or other conditions that cause customer displeasure. Disputed receivables are a window to business problems no due diligence investigator should overlook.

Receivables also identify customers critical to the success of the business and the degree of dependency upon such customers. Identification is the first step prior to evaluating the collectibility of their receivables and the probability of continuance as customers. Key customers known to have financial problems, subject to being acquired with the supplier relationships changed, known for sharp business practices or having reputations for frequent litigation should be evaluated. The cost of preserving key customers in the form of price concessions, generous credit terms, excessive service and sales attention can eventually become too great. Large customers are sought by nearly every business and the ongoing relationships with the customers become critical assets of the business not appearing on the balance sheet. The due diligence questions concern the health of these assets.

At some point an outstanding receivable must be deemed uncollectible. This could be relatively soon if a customer had a valid claim or complaint against the business, went bankrupt, was incarcerated or simply disappeared. It could also be a long period of time before the business became convinced further collection efforts would be fruitless. The criteria used by a business to decide when a receivable is uncollectible is important because premature write-offs depress income and create a hidden asset. Failure to write off bad receivables also is a device for propping up income. Excessive write-offs can indicate failures by those responsible for granting credit. Extremely low bad debts can in some cases indicate excessively stringent credit policies that adversely affect revenues. When reviewing write-offs an investor can identify patterns that affect reported income and gain further insight into past operations of the business.

Most businesses usually establish a reserve for bad debts once a year, and adjustments are made when warranted. If there are inadequate reserves, the write-off will be a direct charge against current earnings. Since the amount of the reserve has a dollar-for-dollar impact upon reported income, an investor will want to know if the reserves were set to realistically estimate uncollectible receivables or to inflate or deflate income.

Retentions are agreed-on amounts held back by a customer for a period of time after a job is delivered or completed and are usually recorded or buried in the receivable account. Their purpose is to provide an incentive to the seller to ensure that the equipment or project is completed according to specifications and performance is satisfactory. Retentions can represent very large sums and an investor should determine if and when they will be collected. Retentions held beyond the scheduled time of payment because of customer dissatisfaction may be a warning of very serious problems. A business's liability is rarely limited to the amount of retention.

Receivables from shareholders and employees or businesses they control may result from less-than-arm's-length transactions and should be investigated fully. Are these isolated events or reoccurring? Is the amount of each receivable an amount that would have been charged anyone else or is it a discounted price? Are the terms of payment customary or were special advantageous terms set up for the debtor? How long have the receivables been outstanding and when if ever does the debtor plan to pay? Do the receivables all have adequate documentation? Answers to these questions will be necessary to establish the value of the "insider" receivables and provide information for the investor's negotiations. The debtors, if current shareholders, will be intensely interested in what happens to the receivables if someone new controls the business.

If the business used "percent of completion" accounting, there will be a separate receivables account, usually called "unbilled receivables." The account covers work completed according to the business's percent of completion calculations but for which the customer has not been invoiced. The amount in the account for each job is a function of management estimates of the original cost for the job, current estimates of the total cost of the job and the percent of completion. This obviously requires considerable estimating and even with the best of intentions, errors in judgment and the unforeseen occur. If management wants to inflate income, it can easily be accomplished with high estimates of the percent of completion and low estimates of the remaining cost to finish a job. The reverse will deflate current income.

Whenever percent-of-completion accounting is used, all aspects should be studied during due diligence because of the opportunity for management to increase or decrease income or even be unaware of true conditions. An analysis of percent-of-completion accounts can best be accomplished by an accountant teamed with someone knowledgeable in the industry who can evaluate the status of every job or sample jobs.

Billing a customer before a product is shipped or a service performed will record revenues prematurely. Holding open a month is another technique to inflate revenues in which shipments actually made during the early days of the month are all billed as being shipped on the last day of the prior month. "Phantom sales" are simply recording sales that never happened.

Subsidiaries and divisions of companies that have strong budget controls are particularly susceptible to premature billing techniques because the managements are under pressure to perform according to their budgets. The corporate managements may wink at the practices because they want the more favorable results. Since premature billing will influence the financial results and distort aging reports, an investor must determine the extent of the practice and the effect upon the financial statements. Existence of the practice will indicate there may be many other accounting practices with the same purpose.

CHAPTER 33

Inventory

Inventory presents a difficult due diligence challenge because it may be under- or overvalued and the chances of knowing its precise value are remote. The final value will be based on information prepared by accountants and used by the parties to reach an agreement incorporating a value they can accept. Even when management strives for realistic inventory values, the actual values may remain unknown until future sales occur. Managements intent upon manipulating financial statements find inventory an area of extreme opportunity, and it is one of the most frequently used means to inflate or reduce income.

Questioning management and reviewing reports and financial statements are important but should only supplement actual counts and physical inspection of the inventory and inventory records. Verification of the inventory both in count and price is essential and preferably observed by independent auditors. The overall statistics, trends and other information are vital to the study but will not provide sufficient data for comfort in the absence of on-site inspections. Inventory may conveniently be in one location, numerous locations, in transit or on consignment and so complicate the task of verification. Knowledge of its location is not only essential for verification but for studies conducted as to the cost of maintaining inventory at specific locations and the impact of the inventory level on sales.

A business's total inventory is important to know, but the information of greatest value is the inventory by product line. The amount of capital committed to maintaining an inventory for a product line is a key element in evaluating profitability or lack thereof.

The number of inventory turns is a measure of how well a business is being managed in relation to others in the industry. Unfortunately, inventory turns is one of those business statistics such as "PE ratio" and "return on investment" for which there are no universally agreed-upon formulas for calculation. Whatever formula the investor normally uses is appropriate for comparison purposes.

The inventory total recorded on a financial statement can be extremely misleading as to what will be the required in the future. The year-end total for a seasonal business may constitute a high or low point for the year. Declines in inventory can reflect excellent management practices or a program of inventory liquidation to meet immediate cash needs that cannot be sustained. A buildup of inventory during the year can be a prelude to forecasted sales increases, the result of a failed sales program or a scheme to inflate income by building inventory. By requesting information on the highs, lows and trends in the inventory, an investor can gain insight into the nature of the inventory and management practices and obtain the basic data for cash-flow projections.

Physical inventories are not a guarantee of value but are an important component of verification of the inventory's existence. Once inventories are taken and priced, the total value is compared to the value on the business's accounting records. Adjustments upward or downward bring the books into conformity with the true inventory and have a direct dollar-for-dollar impact upon the earnings of the business for the year. An absence of year-end adjustments is the hallmark of good inventory systems, while significant adjustments indicate serious problems may exist. An investor will want management's explanation of adjustments and should conduct an adequate study to confirm the explanation or find the true causes.

Definitions used in valuing inventory can have a material effect upon the reported profits of the business. Judgment, discretion and knowledge of the business and industry are necessary to create reasonable and defensible definitions and practices. The definitions of "obsolete," "slow-moving" and "excess" require careful review. Other categories of inventory of doubtful or less-than-full value are returned or defective goods, overruns and scrap, all of which management must define and value on the financial statements. How management defines, values and disposes of each applicable category of inventory is of critical importance in valuation of the inventory. Only after an investor probes the definitions and learns how and when these classes of inventory are disposed of will he begin to understand the nature and value of the inventory.

How easily inventory can be identified and located will partly determine the ease with which it can be verified. In some cases only an industry expert, or with sophisticated tests, as is the case with certain commodities and chemicals, can the composition and quality of the inventory be verified. Poorly organized warehouses and work places will complicate an inventory valuation. Well-managed businesses have easily identifiable inventory in well-marked locations or bins that are recorded. By reading the records, it should be possible to learn the quantity and location of any part, proceed without difficulty to the location and find the parts. Ease of identification and confirmation should comfort an investor.

Managements of privately held businesses more interested in cash flow than reported income may devalue their inventory by setting up contingency reserves and expanding the categories of obsolete, excess and slow-moving. Since ad valorem taxes are based on the inventory value on a given date (usually December 31 or January 1), some businesses relocate all or part of the inventory to facilities out of the jurisdiction of the local tax authorities. An investor needs to know if these practices exist and what is the related impact on the financial statements. Write-offs of inventory not disposed of and eventually sold will reduce future sales costs and increase profits. Relocation of inventory for a few days to avoid taxes is of dubious legality and the relocation costs may be greater than the tax savings.

LIFO is costing inventory on a last-in, first-out basis and FIFO is costing on a first-in, first-out basis. LIFO costing came into heavy use during the 1970s, a time of rapid inflation. The concept was to balance inflationary revenues against the current costs to avoid reporting excess profits not based on actual volume increases. The effect was to create a reserve of delayed income and tax obligations with the book value of inventory less than the current replacement cost of the inventory. The existence of a substantial LIFO reserve can be viewed by an investor as a hidden asset but also one with eventual tax liabilities. However, the value of this asset should exceed the potential taxes unless, during his negotiations, the investor ends up paying for the reserve. Whenever a significant LIFO reserve exists, professional accounting and tax advice will be required.

Purchased parts and products held in inventory for resale may be returnable to the original vendors. Vendor fees for accepting return of merchandise are called restocking charges and typically range from 10 to 20 percent of the original price. Some vendors will not refund cash but give credit toward future purchases. The right to return is of limited value for most manufacturing businesses, but it can be very important for distribution businesses. An investor will find comfort and believe he has some protection of the inventory's value if it largely can be returned. Controversy over the value of slow-moving or excess inventory during the investment negotiations may be resolved by agreeing to return the inventory.

Since inventory by accounting standards should be valued at cost or market value, whichever is lower, the question arises as to how market value is determined. Have tests actually been made and market value standards applied? For most businesses market value tests will have little or no effect, except for discontinued products and others being sold at extreme discounts. However, businesses with large inventories of commodities, such as grain, oil or chemicals, can experience price declines that force write-downs. An investor will want to know if a market value test is being applied to inventory. Have write-downs occurred in the past? Is the inventory of a type where write-downs are probable in the future?

Merchandize returned to the business is usually returned to inventory if it is in suitable condition for resale. Returned defective goods should not be in inventory at full value. However, if a business utilizes independent marketers such as dealers and distributors, they may have the right to return goods they have difficulty in selling. Unrestricted rights to return merchandise can constitute a serious hidden potential problem for any business, but a particularly serious one for those in the fashion industries, those having frequent model changes or subject to technological obsolescence. During due diligence an investor will want to know both the historical level of returned merchandise and the potential for increased levels. He'll want to know what happens to returned merchandise and the accounting entries used to record returns. For most, businesses returns are at worst a minor problem but there have been enough spectacular exceptions to justify careful review.

Inventories are taken by employees of the business and the inventory totals and values remain the work product of the business. The auditor's role is to observe the inventory and express an opinion on the result. The auditors may observe a complete count of the entire inventory or only verify selected samples. Sampling techniques can be very sophisticated and statistically valid. However, sampling is not a complete count and there is a greater chance of error. It also is a system that can be manipulated by unscrupulous managements. An investor should satisfy himself that any sampling utilized was adequate to determine the inventory's existence and value. A review of the auditor's work papers and test count sheets can be helpful in identifying problems.

If any improprieties of management relative to the count and value of inventory are discovered, an investor should assume there is far more he has not discovered. Efforts to blame problems on underlings should be discounted because employees normally do either what they are told or what they perceive management wants. An investor discovering outright fraud will be best served by seeking other investments.

CHAPTER 34

Fixed and Other Assets

Assets other than current assets may be the business's most important and valuable. Facilities, production equipment, office and systems equipment are all critical components without which the business could not function. Major tangible assets should be identified along with their value as reported on the financial statements, their estimated market value and importance to the business. Intangible assets are those primarily visible only on the balance sheet, such as goodwill, capitalized expense, customer lists and trademarks. Intangible assets may have great value or even be undervalued, but many are worthless. Determining the origin of each intangible asset is helpful to estimate current value.

Fixed assets may appear on a balance sheet as several line items or an all-in-one general category of "property, plant and equipment" (PP&E). Regardless of how broadly described, this is a reasonable starting place. Using the balance sheet summary, the due diligence investigator can request the records supporting the individual components. They should disclose the original cost as well as the amount of depreciation taken and that remaining. A review of the financial records coupled with visual inspection of the assets is an essential part of due diligence.

A perfectly managed business will have accurate, up-to-date records identifying each fixed asset, its original cost and the depreciation taken to date. However, fixed-asset records often are poorly maintained, dated and do not accurately reflect the actual assets. Significant assets may have been acquired but not recorded and others sold, scrapped or discarded and not removed from the records. If physical inventories of assets are infrequent or never made, that permits the perpetuation of recording errors. If the fixed-asset records are in poor condition and the asset values represent a significant portion of the total value of a business, an investor should insist upon a physical inventory and updating of the records to a quality that management can warrant.

A business may own valuable assets for which no value is reflected upon the financial statements. The assets may have been fully depreciated or originally treated as current expenses rather than capitalized. To delay taxes, private businesses are notorious for recording as current expense assets that should have been capitalized. Managers of divisions and subsidiaries of large corporations often circumvent cumbersome internal capital expenditure procedures with expensed installment purchases or other techniques. Another common type of unlisted assets are those worth little individually but cumulatively have considerable value. Hand tools, measuring equipment and expendables such as grinding wheels and safety equipment are examples. Assets with no recorded value can have both substantial market value and be necessary to the operation of the business. Unrecorded assets usually are given little value as collateral, but one can assume they will be discussed in the investment negotiations.

Different depreciation and amortization methods may be utilized for financial reporting and tax purposes. Accounting procedures, tax regulations, useful life of the assets and management objectives all affect the methods chosen. Knowledge of what methods and schedules for depreciation and amortization have been used and the rationale for their selection is essential. An investor normally sees a financial statement first and tax returns later and may be disappointed to learn that far less depreciation remains for tax purposes than first believed. An investor should calculate if the financial results would have been substantially different if his own policies had been employed.

The depreciated book value of assets may have little relationship to the actual market value and be high, low or even approximate market value. However, assets can have little market value but still be of critical importance to the business. Examples are highly specialized machines and process equipment designed for a particular business that would have only scrap value for others or leasehold improvements impossible to relocate or sell. However, there may be assets with market values well in excess of their book value with real estate, patents and trademarks the more obvious possibilities. An investor should learn the market value of the business's assets and not rely totally upon balance sheet values.

Independent appraisals may have been secured on the entire business, real estate or any assets or group of assets for a variety of reasons, but most commonly these are obtained in contemplation of selling or to satisfy lender requirements. How independent are the appraisers and how valid the results are always open questions, but most appraisals can be helpful, because they should contain an accurate description of the appraised assets as well as opinions of market value. As part of due diligence, copies of any existing appraisals should be requested along with information on their original purpose.

Intangible assets appear on a balance sheet until fully amortized as opposed to tangible assets, whose original cost may appear until sold or scrapped. Intangibles are items such as goodwill, capitalized expenses for R&D, start-up or acquisition costs and the cost of acquired intangibles such as non-competition agreements, customer lists, trademarks and so on. Many intangible assets actually have little or no value and their primary purpose has been to record acquisitions, improve the income statements and/or create tax advantages. New managements may elect to write off all intangibles at one time and so record a large one-time charge rather than continually explaining their presence. Regardless of the rationale to justify intangibles, many either are assets of little value or ones that under changing conditions could become worthless. An investor will want to be fully informed of these ephemeral assets. Their true value and the amortization methods utilized will be an almost certain topic for negotiations.

"Other Assets" is a category usually not relevant to current business operations. These items can be almost anything and there are no precise guidelines limiting inclusion. Possibly the most common category of assets is the residue from past ventures and contemplated ventures of the business. Leased or unoccupied real estate, machinery awaiting sale and various investments can all be found in the "other assets" account. Tax refunds due may appear as other assets. Each asset tends to have a tale of its own that will give an investor further insight into the business. The investor will also be faced with comparing the book value with an estimated realizable market value.

Subsidiaries and joint ventures may be reported only as an asset on the balance sheet and their revenues, expenses and income not consolidated. The result is a single number indicating the value of the investment for financial reporting purposes and a number likely to have little correlation to the investment's fair market value. An investor can best learn the value and problems of an unconsolidated subsidiary or joint venture by conducting a due diligence review comparable to the study being conducted of the parent company.

Businesses tend to acquire a large amount of baggage unnecessary to the basic objective of operating for profits. Assets that could be sold without affecting the operations in any material way are part of this baggage. Most will be identified in other due diligence activities, but a list of such assets along with the estimated market value of each is helpful to an investor who believes a sure way to improve return on investment is to reduce the investment. Major assets held for sale and discontinued operations are obvious unnecessary assets and should not be retained. Other assets commonly considered superfluous are lavish headquarters, executive dining rooms, art collections, recreational facilities used only by management, boats, aircraft and vehicles exclusively for personal use and any other items that may be a pleasure to have but not necessary.

There is a tendency for some executives to confuse and intermingle the businesses's money and assets with their own. If they own the entire business and there are no minority shareholders, this is not a problem other than ones relating to taxes. If the business is sold or refinanced there may be an issue of what is included or excluded from the transaction or what may be included as collateral.

CHAPTER 35

Liabilities

Due diligence requires verification of liabilities both listed and not listed on the balance sheet. To achieve a level of comfort the investor must gain adequate knowledge of the business's liabilities. Since unknown liabilities can emerge after the investment is consummated, the due diligence investigation should reduce this concern to a reasonable and acceptable business risk. It's virtually impossible to prove there are no other liabilities, but it is possible to reach a point where further concern or fears would border on the irrational. Just as identification of liabilities is important, investors should be wary of overemphasis on liabilities and what is wrong with a business rather than its attributes.

The checklist questions associated with this chapter are for use in evaluating and summarizing liabilities not covered elsewhere. Loans and other formal debts, taxes and other unrecorded liabilities are referred to in other chapters and sections of the checklist.

Unrecorded liabilities are those that should have been recorded or those in which a probable, undetermined liability exists. Inability to determine the precise amount of a liability is sometimes used as an unacceptable excuse to record no liability at all. A list of all unrecorded liabilities, actual and probable, should be developed for the investor to gain a complete picture. Common areas to search for unrecorded liabilities are litigation, non-capitalized leases, product guarantees, loan guarantees, service guarantees, self-insurance, purchase contracts, employment contracts, severance benefits, pensions and health insurance. These areas are by no means inclusive and each industry may have its own special types of liabilities. Once identified, investors need to determine whether liabilities are valid, estimate when cash outlays will be required and determine probable best- or worst-case exposure.

Accounts payable are primarily current obligations stemming from the cost of doing business, but liabilities such as lease payments and contract labor may also be found in the account. A review of accounts payable can confirm and reveal the companies and individuals with whom business is conducted. An "aging of payables" report should be constructed by classifying all payables by the length of time elapsed since the invoice dates. From an aging report, it is possible to determine the business's practices with regard to paying its bills, including discounts taken. The business's promptness in paying bills can reflect management philosophy and whether the business is cash-rich or cash-poor. The reasons for both late and premature payment of payables should be determined.

Known liabilities that require future cash outlays should be accrued and recognized on the financial statements. It's possible to accomplish this by establishing reserves or by recording the liability. Deferred taxes are the most common liability, but any liability of this type should be recognized when management becomes aware of its existence. The due diligence team must learn the origin and nature of accrued liabilities, verify that the amounts recorded are reasonable and determine when cash outlays will be required. The reasons for management not recognizing and recording any obvious and not-so-obvious liabilities should also be determined.

In well-managed businesses, known liabilities are reflected in the financial statements at the close of each accounting period. These businesses employ a discipline and consistency of policies and procedures that ensure liabilities are recorded without concern for their impact on the reported profit or loss. However, every executive understands that delays in recording liabilities can temporarily inflate income. Often this is done with the expectation or hope that the next month's profits will improve and the delayed liabilities can be inconspicuously absorbed. Any delayed or premature recording of liabilities will have a denigrating effect upon the statements and, if discovered, should trigger an alarm and the question, "What else are they doing?"

Businesses have a legal obligation to withhold and collect a variety of taxes and remit the funds to the appropriate government agencies. Failure to do so on a timely basis can result in severe penalties, fines and criminal charges for flagrant violations. Sloppy systems and honest errors are seldom considered satisfactory excuses to avoid penalties, and managements that divert any of these funds even temporarily may find themselves personally responsible and in serious trouble. A review of the systems, collection and remitting of these funds should be conducted to verify there are no present violations and to determine whether any occurred in the past. If such occurred, what was the outcome? Most businesses rigorously comply with all withholding and collection requirements, but since the penalties are so severe, this facet of the business cannot be overlooked.

A business may sell an asset on an installment basis expecting payments to be received over a period of time. Since there will be doubts regarding all payments actually being made, there is also uncertainty that the sale profits will be realized. Conservative financial reporting requires the unpaid portion of the note to be recorded as an asset but a liability should also be created to offset premature recognition of profit. As payments on the note are received, the liability is reduced proportionately. During due diligence, the existence of such a liability indicates conservative accounting and a note requiring study as to the probability of full collection. The longer the note has been outstanding, creating a repayment history, the easier it is to assess its value.

Regardless of the type of business or its stated mission, a business can and frequently does enter into contracts outside of its normal activities that may require future payments that may not appear as liabilities on the financial statements. The possible types of such commitments are endless, but some examples are: executive severance pay, stock repurchase obligations, contingent payments (earnouts) as part of prior acquisitions, payment of excessive sales commissions resulting from windfall sales, necessity to exercise purchase option on leased assets, settlement of lawsuits and unfavorable results of contract renegotiations. Payments may affect future income and will definitely increase the business's cash requirements. The commitments all need to be identified and included in the investor's financial projections.

The terms of acquisitions often result in obligations to the sellers that continue for years. Not all the obligations will appear in the financial statements and those that do may not be readily apparent. More common continuing obligations are:

- Promissory notes issued as part of the purchase price;
- Employment agreements, some with commission provisions;
- Consulting contracts with former shareholders or executives, including some that expect little or no consulting;
- Agreements on royalty payments, cross-licensing or limited use of trade names;
- Earnout provisions that call for future payments based on future earning levels when agreement on a firm price could not be reached.

The only way for an investor to be certain there are no obligations from prior acquisition agreements is to insist on reviewing the documents of the acquisition and not be satisfied with verbal assurances.

CHAPTER 36

Backlog and Income Recognition

Making sales, recording orders and maintaining a backlog are basic activities that commence a sequence eventually resulting in a profit or loss reported on the business's income statement. The level of reported income largely determines the tenure of executives and so produces pressures to perform that should continually be kept in mind during due diligence. Lack of profits will eventually cause failure, the loss of the owner's investment and jobs. Profitability influences the market price of shares, spurs hopes to sell more shares and creates opportunities to exercise options and enjoy bonuses. Budgeted profits, earnings projection, growth targets and unbroken records of increased earnings have often caused managements to engage in dubious practices. The demands for performance are so strong that executives may take regrettable actions that should be ferreted out during due diligence.

Many businesses receive orders for products or services to be shipped or provided at a later date. The cumulative total of all unfilled orders is the "backlog" and is an important indicator of near-term business activity. In manufacturing, construction, contract services and hundreds of other types of businesses, executives watch the backlog closely to plan business activities. Comparisons of the present backlog to prior years and current trends in the backlog will give an investor the single best indication of what is happening to the business and the level of business to expect in the near future.

The amount of gross profit in the backlog is a far better indicator of future pre-tax income than the total level of backlog. In fact, total backlog and trends can be extremely misleading without gross profit data. Low-profit work may have been taken to make the backlog appear good or in the belief that increased pre-tax profits could result from a larger volume of business with a lower margin of profit. The composition of the products and product mix can also affect margins. Products with a high content of purchased material or components and little value added can easily affect total revenues but have limited impact upon gross profit. A large order with higher-than-normal material content could help the appearance of the backlog but at the same time contribute far less profits than smaller orders with less material and greater value added and gross profit.

Backlogs can be misleading if viewed only in total without a breakdown as to the delivery dates acceptable to customers. A large backlog could indicate a steady level of work for months or years to come, a crisis in which the business cannot possibly meet promised delivery dates, a temporary shortage of work at present with a large volume in the future or a backlog strung out over so many months that current production levels cannot be sustained. During due diligence a study of when the backlog is to be completed is essential. A good place to start is by determining the 25 percent to be delivered last, the amount of work in progress and the amount finished and ready to ship.

At a minimum, a comparison of the backlog today with that of one year ago should be made. Starting with the prior year's backlog, it is possible to learn the operation levels required to complete the backlog and handle additional orders received during the year. From this information the volume of new orders that must be received during the year to maintain present production and employee levels can be roughly estimated.

Exactly at what point an order is considered an order and becomes part of the backlog is often unclear and may be controversial. A customer paying cash and immediately receiving a product or service constitutes a completed sale unless the customer has the right to receive his money back. However, lags in time between a customer's purchase and the product's delivery make it difficult to pinpoint when the sale be recorded. Are contracts signed but subject to routine approval by others considered orders? Are verbal orders to be followed by written confirmations recorded as orders? Does the verbal issuance of a purchase order number constitute an order? If a contract contains options for further purchases, should any be entered into the backlog? Since backlog size and level of incoming orders is of such interest to management and those engaged in selling, there is a tendency to record orders as rapidly as possible and often prematurely. An investor should review the policies and confirm that the backlog contains only valid orders.

PERCENT OF COMPLETION ACCOUNTING

"Percent of completion" accounting is used when long-term contracts are received on a fixed- or lump-sum basis. The contracts and accounting are typical for government contractors, engineering and construction companies and manufacturers of very expensive capital equipment. The accounting is essential to fairly record the performance of the business and prevent large, unjustified variations in income to occur each month. However substantial contracts may be, management judgment is required and the opportunity exists to delay or accelerate reported income to achieve other objectives. Percent of completed contract accounting has proven to be a primary playground for executives intent to manipulate income.

When a contract is received, it is recorded along with the estimated gross profit. As the job goes into production, the direct expenses and associated overhead are recorded each month with a portion of the estimated gross profit. Depending upon how well or poorly the job is progressing, and while considering remaining gross profits, income or losses are reported. The formula that the business uses to determine the amount of gross profit to be recorded each month is of critical importance because it directly affects pre-tax income.

If managers are conservative in their approach, they may establish reserves to reduce the gross profit remaining on an incomplete contract. The effect of the reserve is to reduce the amount of income recorded each month and provide reserves for anticipated problems. If the problems do not materialize, managers have an exceptional amount of income to report when the contract is completed. With the effect similar to establishing reserves for contingencies, management may elect to delay income by using lower percentages to record monthly income. For example, management may record only 35 percent of total gross profit when a contract is 50 percent complete. Another approach is to use different percentages and timing on different components of the job, based on their value. As an example, in a "design and construct" contract for a chemical plant, 50 percent of the entire gross profit may be attributed to design engineering that occurs at the start of the job and 50 percent of the gross profit recorded when the engineering is complete.

Businesses using percent of completion accounting should have information and printouts showing the status of jobs in progress, percent complete and gross profit remaining. If these do not exist, a prudent investor should not invest until a report is constructed. The reports will indicate how well the jobs are progressing, how much gross profit remains, jobs in trouble and jobs behind schedule, and indirectly provide information on the competence of those preparing the original estimates of gross profits. All such reports should be verified by direct review of sample individual jobs and their records.

After reviewing the policies, job records and summaries of completed jobs and present jobs in progress, an investor should decide the level of trust that can be placed in the present systems and whether additional detailed study is required. For investors considering businesses that employ percent of completion accounting, the degree of comfort they can reach relative to the status of jobs in progress may be the single most important factor in their decisions.

CHAPTER 37

Cost of Sales, Selling and Administrative Expenses

Due diligence should involve gathering sufficient data to analyze and understand the costs and expenses incurred by the business. While the term "costs" usually applies to production-related activities and "expense" to so-called non-production activities such as selling and administrative charges, there is no difference. Ten dollars of wage cost paid to a production machine operator eventually has the same effect upon the business's income statement as ten dollars of expense paid as part of the president's compensation. This obvious fact is often ignored by executives who are zealous in "cost" cutting but largely oblivious of "expenses."

Financial income statements will provide basic information in summary form and are the proper starting points to evaluate overall costs. Most contain separate information on costs of sales, selling expense and general and administrative expense. From the summary information trends should be discernible, but more specific information must be sought on the composition of each category and any significant shifts in the percentage of the components within a category. As an example in cost of sales, wage costs may be declining and material costs increasing with no net effect. In selling expenses, a large increase in support staff or a shift to telemarketing may be occurring, but selling costs as a percent of total sales may be declining. Trends are of great importance to identify the favorable accomplishments of the business as well as alert an investor to emerging problems.

Gross profit is the profit calculated by subtracting cost of sales from revenues. They are profits before selling, general overhead charges and administrative expense (SG&A) and are primarily determined by two factors—prices received and cost of sales. Higher prices will increase gross profit and lowering of cost of sales will have the same effect. However, total gross profits can increase or decrease while the percent of gross profit remains steady or changes in either direction. During due diligence both the total dollars of gross profit and percent of gross profit should be considered simultaneously. With prior years' data, trends can be discerned and preliminary conclusions drawn. Levels and changes in gross profit are considered by many investors as two of the most important statistical indicators to use in evaluating performance.

Cost of sales consists of material, labor and some overhead, but changes in the composition and relative percentages of each are common. Reducing the cost of sales is a basic management objective, but changes occur at an uneven rate, just as do unavoidable cost increases. However, changes in the relative percentages of each component of cost of sales constitutes conditions an investor should investigate. The investigation may reveal that management is performing well or problems exist that are intractable or being ignored.

For any meaningful evaluation of cost of sales and comparisons with industry averages or comparable business, an investor must know precisely what labor costs and overhead expenses are included. The variations between businesses as to the composition of labor and overhead are substantial. If multiple product lines share facilities, then the method of allocating the shared overhead expenses becomes an issue. This may be a very controversial matter among operating managers who are convinced they are charged for too large a share of the overhead. Non-cash expenses such as depreciation and amortization should be given special attention, since how they are recorded is extremely variable. No investor should draw conclusions regarding cost of sales in the absence of information on its content.

If the percentage of gross profit is identical month after month, an investor should be extremely wary. For most businesses there is at least some slight change up or down and trends do appear. Identical percentages could indicate the application of a uniform percentage to sales revenues and backing into an artificial amount for cost of sales. A largely outmoded accounting system in the retailing and distribution business used uniform gross profit percentages and made adjustments after physical inventories were taken. The result was interim financial statements of limited value. Any discovery of a uniform gross profit percentage should be an alarm for an investor.

Selling expenses incurred in marketing the business's products or services typically include the compensation and expenses of salesmen, staff marketing personnel, sales management, advertising, commissions to independent marketers such as distributors and representatives, public relations for marketing purposes and any other activities that are part of the marketing effort. Managements continually question whether selling expenses are justified. Would increasing marketing expenditures result in greater profits? Could marketing be more effective if different methods were used? These are also questions for which an interested investor should seek answers. The statistical information on amount and percent of sales expense and any trends makes possible comparisons to industry averages and other comparable businesses and intelligent questions to management.

"General and administrative" expenses are the cost of management, the corporate office, personnel assisting management, legal expenses and any other expenses not classified as cost of sales, selling expenses, extraordinary charges or interest expense. The broad category of general and administrative expenses, in addition to obvious corporate management expenses, can and usually does include a diverse group of other expenses the business has incurred that do not conveniently fit anywhere else. Due diligence should include an analysis of all administrative expenses.

If the business has a number of divisions or subsidiaries, depending upon management's policies, corporate expenses may be charged directly to the operating units or allocated in some manner through the use of charges or "management fees." Other managements prefer to retain corporate costs at the parent company level and not charge operating units management fees, in the belief that better control can be maintained and controversy with operation managers avoided. Prior to an investor making comparisons or evaluating trends, this subject of corporate allocations must be understood.

The diversity of expenses found in the broad category of "general and administrative" require an effort to understand all aspects of its composition at both the corporate and operating unit level. Armed with this information, an investor is in a much stronger position to plan a merger of operations, and/or reduce expenses.

CHAPTER 38

Intercompany Transactions

Multiple business units with common ownership or control have evolved to accommodate diversity and growth, spread risk, facilitate management and maintain financial controls. Unfortunately, intercompany transactions can be a source of controversy, complex or misleading financial reports and, in extreme cases, an opportunity for deception. Intercompany transactions have been a favorite playground for those wishing to manipulate the books.

Whenever there are multiple business units controlled, owned or influenced by a common entity, the relationships must be clearly defined from both an operational and a financial perspective. Is the relationship with the parent one of tight or loose control? Do the individual units conduct business between themselves and how are such transactions recorded in the financial statements? Do policies, methods and approach to recording intercompany transactions reflect a desire to accurately record income or losses by each business unit? Are policies designed to benefit the business as a whole rather than individual units? If statements are audited, consolidating income and balance sheets should indicate intercompany transactions.

Intercompany sales are the sales of products and services from one business unit to another. Some businesses negotiate intercompany sales between units on an arm's length basis without influence of the parent. Products and services purchased may be paid for by check. The other extreme is when all intercompany transactions are controlled by detailed policies and only accounting entries are made to record the transactions without cash changing hands.

The investor should identify intercompany sales and learn the policies and practices influencing pricing and accounting for the transactions. Each line item on the financial statements involved must be identified. How is income on each transaction recorded? Is income inflated or duplicated and not eliminated in consolidated financial statements? The business purpose for the intercompany sales should also be explored to determine if sales should be reduced, as would be the case if an unaffiliated supplier with a much lower cost was available. Not to be overlooked is the possibility that low existing intercompany sales are an indication that a great opportunity exists for expansion of such sales.

Transfer pricing is the practice of pricing products or services in intercompany sales in a manner that reduces or increases profits for either the seller or the buyer. The purpose is to reduce or avoid taxes or tariffs in subsidiaries in different countries. These schemes often are secretive, require a high level of sophistication and may be illegal, since governments resent any loss of revenue. An investor needs to identify any transfer pricing, its propriety and any possible liabilities or penalties. Since the purpose of transfer pricing is to artificially allocate profits, there may be difficulty in accurately evaluating the profitability of each business unit involved.

Management fees are charges assessed to subsidiaries and divisions by their parent organization as a means of allocating the cost of the parent organization. The fees may also be a means of taking cash from the operating units. The amount of charges may be totally arbitrary or be based on formulas such as a percent of invested capital, sales, profits or a combination of these and other factors. Regardless of the formula used, some operating units will consider the charges unfair. Rational and equitable management fees are usually more of a goal than actual fact. Consequently, the formula may change from year to year in an effort to reduce controversy and improve the system. The investor needs to understand the system used and identify the amounts charged each unit. Only by placing a value on actual services provided by the parent and comparing that value to the fees charged is it possible to determine the profitability of each operating unit.

Intercompany loans are transactions recorded on the financial statements as loans between the parent and a subsidiary or between two subsidiaries. The transactions may or may not require that cash change hands. There are many reasons why loans are recorded and/or made with the parent or another subsidiary serving as lender to a subsidiary. Cash advances as loans to subsidiaries in other countries may have tax, repayment or repatriation advantages over equity investments. An accumulation of unpaid receivables or management fees may have tax advantages if converted to an interest-bearing note. Treating cash advances as loans assists in the measurement of each unit's profitability as though it were an independent business. Loans from foreign subsidiaries to the parent may be a means of avoiding or delaying taxation on dividends.

The investor should identify every loan to learn of the reasons for their creation and what plans exist for repayment. There may not be plans or capability for loans to ever be repaid. The next step is to secure copies of the loan documents. These documents may be complete and appropriate for an arm's length transaction, minimal with casual or incomplete execution, or nonexistent. While most intercompany loans are proper business transactions, an investor should be alert for improprieties.

Intercompany investments are transactions recorded on the balance sheets of parent and subsidiaries as investments and equity. These transactions may range from minimal amounts necessary to establish a new subsidiary on up to huge amounts needed for an unconsolidated acquisition. It's important to determine the origin and purpose of intercompany investments and review the documentation. The market value of each investment should be estimated and compared to the value on the financial statements. Equity investments in foreign subsidiaries and joint ventures require particular attention.

Transactions that have occurred only once or infrequently, whether product sales, loans or investments, should be scrutinized. Sales of subsidiaries or major assets, unusual loans or transfers of inventory need to be studied as to purpose and for possible distortion of the financial condition of the business units involved. Suspicions should grow the closer the transactions are to the close of a fiscal year. While most transactions of this type have a valid business reason and are perfectly proper, intercompany transactions have been used by clever scoundrels. Investors need to view unusual or non-recurring transactions between controlled business units with caution and not cease their investigation until the documentation is reviewed and all aspects understood.

Divisions and subsidiaries are usually not self-contained business units and they rely upon their parent for certain functions. The more common functions provided are legal services, cash management, accounting systems, portions of the accounting functions, information systems and data bases, research and development, assistance in labor relations and human relations, credit services, treasury functions and joint marketing assistance. An investor seeking to acquire a subsidiary or division should learn precisely what is being acquired and what services will have to be replaced or what will be the cost of their continuance. In most acquisitions the investor will be expected to replace all of the services received from the parent.

CHAPTER 39

Investment Questions and Issues

There still remain due diligence questions relative to participants in the proposed transaction and the business's value. All professionals, organizations and government agencies that may influence or can affect the investment decisions should be identified. Data useful in estimating the relative value of the business should be reviewed. Information on the business that may have been previously overlooked should be sought, even if it involves locating third parties whose approval must be secured before the investment can close.

Third-party approvals are those required from individuals, businesses, institutions and government agencies who are neither the buyer, seller nor investor. In some cases the third party must approve the entire transaction and in others only one segment. A search for such parties and an evaluation of the time, procedures, difficulty and strategy for securing their approvals should commence early in the due diligence process. The type and structure of an investment will affect the approvals required. If the investment is a purchase of selected assets and liabilities of a going business, approval may be required of lenders and creditors, and to transfer all contracts in effect and government permits. Contracts includes leases, customer orders, purchase orders and licenses. In stock acquisitions approvals may be required from lenders, government anti-trust regulators and licensors.

Consultants provide highly specialized skills for projects of relatively short duration where it would be impossible or impractical to employ full-time employees. They provide businesses with knowledge and skills often unavailable by any other means. Consultants are not employees and are considerably more expensive, often commanding large fees. The investor should identify the problems consultants were hired to solve and compare their costs with the results. If consultants are currently under contract, the value of the project, its cost to complete and the ramifications of halting the work should all be studied. Whether consultants should be retained after the investment is complete requires an early decision.

Most think of investment bankers as professionals in financial matters who are associated with large, well-known Wall Street investment banking firms. These certainly are investment bankers, but there are thousands of small regional and local firms and individuals specializing as investment bankers. Some businesses keep investment bankers on a retainer basis to be called when needed but most work on a project-by-project basis. Whenever investment bankers are present, the investor should determine their role, responsibilities and terms of engagement. Their fees are usually substantial (many believe exorbitant) but they provide services not readily available from other sources. They also are accustomed to taking adversarial positions and so it's essential for the investor to learn their expected role and function.

Professionals retained over a period of time may become entrenched confidants to key owners or executives and their views and advice are given great weight. Whether their views represent wisdom or self-serving nonsense is debatable, but their presence and influence is a fact not to ignore. These confidant roles tend to develop because the professional has valuable perspectives and the detached view of an outsider. An executive may feel more open to discuss matters with someone not involved in day-to-day affairs. As negotiations progress, the investor will undoubtedly learn of the existence of any confidants to key executives or shareholders. Since they can have so much influence, the investor will be wise to meet with them directly, if such is possible.

As part of their services professionals provide interim and final reports describing the scope of their assignments, observations, conclusions and recommendations. The reports become the property of the business and copies should be requested. Problems or programs considered so severe or pressing as to merit the involvement of outside professionals are ones of which the investor should be aware. A comparison of the reports to current conditions will indicate if recommendations have been accepted and the level of progress accomplished to date. In all cases reports by professionals should be tempered by the possibility that their conclusions and recommendations are not always wise or practical.

Formal business valuations are conducted by individuals or companies that claim to be expert in business appraisals, but there are wide differences in their competence, opinions and, often, conclusions. Business valuation is an extremely subjective activity. Valuations may have been conducted for tax purposes, to value ESOP shares, to set prices on minority share sales, to value an estate, resolve divorce settlements and because the shareholders wanted an opinion on the value as part of their decision to sell or bring in investors. The existence of a valuation, regardless of its purpose, is likely to influence any negotiations and a copy should be requested. If the value is one the investor can accept, it may help the proposed transaction. If the appraisal is too high, the investor can attempt to discredit it with his own arguments or with another appraisal. Most appraisers, if properly motivated, can usually find fault with the work of others. An appraisal's greatest value to an investor may be a detailed description of the business that should be factual and which may contain information previously unknown.

The prices for which comparable businesses have recently been sold would be an indication of the market value of the business under study. Unfortunately, no two businesses are identical and it is difficult to obtain the exact price paid for a private business. Private company sales are not only private, they frequently have prices complicated by combinations of cash, debt, leases, consulting and non-competition agreements. For public company sales, determining the price is easier because they are usually sold on a price-per-share basis. It is not uncommon for extremely inaccurate reports to circulate regarding prices paid for both public and private businesses. Regardless, an investor would be wise to attempt to determine true prices paid for comparable businesses. Such market prices can assist in deciding if the values discussed in negotiations are realistic.

Comparable companies can provide other valuable information to use in evaluating a business. Gross profit margins, return on investment data, market size, markets served, and administrative costs are some of the more important details that an investor can use for rough comparisons.

At least initially in the due diligence process, management will know far more about the business than the investor and should have strong views as to what "probable" good or bad events are likely to occur. A "probable" event can be defined as one that management worries might happen or believes will happen. A good question to ask management is to list probable good and bad events, a task that may help identify unknown factors not discovered in other phases of the due diligence process. It will also provide another opportunity to review previously identified, significant possible events. The investor must evaluate the degree of risk associated with probable bad events and ascertain the available defenses. For probable good events, the investor should guard against counting on their occurrence and use sparingly the possibility to promote the deal to himself or others.

The Critical Questions for Business Decisions

CHAPTER 5. BUSINESS DESCRIPTION AND BASIC INFORMATION

1. Date of study. (Date documents received and record sources.)

2. Names of persons conducting the due diligence study.

3. What is the legal name of the business? Does it more commonly operate under a shorter or different name?

4. What is the address, telephone and FAX number of the business's headquarters and/or the owner?

5. What are the names, telephone numbers and addresses of the principals involved in negotiating this transaction?

6. What are the names, titles and telephone numbers of executives and others providing information for this due diligence study?

7. Request copies and review as many of the following documents as possible prior to conducting due diligence activities.

- Descriptive company brochures.

- Five years of financial statements.

- Five years of tax returns.

- Last 12 monthly financial statements.

- Five years of annual reports, proxy statements and SEC filings, if public.

- Dun and Bradstreet report.

- An organization chart showing personnel and reporting relationships.

- Reports of security analysts if a public company.

8. What is the business's history? Request copies of any prepared histories that may be available. Include the founders, ownership, products, locations, acquisitions, significant events and other milestones.

9. When was the business founded? When was the business incorporated? Where is the business incorporated?

10. List all subsidiaries, percent of ownership, names of their directors, managers, addresses and their activities.

11. List all divisions, names of their managers, addresses and their activities.

12. List all joint ventures or partnerships, names of partners or directors, managers, percent of ownership, addresses and their activities.

13. List all minority investments in operating businesses, percent of ownership, addresses, activities and history.

14. In what states and foreign countries does the company conduct business? Is it properly licensed and in good standing in each?

15. Request or prepare a corporate organizational chart showing the owners' legal relationships to each subsidiary, division, joint venture, partnership or minority investment.

16. How much are the professional fees of attorneys, accountants, investment bankers, consultants, brokers, finders, actuaries and so forth estimated to be? Identify all professionals involved, their estimated fees and who will pay the fees.

17. What is the purpose of this due diligence study? Who requested and authorized it?

CHAPTER 6. CRITICAL EARLY QUESTIONS

1. What is the quality, competence and depth of management? Identify managers or other key employees who will remain with the business, depart, or whose tenure is unknown after this transaction. Identify any key vacancies.

2. Identify and determine causes of any significant trends or changes in revenues, profits or financial ratios.

3. What has been and what will be the cash flow for five years, past and future? Request copies of management forecasts.

4. Do you understand the financial statements? Systematically study each line item on the balance sheet, income and cash-flow statements for the last annual and monthly financial reports. Review the notes to the statements. Request information on any aspects not fully understood.

5. List all significant income for the current and each of the past five years that could be considered as extraordinary and non-recurring. Identify operating and non-operating income.

6. Is there any portion of the current income stream that for any reason will cease or be drastically reduced in the next five years? Are there large contracts about to expire or subject to termination?

7. List all significant expenses for the current and each of the past five years that could be considered as extraordinary and non-recurring.

8. Are there any unusual and/or extraordinary expenses that are known to have a high probability of occurring in the next five years?

9. During the past five years what new product lines, divisions and acquisitions have been added to the business? What was the rationale for each addition? What has been their revenue and operating profit each year? Are forecasts being achieved?

10. During the past five years, what product lines or business units have been sold, spun off or liquidated? What revenues and operating profits did they account for in each year? What was the cause or rationale for each deletion?

11. What were the capital expenditures for the past five years? What are planned for the current year? Compare actual expenditures to budgets and depreciation levels. What are planned and/or will be required during the next four years? Is there a policy of minimum return? Request copies of management's plans. Identify critical assets that will have to be replaced.

12. Who controls the business? Is there one large owner? Where is the voting power? Do coalitions of shareholders exist? Are there any voting trusts? Are negotiations being conducted with the individuals who can commit and deliver upon their commitments?

13. Identify known or suspected significant problems, in any aspect of the business, requiring special study or evaluation.

14. Do any shareholders or key executives have a propensity for litigation?

15. Have the major shareholders or key officers engaged in serious discussions or negotiations within the past five years to sell the business? If yes, what were the full circumstances, including reasons for failure? Has this deal been shopped? Are other potential buyers considering the business?

16. Why is this business for sale? Is financing needed or are securities sales desirable? What is the motivation for this contemplated transaction?

17. Does the company have any anti-takeover defenses or other barriers to the deal such as loan covenants or buy-sell agreements?

18. Are any subsidiaries, divisions or other major assets of the company scheduled or being considered for divestment? If yes, list and describe circumstances.

19. What is the risk of employees at any level leaving and taking with them management, professionals, customers or confidential information? Have there been prior incidents?

20. Is there any indication of illegal activity, gross improprieties, deceitful accounting or dishonest management practices?

21. Has management taken steps to improve the appearance of the business by accelerating income, deferring or delaying expenses, cancelling bonus programs and so on, primarily to impress investors?

22. Does this business conform to the investment or acquisition criteria of the investor?

23. What expenses, if any, may be eliminated if this contemplated transaction occurs? Estimate annual savings.

CHAPTER 7. CAPITAL STRUCTURE AND OWNERSHIP

1. How is this business legally structured?

Regular (C-Corp) Corporation?

S Corporation?

Partnership?

Product Line?

Limited Partnership?

Other?

Sole Proprietorship?

Division?

Product Line?

Limited Liability Company?

Combination of above?

Request copies of articles of incorporation, bylaws, partnership agreements or other documents creating the business.

2. Find out:

Number of common shares issued.

Number of treasury shares.

Number of common shares authorized.

If there is more than one class of common, describe.

3. If the common stock is publicly traded: What is recent price per share, date of price, four-year price range, book value of common share as of what date, and average monthly or weekly volume of shares traded?

4. Has the company issued any bonds, preferred shares, warrants, debentures, convertible securities or any other type of security?

If the answer is yes to any of the above, request documents creating the security, history, names of owners or holders and amounts outstanding. If any of these are publicly traded, ascertain the current market price and the history of price and volume.

5. If a private company, what ownership transfers of its securities occurred and at what price during the past three years? Who were the buyers and sellers?

6. Request a list of all shareholders, partners, limited partners or other type owners and the number of shares, securities, units or other forms of ownership held.

a. Will any be difficult to locate?

b. What is the reputation of the major holders?

7. What has been the company's dividend policy and payment history for the past five years for all securities? Are current practices expected to continue?

8. Has the company defaulted in the past or is it now in default on any debt or security covenants? If yes, what actions have the security holders taken or threatened? What is required to cure the default?

9. Do any debt agreements or securities contain provisions that could affect control of the business or restrict sale of shares?

10. Does the company have any stock buy-back obligations to its shareholders? Request a copy of the agreements. How will buy-backs be financed?

11. Do any shareholders have obligations or preferential rights to purchase other shareholders' or new shares first? Request documents, including "buy-sell" agreements.

12. Has the company had, or are there any, stock repurchase programs in progress? Have options or warrants been repurchased?

13. Determine the reasons for any changes in the number of shares authorized, issued or in the treasury during the past three years.

14. On what stock exchanges do the company's securities trade? Who are the market makers? Request copies of reports on the business or industry written by security analysts.

15. Are any securities registration statements in progress or being contemplated? If yes, what is purpose and effect upon this transaction?

16. Does the company have an ESOP plan? If yes, request full information on its history and current status, including the reasons for establishing an ESOP plan.

17. Have shares for the ESOP plan been valued realistically? Demand copy of appraisal.

18. Are there active and vocal dissenters to present management or controlling shareholders? Are they likely to oppose or support this transaction?

19. Describe the last two shareholders' meetings. What was the attendance, atmosphere, events and so forth? Have there been any special or delayed meetings?

20. In general, are shares higher or lower in price or value than when most shareholders acquired their shares? If possible, determine the tax base for major shareholders.

21. Are minutes of shareholders' and board of directors meetings up-to-date? Request and review.

22. Does the business maintain a financial public relations program? Who meets and communicates with security analysts?

23. Is there a formal or informal program of informing and nurturing

shareholder relations? Are shareholders given discounts on the business's products or services?

24. What major shareholders, officers or directors have bought or sold shares in the past two years? List all trades during the past two years reported as "insider trades."

25. Have any securities, options or warrants that were not part of a formal program been given or sold at a discount?

26. Are there any stock options outstanding? If yes, request a copy of the plan, list of option holders and amounts each holds.

27. Request a list of company directors. Determine their background, business affiliations including other board memberships, and length of time on the board.

28. What are the terms of office for the directors? Is voting staggered? What were the reasons or circumstances that resulted in the election of each member to the board of directors?

29. Have any board members resigned or not stood for reelection in the last three years? If yes, why?

30. How often does the board of directors meet? Where?

31. What compensation do the directors receive? Include fees for meetings, salaries, options, pension benefits, termination pay, perquisites and other items of value.

32. What is the board's role in running the business? How often does the board disagree with and overrule management decisions and/or recommendations?

33. Does the board have committees such as an audit and compensation committee? If yes, how active are the committees? Who is on each? Request copies of any recent committee reports.

34. Are there any splits or factions within the board?

35. How are the directors protected from liability?

36. If the company has subsidiaries, do the subsidiary directors have any role in overseeing the subsidiaries? Does the company have directors appointed to joint ventures or minority investments?

37. If there are subsidiaries, joint ventures or partnerships less than 100 percent owned by the company, request full information on the other shareholders or partners, including their rights, value of their investment and status of relations with them.

CHAPTER 8. MANAGEMENT

1. Request a list of all officers and key employees, their titles, ages, lengths of service, brief job descriptions and background information.

2. Request complete compensation information for the past three years, current year and future commitments for officers and key employees. In-

clude information on salaries, bonuses, options, severance, golden para-chutes, retirement benefits, loans and so on.

3. Determine the total cost for each of the business's three top executives. Include direct compensation, stock options, fringe benefits, perquisites, travel and entertainment expenses and secretarial or other employee assistants.

4. Rank the officers and/or executives in order of actual authority or power within the business. To whom do employees look to make the major decisions? Has one executive imposed a management style and business philosophy upon the organization?

5. If any directors, officers or key employees have been in their present positions for less than two years, determine the factors influencing their selection and the reason for the vacancy.

6. Are there presently any unfilled executive positions? Determine if any directors, officers or key employees are to change positions, quit, retire or be terminated for any reason, including health problems, during the next 24 months.

7. Are there logical successors for the most important officers and/or managers?

8. What is the CEO's estimate of the overall strength and depth of the management?

9. What is the level of nepotism in this business? List all relatives of shareholders, officers and directors employed in the business and their positions and compensation. Does the company have a formal policy on nepotism?

10. Are there officers or employees who could severely damage the business if they left the company on a hostile basis?

11. Are any officers or employees so important to the business that they are nearly irreplaceable and that if they suddenly left, the business would be severely damaged?

12. Are there any officers or salaried employees who do not work full-time for the company? If yes, request an explanation including amounts paid to each.

13. Are there any shareholders, employees, directors or consultants who are paid for little or no work? If yes, secure explanations and amounts paid.

14. Do any officers or key employees have hobbies, investments or business activities that prevent their devoting full time to their positions?

15. Are there any officers, employees, directors or consultants who are knowingly paid excessive compensation? If yes, request explanations and the amounts paid.

16. Is there any evidence of past or present management or shareholder conflicts of interest, such as owning an interest in a business that conducts

business with this one, co-investment or property sales to or from share-holders, officers or employees or their relatives?

17. What perquisites other than normal fringe benefits do officers, directors or key employees receive? Is there an executive dining room? Estimate value of the perquisites. What special perquisites are enjoyed exclusively by the CEO and/or the largest shareholders?

18. List any company-owned or leased recreation lodges, facilities or boats. If the business leases or owns aircraft, determine the use by key executives. What percent is for personal use?

19. Are any executive shareholders paid excessive bonuses in lieu of dividends? Could there be any excess compensation tax violations?

20. Do any officers, directors or key employees have national or international recognition or prominence for any reason in any field?

21. What is the general reputation of management? How is management viewed by customers, employees, shareholders and the general public?

22. Have any major shareholders, officers or directors been associated with any businesses that failed? Have any been involved in scandals of any sort?

23. Has the business's organization been relatively stable or have major internal reorganizations occurred during the past two years? Are any internal reorganizations in progress or being planned?

CHAPTER 9. PRODUCTS AND SERVICES

1. List all products and/or services sold by the business and the total revenues and gross and pre-tax profits each represents. Request data for last three years and year-to-date. Request copies of product literature and catalogs. Request copies of any studies on profitability of products or services.

2. Estimate remaining market life and growth potential of the major products and services. Prepare five-year forecasts.

3. Are any products or services threatened with technological obsolescence? Are any products subject to fads or fashion?

4. Does the business have products or services that are under consideration or scheduled to be phased out?

5. Are sales of assets and "involuntary conversions" a normal part of this business's sales activity? If yes, determine revenues and profits.

6. For each line, what percent of annual revenues and profits are for after-sale service, maintenance or enhancements?

7. For each line, what percent of annual revenues and profits are spare or replacement parts?

8. For each line, what percent of annual revenues and profits are expendables?

9. Does the business have any contracts with customers that may be

difficult to fill for any reason such as pricing, available raw material, delivery or meeting specifications?

10. What products, services or processes are scheduled to be introduced in the next two years? Are any behind schedule? What is the cost of development and introduction for each? What revenues and profits are forecast for each?

11. What product guarantees are normally given? Request copies of guarantees or warranties.

12. How is product service provided, managed and charged?

13. Has any product been recalled or are any under consideration to be recalled? Have any alleged defects resulted in personal injuries?

14. Are warranty costs, claims and exposure a significant factor in this business's operations?

a. Request a list of the major causes of warranty claims.

b. What is the estimated total current warranty exposure?

c. What is the amount reserved for warranty claims and is it adequate?

d. What has been the cost for warranty claims in the current year and three prior years? Identify trends and causes.

15. Are there substantial seasonal variations in the level of this business? If yes, determine how it affects all aspects of the business, production and inventory levels, employment, cash flow, profits and so on.

16. Is all or any portion of this business's continued operations subject to the renewal or continuance of any government permits or licenses? Request a list of all permits, licenses, consents, orders or authorizations from governmental or regulatory authorities.

17. Is any portion of this business dependent, either directly or indirectly, upon government subsidies or grants?

CHAPTER 10. R&D AND TECHNOLOGY

1. Is this business engaged in research and development? If yes, how is the cost recorded on financial statements?

2. Describe the business's R&D program, including objectives, expenditures, manpower and results. Identify R&D contracted out, number and names of contractors. List significant new products introduced in the past three years. Request copies of budgets and plans.

3. What products, processes or services are under development and what is their expected date of commercial availability? Will any replace existing products?

4. Are timetables being met? Describe any R&D programs significantly behind schedule.

5. How is R&D organized and structured within the business? Who is

directly in charge of the R&D program and what is the person's title and background?

6. Describe any technology or know-how, not patented or licensed, which is critical to the operation of the business or gives a competitive advantage.

7. How many graduate engineers, scientists or other professionals are employed in research or development work? How many have Ph.D.s?

8. During the past and current fiscal year, what was and is the estimated royalty or license income of the business? What is forecast for the next five years? Request copies of all licenses.

9. During the current fiscal year, what is the estimated amount to be paid to others for royalties or license fees? How long will these obligations continue? Request copies of all licenses. Are fees being paid for technology no longer in use?

10. Are there any licensing agreements critical to the company's financial success either as licensee or licensor? When do they terminate?

11. List patents owned or licensed by the business, their date of expiration, and describe their purpose and application. Which patents are active and of real value? Are any being challenged?

12. Do any businesses, individuals, employees or former employees have any rights or royalty income from patents used by the business?

13. Does the business have disputes of any kind with inventors?

14. Are the products being developed subject to government approval or that of independent laboratories?

15. Describe any research funded by the government. What is the magnitude of funding, probability of continuance, and what are the prospects for future funding?

16. Are patents all owned by the business being studied or are they owned by an affiliated company?

17. Does there exist within the business any controversy over the viability or safety of either products under development or those already on the market?

18. What security measures are taken to protect R&D and intellectual property?

19. Is this business in an industry where theft of R&D and trade secrets has occurred?

20. Has the business been accused of stealing trade secrets or has it accused others of stealing its trade secrets?

CHAPTER 11. REAL ESTATE AND FACILITIES

1. List all real estate owned or leased by the business and for each request the following information:

a. Address and legal description if available.

b. Description and use of facility.

c. If owned, date of purchase, price paid and cost of improvements. Estimate market value and current tax base and/or depreciated value.

d. If leased, terms of lease and expiration date and probability of renewal. Describe any leasehold improvements and depreciated book value. Identify the landlord and describe relationship with same. Would loss of the lease damage the business?

e. Number of employees.

f. Square feet of space under roof. Separate by type, that is, office, factory and so on.

g. Total acreage.

f. Age of facility and general condition? Is there compliance with applicable codes; fire, safety, provisions for handicapped, structures and so on? If not, estimate cost to comply.

i. Mortgages, if any, and amounts. Compare actual balance to amount reported on the financial statement.

j. Known or suspected environmental problems.

k. Request or take photographs of key facilities.

l. Does the business presently lease or sublease to others? Identify tenants and terms of lease.

m. What are the tax appraisal and annual ad valorem taxes? Has or should the appraisal be contested?

n. Are property taxes current or delinquent?

o. Is maintenance excessive? Are major repairs required?

p. Estimate difficulty of marketing the property if desired or necessary.

2. Is any of the real estate for sale or lease? If yes, why, for how long and what is the asking price?

3. Are negotiations in progress or contemplated near-term to acquire or lease new facilities? If yes, why?

4. Are new facilities under construction? If yes, why? How are they being financed?

5. Are any of the facilities shut down, vacant or only partially utilized? If yes, why?

6. Do shareholders, officers or employees own any real estate or equipment leased by the company? If yes, describe in detail, including a comparison of rents paid versus normal area market rates.

7. Does the business have clear title to the property it believes it owns? Is there title insurance? Have there been property boundary surveys?

8. Have any appraisals of company-owned real estate or leases been

conducted within the past four years? Request copies. Why were they conducted?

9. Are there any significant advantages or disadvantages the business experiences as a result of its facility's locations? Are any in high-risk areas subject to thefts, vandalism or riots?

10. Are present facilities adequate? If more are required, when? Can present facilities be expanded to accommodate growth? What will be the cost and source of financing? What are the alternatives?

CHAPTER 12. MARKETS, COMPETITION AND CUSTOMERS

Note: Subscribe to industry trade publications and request back issues. Request industry or competitor studies conducted by security analysts.

1. What are the markets and the main type of customers? Estimate separately the size of the domestic and international markets for each product line or service.

2. What is the business's market share for each product line or service? Is the market share for each growing or declining?

3. Are the markets growing or declining? Locate or develop estimates of future market sizes.

4. Does management plan to enter any new markets?

5. Are there demographic trends affecting this business?

6. Where are the business's main geographical markets? Are there plans to expand into new geographical markets? Has the business withdrawn from any market?

7. What is the general state of the industry for each product or service line? What are the significant trends, if any, in the industry in marketing approach, products or services, manufacturing, government regulations, international activities and so on?

8. Are there acquisitions trends within the industries in which this business functions? Have any competitors been sold or reported to be for sale?

9. Identify the major competing businesses for each product line or service. Compare the business studied with the major competitors and their market shares. What advantages does this business have over competitors and what advantages do competitors enjoy? Cover such items as design, costs, methods of marketing, pricing, discounts, services, quality, delivery and so on. Request Dun & Bradstreet reports on competitors. To what degree is foreign competition a factor?

10. Are any competitors engaged in expansion programs? Are any competitors having major problems? How difficult is it for new competitors to start up and enter the market?

11. What is management's opinion of its marketing methods and cost of distribution compared to competitors?

12. What do competitors think of this business?

13. Have any competitors been formed, or are any now being managed by former employees?

14. Is the business obligated by, or does it hold, any non-competition agreements? Have any of importance recently expired?

15. For each product or service line list the 10 largest customers and percent of sales they represent. Are any in danger of being lost? Does the company have disputes with any of these customers? Are any key customers experiencing financial or other difficulties that could reduce or eliminate their purchases?

16. Identify for each product line or service the major new customers added in the last three years.

17. Identify the major customers lost in the past three years and describe the circumstances. Has the company been terminated on any jobs or contracts before completion?

18. How do customers view this business?

19. In which segment and at what level in the customer's organization is the buying decision made?

CHAPTER 13. MARKETING

1. What is the method of selling and distribution for each product line, such as direct sales, distributors, manufacturer's rep, catalogs, telemarketing, and is management satisfied with the effectiveness of its strategy?

2. List the countries in which the company conducts business on a regular basis. Request a list of foreign representatives and sales outlets and the annual volume of business of each for the past two years.

3. What was the dollar volume of international sales by country for each product or service line during the past fiscal year, and what is expected during the current year?

4. What was the dollar volume of government sales for each product or service line during the past fiscal year, and what is expected during the current year? How are these products or services marketed and to which agencies or departments? Are any contracts subject to renegotiation?

5. Does this business have an overall marketing plan and strategy? If yes, request copies. How does this marketing strategy differ from competitors'?

6. Describe any major changes in the marketing methods in the past 24 months.

7. Determine the role, strategy and importance of the following in the marketing program. Why do customers buy the product or service?

a. Pricing

b. Delivery

c. Quality

d. Credit

e. Post-purchase service

f. Installation services

g. Made-to-order products

h. Advertising and product literature

i. Technology level

j. Rebates

k. Compensation for reps and distributors

l. Tariffs

m. Distributor or dealer financing

n. Customer financing

o. Diversity of products or services

p. Personal relationships

8. Describe the marketing organization. Request or sketch a chart. Clearly identify all inside support personnel. Request resumes and compensation data on management and opinions on their performance and potential.

9. Compare the typical salesperson's education and experience with what management would consider to be ideal. Is there a sales training program? How difficult is it to employ new salespeople?

10. Request a list of salespeople currently employed, their sales volume and compensation. Request a copy of their compensation plan.

11. Does the business provide or arrange financing for customers? If so, describe in detail. Is this financing with or without recourse? If yes, what is the exposure to the business? What is the source of financing?

12. Does the business lease its products? If yes, what are the terms, sources of financing, disadvantages and advantages?

13. Is all or any portion of this business's marketing rights to any product or service dependent upon franchise, distributorship, representation or other similar type agreements? For each, estimate the probability of its continuation.

14. Does the business provide financing or financial guarantees to distributors, agents, retailers or dealers? What is the record and probability of recovering funds advanced and maximum financial exposure?

15. Request a list of distributors, dealers or manufactures' representatives selling the products or services of this business and the volume of sales each was responsible for during the past year.

16. What rights do distributors, dealers and retailers have to return unsold merchandise?

17. Is this a business where departing executives or salesmen are likely

to take their customers with them? Has this happened? What defenses does the business have?

18. Is there an active market for used equipment manufactured by the business? If so, how does the company participate and how is it affected?

19. Does this company conduct business in countries where bribes and unusual commissions are commonplace?

20. If the business is a franchisor or franchisee, what is the total number of franchises, annual turnover of franchise ownership and failure rate? Identify areas of controversy or litigation between franchisors and franchisees.

CHAPTER 14. PRICING

1. What is the business's general philosophy or approach to pricing? Does it have pricing policies? If yes, request copies.

2. How are prices actually determined? Who is responsible? What are the primary factors influencing pricing, such as cost, competition, production capacity, inventory levels, backlog and what the market will bear?

3. How are competitors' prices ascertained or estimated? Has there been or is there any evidence of price collusion or fixing in the industry?

4. What are the normal terms and discounts given on products and services sold? Are price lists rigid or only a starting point?

5. What cost system is used in pricing? Are overhead allocations reasonable?

6. What is the history of price increases or decreases and the probability of future revisions?

7. How easily can cost increases be passed on as price increases?

8. Does the business under- or overprice its products or services? Could prices be increased? Would decreasing prices increase volume and profits?

9. Is this business in an industry with a history of price wars? Are any in progress or threatened?

10. Are any of the business's products under price pressure from generic brands? Does the business sell and price its products as generic brands?

11. Does the business pay "mark down" money guaranteeing minimum profits if goods prove to be slow-moving and difficult to sell? If yes, what is the potential liability?

12. Are distributors or retailers protected from decline in inventory value if the business reduces its price?

13. Does this business attempt to impose prices upon those marketing its products? If yes, review the legality of such practices.

14. Does the business have an individual or department responsible for estimating? If yes, what is its role and performance record?

15. Has the business been, or is it now, involved in barter arrangements or countertrading? What have been the results?

CHAPTER 15. ADVERTISING AND PUBLIC RELATIONS

1. Does the business spend funds on advertising and public relations? What are this year's budget and the expenditures for the last fiscal year? Request copies of budgets and plans.

2. What are the primary advertising activities and overall policies and objectives? Identify the personnel.

3. What is the name of the advertising agency used and what are its annual billings to the business? Has the advertising agency been changed in the past five years? If yes, why?

4. Compare the advertising program to the major competitor's.

5. Identify the media, including all publications in which this business has advertised in the past two years. Request copies of advertisements, video tapes, recordings and all product literature.

6. Has the business ever been accused of deceptive advertising?

7. List all trade names, trademarks and logos and management's estimate of their importance. Are they registered or copyrighted?

8. What are the role and purpose of the public relations program? Describe its activities, recent and current assignments.

9. Does the business retain a PR firm? What is its name and function? Has the PR firm been changed in the past five years? If yes, why?

10. Does PR include lobbying government agencies, bodies or officials? If yes, describe in detail.

11. During the past five years has this business or its shareholders or officers received major media attention for any reason, favorable or unfavorable? Request copies of any news articles.

CHAPTER 16. MANUFACTURING

1. Identify each manufacturing facility and warehouse, its location, principal activities and products produced. Request copies of brochures describing the manufacturing facilities and capabilities.

2. Request internal financial statements for each manufacturing operation. Request copies of all internal reports utilized by manufacturing management regarding output, efficiency, costs, variances, safety and so on.

3. Identify the executives responsible for each manufacturing location. Request career summaries and evaluate performance and potential. How long has each been in his present job?

4. Are products being produced and shipped on schedule? Are any large orders or projects behind schedule? Are any significant cost overruns occurring?

5. What is the overall quality, age, state of the art and condition of machinery and processes used in manufacturing? Is any nearing the end of its useful life? Compare the machinery and processes with competition.

6. What were the total capital expenditures for machinery and equipment for the past four years? What are planned for the next two years? What new manufacturing facilities or major machines are under construction or on order?

7. Is the equipment used in manufacturing specially designed for one application or is it more "off-the-shelf"?

8. Certain key manufacturing activities are readily measurable, and the presence of unfavorable statistics should trigger intense due diligence study.

a. Production—measured in dollars or units per man hour level or declining.

b. Back orders—high present level and/or increasing.

c. Scrap, rework, returns—high present level and/or increasing.

d. Variances—erratic, high or unfavorable trends.

e. Material costs—high and/or increasing trend.

f. Wage costs—high and/or increasing trend.

g. Down time—high level and/or increasing trend.

h. Shipments—disproportionate amount in last week of month.

i. Inventory—total inventory or segments high and/or increasing.

j. Maintenance costs—high level and/or increasing trend.

k. Employee turnover—either management or employee at high level.

l. Accidents—at high level and/or increasing.

m. Overtime—at high level and/or increasing.

9. Describe the manufacturing organization, identifying the responsibilities and functions of each major department. Request organization charts.

10. Describe any critical manufacturing machines or processes dependent on licenses, leases or other contracts.

11. Evaluate the effectiveness of the quality control function. What is the reputation for quality? Is there a formal written quality control manual? Has ISO 9000 compliance been received?

12. What is the average hourly direct wage cost of manufacturing employees? What is the average hourly wage cost with factory overhead applied? How does this compare to the competition?

13. At what percent of capacity is each manufacturing plant operating? What is considered the break-even point? What is the present work week? How much overtime is currently being worked?

14. Are freight and transportation costs a significant factor in this business? Does this business have any transportation advantages or disadvantages compared to competitors?

15. If special orders and change orders are a regular part of this business, are all costs captured and customers charged?

16. What is the backlog? Is manufacturing working mainly from firm orders, a sales forecast or to maintain inventory levels?

17. Is maintenance and repair adequate? What will be this year's expected costs and how do they compare to prior years?

18. How much labor or service is sold to customers as a separate charge? What are the business's hourly billing rates to customers, if applicable?

19. Are utility costs significant? How do utility costs compare with competitors'?

20. Describe, request and develop opinions of the plant layout and work flow.

21. Describe the use of, and potential for, subcontracting and reasons for such. Could any work now subcontracted be economically returned? Is subcontracting a source of controversy? Could any subcontracted work be supplied by the investor? Does the business have products or parts manufactured abroad? If yes, what are the advantages today, if any?

22. Has the company relocated any manufacturing operations within the past three years? Are any such moves under active consideration?

23. Describe the material control, production, planning and scheduling systems. What computers and software systems are used? Is management satisfied with the systems?

24. What in management's opinion are the three greatest strengths and three most significant problems in manufacturing?

25. Describe any programs and the results to reduce costs, increase efficiency, improve quality or morale.

26. Is management obsessed with direct-indirect labor ratios?

CHAPTER 17. PURCHASING

1. What percent of the sales dollar is purchased material or outside services?

2. Determine and describe the status of the purchasing function and its actual control over purchasing.

3. Who is responsible for purchasing and what is the purchasing organization? To whom does the individual responsible for purchasing report?

4. Are there active programs or objectives to aggressively reduce the cost of purchased materials and services? Request copies of program reports.

5. List the major and critical suppliers, the items supplied and annual purchases.

6. Have long-term supply contracts with vendors been negotiated? Request a list of all long-term supply contracts and copies of those most important.

7. Describe any sole-source supply situations.

8. Describe any unusual or significant purchase commitments made or soon to be made.

9. Describe any vendor relationships that may involve conflicts of interest. Do management or shareholders have a financial interest in any supplier?

10. Describe any unusual payment terms or vendor financing. What is the cost of extended payments permitted by vendors? Is the business locked into a vendor because of financing?

11. What is the business's policy with regard to employees accepting gifts and entertainment from vendors? Is it written?

12. What is the training and experience level of those involved in purchasing? Could they be considered professionals?

13. Is purchasing largely the responsibility of one individual subject to little review?

14. Are purchase orders issued before purchase commitments become a contract? Request copy of standard purchase order form.

15. Have any purchasing employees been suspected, accused or discharged for improprieties in the past five years? Is there any history of kickbacks, excessive gifts or other valuable benefits from suppliers?

16. What controls exist on purchasing decisions and procedures?

17. Do import tariffs affect purchasing decisions?

18. Does the business use systems to automatically reorder from suppliers?

19. How do vendors view this business? Do any refuse to quote when the business requests?

20. Could this business be adversely affected by fluctuations in commodity prices?

21. How are freight and transportation purchased? How are costs controlled? Who is responsible?

22. How significant are transportation costs in the receipt of raw material and parts or the shipment of finished goods? Does the business have either a competitive advantage or disadvantage?

CHAPTER 18. HUMAN RESOURCES

1. What is the number of full-time employees? (Exclude contract, part-time and temporary). Break down the total by country and business unit in which they are employed. Request lists, if needed, of employee names, job titles, compensation and other necessary information.

2. What are the total numbers of sales, administrative and executive employees? Request list of employees if needed.

3. What is the total number of professional employees?

4. What is the total number of hourly full-time (non-exempt) employees? Are there wide seasonal variations?

5. What is the total number of temporary employees?

6. What is the total number of contract employees?

7. What are the use and total number of part-time employees?

8. How many job openings exist at each level? Is a shortage of employees in any area adversely affecting the company's operations? Are any anticipated? Is employee turnover a problem?

9. Are any significant layoffs or closings in progress or being contemplated? Have any occurred in the past year?

10. Request copies of all personnel manuals, employee manuals or other documents describing benefits rules and other terms of the employment relationship. Can any be or have been interpreted as employment contracts?

11. How does the business select and recruit executives? Does it use executive search firms and psychologists? What fees were paid during the last 12 months? Is there a policy of promotion from within?

12. Which employees have been required to sign non-competition agreements and/or confidential information agreements? Have any refused to sign? Request copies of forms. Has there been any litigation or threatened litigation by or against former or existing employees over the agreements?

13. What training, formal or informal, is provided employees? Describe all programs at all levels. Does the business reimburse employees for tuition for college courses?

14. What are the policies on use of company automobiles and aircraft?

15. What has been the business's safety record? Describe any safety programs. When was the last OSHA inspection and what were the results? What were the worst accidents in the past five years? List all accidents involving fatalities in the past 10 years. Does the business have someone in charge of safety?

16. What has been the business's workmen's compensation costs for the past three years? Is this, or is it likely to be, a significant problem area for the company?

17. Are there any occupational health problems common to this industry?

18. Request a breakdown by age of the employees. Does the business have any programs to encourage or force early retirement?

19. Does this business employ minors or illegal aliens?

20. Is this business in an industry known to employ minors, illegal aliens and have frequent violations of labor laws?

21. Are prospective employees given physical examinations and tested for drugs? Does the business use psychological testing?

22. If the business utilizes consultants or contract labor on a regular basis, has their relationship been studied to verify that they should not be classified as employees?

23. What are unemployment compensation costs? Is this a significant cost factor?

24. Are employees tested for drugs? What is the business's substance abuse policy? Is this a problem area?

25. Does the business have a policy and program of social responsibility to hire and promote minorities, women and those over 40 years of age? If yes, what has been the result?

Unions

26. List unions with bargaining rights, location and date contracts expire. Request copies of all union contracts.

27. How does management characterize its union relations? Does management have experienced and objective personnel handling union officials?

28. Does management expect serious difficulties in negotiating any of the next union contracts?

29. Do the union contracts contain restrictions on subcontracting or relocation?

30. Does the company negotiate its own contracts or is it part of a multi-employer agreement?

31. List any union representation elections held in the past three years and describe results. Have there been any attempts to organize in the past three years?

32. List any union decertifications in the past five years. Have there been any attempts?

33. What has been the strike history at each location?

34. What arbitrations were held in past 24 months?

35. What are the most troublesome aspects of each contract?

36. What is the level of unionization in the industry? Are any major competitors organized?

37. What are the national and local reputations of the unions representing employees?

38. Have any unfair labor charges been filed against the business in the last six years? If yes, describe outcomes.

39. Does the business provide supplemental unemployment benefits (SUB)? If yes, how are they funded and what is the present status of the fund?

CHAPTER 19. EMPLOYEE COMPENSATION AND BENEFITS

1. What in total are employee benefit costs? Are present and former employee benefit costs, including insurance and pensions, higher, lower or about equal to the competition?

2. List all retirement plans in effect or announced, including multi-employer plans. Indicate who is covered by each plan. Describe benefits. Describe method of funding and annual cost. Describe in detail the amount

of unfunded past service liability if any. Request actuarial valuations, trustee reports, IRS letters of determination and copies of all plans.

3. What health and life insurance benefits are provided current and retired employees and their dependents? What is the cost for active employees? What is the cost per retired employee? Request copies of plans or policies. Does the business use a carrier or is it self-insured?

4. List all profit-sharing plans in effect and describe in detail who is included and the history of amounts paid. Request copies of plans.

5. Describe any bonus or incentive plans and who is covered. List amounts paid and due. Request copies of plans.

6. Describe any deferred compensation plans in effect and who is covered. List amounts paid or due each participant.

7. Describe any ESOP stock purchase or savings plan. Request copies of the plans.

8. Describe any stock option or bonus plans. Who is included and what obligations are outstanding?

9. Does the business have a 401K plan? Request a copy of plan.

10. Describe any benefits and funding source for any terminated or retired employees, such as salary continuation, insurance, club memberships and so on. Who is currently receiving such benefits?

11. List employees who have employment contracts and the date each contract expires. Request copies.

12. What are the business's severance pay policies, practices and obligations? Will a change of ownership trigger any severance pay obligations?

13. What are the vacation and sick leave benefits? Can these be accumulated from year to year if not taken? If accumulation of benefits is permitted, what is the quality of the records? How are these benefits funded and accounted for in the financial reports?

14. Has the business had any full-employment or no-layoff policies?

15. Is the business's general compensation policy to be competitive, pay higher or lower than area rates?

16. Are the business's pay scales or rates and benefit costs higher or lower than competitors'? Is this a significant factor?

17. Does the company have a formal salary and/or wage administration plan? How are jobs ranked and wages set? How are executive salaries and compensation determined?

18. Have any benefit plans been introduced, terminated or substantially modified within the past three years? If yes, what was the reason and result?

CHAPTER 20. CORPORATE CULTURE

1. Assume the investor's management philosophy and style are the norm and identify significant areas of deviation from this norm in the business under study. Review approach to employees, customers, community

and others of importance. Have management philosophies resulted in policies and practices that most dispassionate observers would consider to be extreme, excessive or atypical of customary business practices?

2. What is the racial and ethnic composition of management and the work force? Has this been a source of conflict or is it expected to be in the future?

3. What is the religious composition of management and employees? Has religious affiliation affected employment and promotions either overtly or covertly?

4. What are the decision-making and approval procedures for making charitable contributions? Is there a donation and contribution budget? If yes, request a copy.

a. Do large shareholders or key officers influence the business to make large contributions to their favorite charities?

b. What were the actual donations in the last 12 months?

c. Are any shareholders or executives active in major charities?

d. Does the business make contributions to religious organizations?

5. During the past four years has the business made political contributions in cash or in kind either directly or indirectly? Describe the methods of contributing, the amounts and to whom.

a. Have any key shareholders or executives personally made significant political contributions during the past four years?

b. What has been the purpose of the contributions and actual or anticipated benefits to the business?

c. Has an effort been made to comply with federal and state laws governing political contributions?

d. Is any income of this business dependent upon an elected official remaining in office or being replaced?

e. Does the business have a political action committee (PAC)? If yes, describe its activities, method of funding and contribution record.

f. Are any officers or key employees holders of elective offices either in government or a political party or recipients of a political appointment? If yes, name them.

g. Is the great majority of the management of one political persuasion? If yes, describe?

h. Does the business employ or retain a political lobbyist? If yes, what have been the costs, purpose and result?

i. Do any major shareholders or key executives have a close relationship with any high-level elected officials?

6. Has the business made investments or purchased from vendors because of social, political or religious considerations?

7. Does the business have a code of business conduct or some other policy statement covering ethical practices? If yes, request a copy.

8. Is this business engaged in any management innovations or fads?

CHAPTER 21. LEGAL

1. Detail all claims, actions, suits, arbitrations, investigations, disputes or other proceedings against the business that are pending, threatened or anticipated. Review all relevant pleadings, documents and files. Estimate legal costs, dates of resolution and amounts, if any, of losses.

2. Detail all claims, actions, suits, arbitrations, investigations, disputes or other proceedings by the business that are pending or anticipated, against others. Review all relevant pleadings, documents and files. Estimate legal costs, dates of resolution and probable amounts recovered.

3. Is the business or any of its officers or directors subject to any fine, penalty, order, writ, injunction, restraining order, agreement, or decree of any court, department, agency or instrumentality or settlement agreement? If yes, has there been any default? Request copies of all relevant documents.

4. Request a copy of all settlement agreements relating to any claim, action, suit, arbitration, investigation, dispute or other proceeding against the business that is in the process of being settled or has been settled within the last five years.

5. What law firms and attorneys are used by the business? What were the business's legal expenses for each of the past three years? Itemize amounts paid to each firm and/or attorney. What legal work is performed in-house?

6. What reserves have been established for potential litigation losses, and are they adequate?

7. Request a copy of all letters sent during the last three years from the attorneys for the business to the business's independent public accountants concerning litigation and other legal proceedings.

8. Describe in detail any past, current or anticipated litigation against any officers or directors of the business.

9. Has the business or any of its key employees, significant shareholders, officers or directors ever been charged with criminal activity?

10. Describe all claims, actions, suits, arbitrations or other proceedings brought by shareholders of the business that are pending, threatened or anticipated against any director or officer of the business.

11. Describe any claim against or liability of the business on account of product warranties or with respect to the manufacture, licensing, sale or rental of defective products. Is there any basis for any such claim? Identify claims that are fully insured.

12. Have there been any investigations or inquiries by the Consumer Product Safety Commission or by any other federal, state, or local agency

or governmental entity with respect to products manufactured or sold by the business or with respect to products that are similar or of the same type as products manufactured or sold by the business?

13. Detail all pending worker's compensation claims and all such claims that have arisen in the last three years. Is the business aware of any events that would cause its worker's compensation insurance premiums to increase or of any notifications of increases or possible increases?

14. Describe any claim, action, suit, investigation, dispute or other proceeding against the business that is pending, threatened or anticipated, relating to any violations or alleged violations of any laws, rules or regulations. Give particular attention to those relating to: taxes, the environment, occupational safety and health, foreign corrupt practices, sexual harassment, age and racial or other types of discrimination, wage and hour laws, child labor laws or employment of aliens.

15. Has the business complied with all laws, rules, regulations and orders of regulatory agencies relating to the operation of its business, in which failure to comply would be materially adverse to the business? During the last three years, has there been any action instituted against the business by any governmental entity, board, bureau, agency, instrumentality or other tribunal for any violation of any laws?

16. Describe all suits, claims, disputes, or other proceedings involving the infringement or alleged infringement of any of the business's permits, licenses, franchises, certificates, trademarks, trade names, patents, patent applications, copyrights, drawings, schematics, designs or other similar proprietary and/or intangible rights. Describe all action that the business is taking to stop such infringement.

17. Describe any claims, suits, disputes or other proceedings involving allegations of infringements of proprietary rights by the business.

18. Has the business or any agent of the business, directly or indirectly, within the past five years, given or accepted any gift or similar benefit to or from any customer, supplier, government employee or other person in a position to help or hinder the business, which (1) might result in damages or penalties in any civil, criminal or governmental proceeding, or (2) if not continued in the future, might materially and adversely affect the assets, business operations or prospect of the business?

19. Has the business or any of its employees been charged with price-fixing, kickbacks, market-splitting or payoffs? Has the business ever been the subject of FTC or other governmental agency investigations?

a. Is the business in an industry where price-fixing, bid-rigging, market-splitting, kickbacks or payoffs have occurred?

b. If the business belongs to trade associations, how are these associations kept free of illegal activities by members?

20. Do the investor and the business operate in any of the same markets? Are there any foreseen anti-trust concerns with the business, if acquired by the investor?

21. If the business has made any acquisitions within the past ten years, are there any disputes with selling shareholders for any reason, including disputes regarding any earnout obligations?

22. If the business or any of its businesses have been sold within the past ten years, what contractual obligations of the business or with former owners still survive?

23. Are there any trends, events, or litigation in the business's industry that would indicate that the business may become subject to substantial litigation?

24. Are there any proposed changes in legislation or government regulation that would have a material effect upon the business?

25. Does the business have in place procedures to keep management informed of new federal and state legislation or areas of rapidly expanding litigation (such as sexual harassment, wrongful discharge, and non-competition restrictions) that impact the business? Is the business in compliance with the "Americans With Disabilities Act" and the "Family and Medical Leave Act of 1993"?

CHAPTER 22. INFORMATION SYSTEMS

1. Request a list of all information systems and functions in the business that utilize computers. List types of machines, software, their age and number of units.

2. Does the business have valid licenses for each system of software? Are there restrictions on transferring any licenses if there is a change in the control of the business?

3. Are computers and other hardware leased or owned?

4. Identify software licensed, leased, developed in-house and owned or developed with source code purchased.

5. What new information systems are scheduled to be added or replaced?

6. What are the strengths of the present systems? With what aspects of the systems is management dissatisfied?

7. Is the company committed to long-term leases of equipment, software, systems and/or services? What are the penalties for cancellation?

8. Have any new major systems been installed in the past year? Why were they installed and have they worked as planned? What has been the success in installing new systems?

9. Does the business have an overall strategic plan with objectives to coordinate, integrate and standardize its information systems? If yes, request a copy.

10. Who is in charge of information systems? If there is one individual, what is his authority and responsibility? Does this person approve purchase, licensing or lease of software and hardware to assure compatibility and compliance with overall objectives? Does this person prioritize software development and establish standards?

11. Is there a central database? Are there plans to establish a central database? Is there networking in the business?

12. Has the business contracted out entire departments or functions of information systems? Does the business use service bureaus or contract out software development? Identify the contractors and evaluate costs, benefits and levels of satisfaction with their performance. Request copies of the contracts.

13. What are the backup and disaster recovery procedures and programs?

14. Has the business conducted any studies to determine if the cost of information systems has been offset by cost reductions or increases in productivity? Request copies.

15. What security systems, procedures or practices are in place to protect information systems? Has the business been a victim of fraud or theft through its information systems? Have software viruses been a threat or problem?

16. Are there any employees involved in information systems whose departure for any reason would seriously impair the systems? Identify any employees thought to have exceptional talent for writing software.

17. Does the business use any special telecommunications systems? Is the equipment leased or owned?

CHAPTER 23. BUDGETING AND PLANNING

1. What are the business's short- and long-term objectives and is there a plan either formal or informal for their accomplishment?

2. Does the business have a system of planning and/or budgeting and forecasting? If yes, request copies of the plans and/or budgets for the past three years and any covering the present and future years.

3. Is planning a separate function from budgeting? How long has either function existed?

4. Are the planning and/or budgeting programs fairly well formalized? Who participates in the preparation and approval process? Are executives experienced and sophisticated?

5. What is the philosophy or attitude of those preparing plans and budgets? Is the approach conservative, realistic, easily attainable or fantasy?

6. How seriously is planning and budgeting taken and is it used effectively by management?

7. How often are plans and/or budgets reviewed and modified during the year after initial approval?

8. Does management have an overall strategic plan? Does it have a "mission statement?" If yes, secure copies.

CHAPTER 24. INSURANCE AND BONDING

1. Request a copy of all insurance contacts or policies in effect. Prepare a list of the coverage, amounts, names of the carriers and premiums. Identify areas where coverage is inadequate or lacking.

2. Are any policies about to expire with renewal refused, difficult or at greatly increased premium cost?

3. Are any policies on a retrospective basis? Is any significant income anticipated from favorable experience?

4. Have any carriers cancelled or refused to renew policies in the past three years?

5. Have there been major losses under any policy in the past three years? Are any claims disputed or unpaid?

6. Is the business self-insured in any areas? If yes, secure full information including the rationale, loss experience, adequacy of reserves, bonding, umbrella policies or other catastrophe coverage.

7. Does the business provide health insurance for its employees? What percent of the premium is paid by the employees? What is the annual cost to the business per employee? How does this compare to competitors' programs?

8. Is the business required to provide bid and/or performance bonds? Is securing bonds a problem? What is the business's bonding limit?

9. Is any bonding of employees required? Have there been any fidelity losses?

10. Is the business presently having difficulty in seeking new insurance coverage or bonding?

11. Does the company carry directors' and officers' liability insurance? If no, why not?

12. Does the business carry key man life insurance? If yes, who are the beneficiaries and what was the purpose of buying the insurance? What is the present cash value? Has the business borrowed against the policies?

13. Does the business carry flood insurance? Has flooding occurred or does a risk of flooding exist?

14. Are any of the carriers reported or rumored to have financial difficulties that could limit their ability to pay claims?

15. Why were the carriers selected that provide insurance to the business? Who is the business's insurance broker?

CHAPTER 25. ENVIRONMENTAL ISSUES

1. Have there been or are there now any EPA or other government environmental suits, actions, audits, studies, investigations or charges involving any locations or activities of the business? If yes, summarize and obtain copies of all suits, reports, assessments, complaints and correspondence.

2. Has the business internally conducted, or employed consultants for environmental studies? If yes, obtain copies of reports.

3. Consider separately each parcel of real estate owned or leased by the business.

a. Do present operations contaminate the soil?

b. Did or do any past operations of present or former owners or tenants of the real estate contaminate the soil? Who were the prior owners?

c. Have any studies involving test borings been conducted? If yes, obtain copies of reports.

d. Do any neighbors have operations that present serious environmental hazards?

e. Are there any known toxic waste dumps in the vicinity of any real estate of the business?

f. Are there any underground or surface storage tanks on the business's property?

g. Are the sewer system and sewage treatment facilities in compliance and adequate?

h. Do any buildings contain asbestos?

i. Does the business use radioactive material or devices?

j. Are any chemicals used in the business's operations that are considered toxic? If yes, list and describe their use and methods of disposal. Where are the dump sites, if such have been or are used?

k. Do any operations of the business release either toxic or non-toxic emissions into the air or water? If yes, list and describe problems that may exist.

l. Are there any discharges of industrial waste water on or from the premises?

m. Is there any waste oil generated from the uses and operations conducted at the premises? Is it being stored and disposed of in compliance with all applicable environmental laws?

n. Are there any PCBs or PCB-containing electrical equipment on or in the premises? Secure copies of all documents relating to the existence or removal of any PCBs or PCB-containing materials on any of the business's premises.

o. Have any hazardous materials been treated, stored, disposed of, incinerated, or recycled on the business's premises or elsewhere by the business or any of its agents?

p. Except for lubricants and motor oils in insignificant quantities, have any hazardous materials ever been spilled, disposed of, discharged or released on or in the premises, or been transported or disposed of by the business, or at the business's instructions on any off-site location?

q. Has the business been accused of disposing of, or disposed of, any waste at a Superfund site?

4. Is the business in violation of any existing environmental regulations? Identify possible violations of which government agencies are unaware.

5. Is there current activity in legislative bodies or regulatory agencies that may lead to regulations that could affect the operations of the business? If yes, explain. Has any legislation recently been passed affecting the business?

6. Has the business established any financial reserves to cover environmental cleanup costs, legal fees or fines? Is there a footnote to the financial statement?

7. What EPA or other government agency permits does this business have? Are there any others it should have, but do not? Have any expired or have waivers been granted?

8. What has the business spent for environmental compliance and remedial work during each of the past three years? What is the estimated cost for the next three years?

9. Who is in charge of environmental matters for the business? Is there a corporate compliance program? Request copies of any procedure or policy manuals.

10. Request the names and addresses of all regulatory agencies with whom this business has had or has direct contact. Obtain names and titles of all executives and representatives of the agencies that have contact with this business.

CHAPTER 26. DEBT AND BANKING

1. List all loans, borrowings and debt securities outstanding and their basic terms. For each debt list the collateral pledged. Request copies of all significant debt instruments. Conduct a Uniform Commercial Code search for liens.

2. List each bank or financial institution that the business has worked with in the past two years. Describe the natures of the relationships. Request a list of all bank accounts and the authorized signers on each account. For each institution determine why it was selected and whether there are any special relationships.

3. Request a list of lines of credit, their cost, limits and amounts drawn down. Are there covenants that have the practical effect of preventing the lines of credit from being fully drawn down?

4. How does the business plan to meet its current and long-term debt

obligations? Is the business seeking new borrowings? Is there an opportunity to refinance at lower cost? Is the business having, or has it had difficulty in seeking new financing?

5. Is this business in default or about to become in default on any debt obligations?

6. Are any cash investments or securities pledged as collateral?

7. What parent company guarantees are outstanding? What is the policy?

8. Are there any personal guarantees on any of the business's debts?

9. Describe the major restrictions contained in any debt agreements.

10. Is there any off-balance-sheet financing?

11. Is the value of the collateral pledged relatively consistent with the value of the loans outstanding?

12. Does the business provide letters of credit? If yes, what is outstanding? Who issues the letters and how are they backed?

13. Is this business paying normal interest rates?

14. How do financial institutions and other lenders view this business and its industry?

15. What financing is provided by suppliers? What are the true costs and obligations?

16. Are there any loans from shareholders or officers? If yes, what are their origins, interest rates, repayment histories and schedules? Are the loans fully documented?

17. Prepare a list of all leases and their terms. Identify those that are capitalized. What renewal and purchase rights and critical obligations exist? Request copies of leases.

18. Has the business received any tax concessions or loans with covenants to locate or remain in a specific location?

19. Has all or any segment of this business ever been in bankruptcy proceedings?

CHAPTER 27. INVESTMENTS AND CASH MANAGEMENT

1. Request a list of all cash investments and securities, both marketable and unmarketable. Compare book price to market price. What has been the business's investment policy and results? Identify all investments in foreign countries. Identify those of a high-risk or clearly speculative nature such as junk bonds, derivatives and non-performing loans.

2. Are there any loans to shareholders or executives? If yes, what are their origins, interest rates, repayment histories and schedules? Are the loans fully documented?

3. How are temporary surplus funds invested?

4. How are investments made? Who selects the investments? Identify

brokers and financial advisors utilized. Does the business receive any supplemental benefits by investing with or through any financial institutions?

5. If there are unrepatriated foreign profits, what are the business's plans for these funds? How have they been used in the past? How are they invested?

6. What evidence is there that this business aggressively manages its cash?

7. Are evaluating customers, granting of credit and receivable collection major factors in the business? Explain. Who is responsible for extending credit and collections?

8. Describe the credit investigation and approval system and policies. Is an outside factoring institution used to guarantee credit?

9. Is this a business where employees handle cash on a regular basis? If yes, have there been any thefts or evidence of skimming? What controls exist to deter theft?

10. Does the business buy supplies and raw materials for cash?

11. Does the business engage in hedging? If yes, describe in detail.

12. What is management's program to avoid losses on foreign exchange? Have there been significant losses or gains? What is the present exposure?

13. Does the business print payable checks and hold the checks to conserve cash or until cash is available?

14. What controls exist to prevent improper or unauthorized checks from being issued?

15. Does the business have any pension, 401K or profit-sharing funds? Where are the funds invested?

a. Who administers the funds? Request lists of all trustees and administrators and their relationship to the business. Who establishes investment policy and makes specific investments? Request copies of fund reports and audits for past two years.

b. What are the assets of each fund? Identify any illiquid assets.

c. Are the funds over- or underfunded? What assumptions, including interest rates, were used in the actuaries' calculations?

d. Is any money from the funds invested in the business or securities of the business?

e. Is any money from the funds invested in ways that could constitute conflicts of interest?

f. What has been the investment performance of each fund?

g. Have any employees or former employees filed suit or threatened suit over any funds performance or investments?

h. Have the business's contributions all been made?

i. If plans are underfunded, what are the company's plans for funding?

CHAPTER 28. TAXES

1. List all governments and government agencies, federal, state, local and foreign, to which tax reports must be filed and/or taxes paid. Secure copies of returns for past three years.

2. Request for each of the taxing bodies the following information: amounts paid to each during the past three years, amounts owed but not paid, any amounts in dispute and any reports not filed on time.

3. When was the last U.S. Internal Revenue Service (IRS) audit and what was the result? What years are still open?

4. Are any IRS, state, local or foreign tax audits in progress or scheduled?

5. When were the last state, local or foreign tax audits and what were the results? Have revisions in federal returns been reflected in state returns?

6. Are there any current or potential disputes with any taxing bodies? If yes, request complete information.

7. Has there been a need and has management made any provisions for claims, tax renegotiation or redetermination? What has been recorded in the financial statements?

8. What is the actual or effective tax rate? Determine the reasons for any differences from the statutory rates.

9. Describe the circumstances and procedures that give rise to deferred taxes. Under what circumstances would deferred taxes become due and payable?

10. Summarize all tax loss carry forwards (NOLs) and/or tax credits and the years of their expiration. What is their origin?

11. Is tax planning a major consideration in how the company conducts its international business? Is tax planning a factor in intracompany sales, loans and other internal transactions?

12. Are there changes being proposed to the tax codes at any level of government that would have either beneficial or a serious adverse effect upon this business?

13. Has the business requested or received any private letter tax rulings from the IRS? If yes, request copies.

14. How do this business's state and local taxes compare with competitors? Are any state taxes considered very high or low?

15. Review the tax status and obligations of all foreign subsidiaries, both active and inactive.

16. Are profits diverted to or from foreign subsidiaries or other affiliated business units to avoid or reduce taxes?

17. Who prepares the business's tax returns?

18. What is the tax basis for each category of assets of the business?

CHAPTER 29. ACCOUNTING GENERAL QUESTIONS

1. In general, how reliable do the financial reports appear to be? Are management and shareholders willing to warrant the accuracy of the statements? Are the statements audited, reviewed or compilations?

2. Name the public accounting firm engaged for the audit and fees paid during the past four years. Identify any other accounting firms used and fees paid. Arrange to have access to their work papers.

3. If the opinion of the auditors is qualified in any way, request full information on the reasons for the accountant's reservations.

4. Have the auditors been changed in the past five years? If yes, request full details.

5. If the company has multiple business units or subsidiaries, do the auditors audit each unit or only give an opinion on the business as a whole?

6. Request copies of any management letters prepared by auditors during the past four years. What steps have been taken to implement recommendations?

7. Describe any major personnel changes in the financial departments within the past two years and reasons for the changes.

8. Describe any financial systems undergoing major revisions. What is the reason?

9. Are there any significant differences between financial statements, tax returns and SEC filings? If yes, describe in detail.

10. If there are multiple divisions or subsidiaries, are accounting policies uniform and formats identical? If not, describe.

11. Are the financial statements for the past five years in essentially the same format so trends and ratios may be readily calculated? Are they in sufficient detail to determine trends in critical expense categories?

12. Does the company have internal auditors? Review copies of their reports. What is the scope of their authority and role? To whom do they report?

13. Are any accounting functions contracted out (other than auditing)?

14. How many days after the close of each month are financial statements produced?

15. Describe the business's overall systems of internal control. Are they adequate? Have the auditors voiced any opinions on this subject? What controls exist to audit and approve expenses of senior executives?

16. Has the quality of the financial statements been influenced by extreme pressure to achieve budgeted targets or management incentive plans?

CHAPTER 30. ACCOUNTING POLICIES

1. Are the annual financial statements prepared in accordance with GAAP and AICPA? If not, list deviations.

2. Describe accounting principles, policies and actual practices employed in each of the categories listed, and their effect upon income. Secure a chart of accounts.

a. Inventories

b. Percent of completion

c. Reserves and allowances

d. Capitalization versus expense

e. Prepayments

f. Payables

g. Inclusion or exclusion of subsidiaries or affiliates in consolidated statements

h. Revenue and income matching and/or recognition

i. Cost accounting

j. Retirement benefits and stock options

3. What differences in results would have occurred if the investor's accounting policies had been applied?

4. Describe the year-to-year consistency of application of accounting policies, principles and procedures. Any changes in the past five years?

5. Do any subsidiaries, joint ventures, affiliates or companies in which there is a significant investment have different fiscal years?

6. Does the business use accounting policies to increase reported income or to hold back or reduce income whenever it can do so?

7. Does the business have pending any requests to change accounting policies and practices? Are there changes that the business may be compelled to make?

8. Has this business been engaged in any programs that could be described as restructuring? If yes, what have been the accounting policies and approach?

9. Have there been any changes in the fiscal year ending for any business unit under study during the past five years? If yes, what was the purpose and effect?

CHAPTER 31. CASH

1. Is the cash restricted in any way? Compensating balances, deposits for bonding and so on?

2. Is any cash in currencies not readily converted into hard currencies or in blocked accounts?

3. Is a portion of the cash due to "front end" mobilization or progress payments?

4. Are cash levels highly influenced by seasonal factors?

5. Is there any cash earned outside the United States in foreign accounts that cannot be repatriated without paying taxes?

6. Are certain levels of cash required by debt covenants either separately or as part of the total current assets?

CHAPTER 32. ACCOUNTS AND NOTES RECEIVABLE

1. Classify accounts receivable by age. Secure copies of internal aging reports. If none available, prepare such a report.

2. How does the business define "current" and "past due" accounts receivable both from a reporting and practical basis?

3. How are discounts, returns, rebates, claims against customers, change orders, installment and consignment sales recorded and the receivable account affected?

4. Are any accounts receivable disputed? If yes, secure the amounts and circumstances.

5. Identify the major customer receivables. What percent of the business does each of these customers represent? Are any considered a collection problem?

6. Describe the method for providing for uncollectibles, including the method for determining when an account is uncollectible.

7. Describe any reserves for doubtful or uncollectible accounts and how they were determined. Does the company have a history of establishing adequate reserves? Does the company overreserve or write off accounts prematurely to delay taxes?

8. Describe any collateralized accounts receivable.

9. Describe any pledging, factoring or restrictions. If factoring of receivables occurs, determine procedure, cost and financial institution used.

10. Describe how retentions, if any, are accounted for. If appropriate, include in the A/R aging. When and how much of the retainage will likely be collected? Are any jobs for which retainage is outstanding in trouble?

11. Describe and quantify any non-trade receivables such as those arising from royalties or sale of assets.

12. Request a detailed list of all receivables and/or notes due from shareholders, businesses controlled by shareholders, management or sister companies. How did they arise, terms and payment history? Are they documented?

13. List all notes receivable, debtors, interest rates, retirement schedules, collateral, liens and legal status, whether up-to-date in payment and reasons for notes.

14. If the business uses percent of completion accounting, determine the methods, accuracy and validity of the "unbilled receivable."

15. Under what conditions do customers refuse to pay receivables?

16. What has been the company's record in eventually recovering written-off bad debts? Is this a "hidden asset"?

17. Have invoices been backdated to accelerate income? Are some months "held open" to include shipments made after the month end? Has the business ever recorded "phantom" sales?

CHAPTER 33. INVENTORY

1. Determine the book value of inventory by location and product line. For each product line calculate the number of annual inventory turns. Determine causes of significant increases or decreases in inventory levels.

2. During the past 12 months, what was the high and low point for the inventory of each product line and in which months did the highs and lows occur?

3. Determine by product line the composition of the inventory, the dollar amount and the percentage of the sales dollar and percentage of total inventory each category represents.

a. Raw Materials

b. Components or Parts

c. Work-in-process

d. Spare Parts

e. Finished Goods

f. Labor and Overhead

g. Manufactured versus Purchased

h. Tools and Supplies

4. How often are physical inventories taken? Are inventories observed by auditors? Are spot checks with sample counts taken during the fiscal year? Are inventories counted in their entirety or are random or representative samples counted?

5. What were the amounts of year-end inventory adjustments by location or product line and in total for each of the past three years? If the adjustments were significant, what is management's explanation?

6. Does management consider inventory reserves to be adequate? How were the reserves calculated?

7. What has been management's policy and practice for defining, valuing, charging off and disposing of obsolete, excess and slow-moving inventory? How much is in each category? Is there a deviation between actual practice and the formal policy relative to the definition, pricing and disposition of each category?

8. Is inventory readily identified, neatly stored and easily located with locations well marked?

9. What is estimated to be the net realizable value of the inventory?

10. Has inventory been aggressively written down or relocated to reduce or delay taxes? Is there evidence the inventory is undervalued?

11. Is any inventory not owned by the business kept on a consignment basis?

12. Does the company have inventory out on a consignment basis? How is this counted and recorded?

13. Is inventory costed on a LIFO or FIFO basis? If inventory is costed on a LIFO basis, what is the amount of the LIFO reserve? Does management plan to keep the LIFO method?

14. Does the business have the right to return inventory to vendors? What are the amounts permissible and restocking charges?

15. What is the inventory control system and is management satisfied with its performance? How accurate are inventory records?

16. Has there been inventory shrinkage due to theft or other mysterious disappearance?

17. How is "market value" determined and applied in valuing inventory at "cost or market, whichever is lower"?

18. Do dealers, distributors or customers have the right to return merchandize to the business? What was the value of merchandize returned during the past year? How are returned goods valued and recorded?

19. Determine or estimate the percent of the inventory that turns very slowly compared to the remainder of the inventory. Is the inventory out of balance?

20. Is any material amount of inventory in transit between business units of the company?

21. Has any event occurred or been observed in which inventory was intentionally incorrectly counted or valued?

22. Does management consider the present inventory to be excessive, too low or within a reasonable range?

CHAPTER 34. FIXED AND OTHER ASSETS

1. Review each category of fixed assets as it appears on the balance sheet and request a description of the major assets in each category, their age, cost and depreciated value.

2. How accurate and complete are the business's fixed asset records? When was an actual inventory of the business's fixed assets last taken? Do assets have an identifying number attached?

3. Identify tangible assets that are fully depreciated or not listed? What is their estimated market value?

4. What are the depreciation and amortization policies used? Are these

the same for book and tax purposes? Identify assets for which the book value differs from the tax value.

5. For each category of fixed assets, how does the depreciated book value compare to estimated market value? Identify the individual major assets that have a material difference between book and market value. Do leasehold improvements have any market value?

6. If there have been any recent appraisals of assets, what were the results? Obtain copies.

7. Does management consider maintenance and repair costs a significant cost item? What were they last year? Are these excessive by industry standards?

8. Identify and describe any fixed assets that were constructed by employees or purchased from affiliated businesses. What was the method of determining their cost and recording their value on the financial statements?

9. Request a list of all intangible assets and the value represented on the balance sheet. What was the origin and original valuation of each intangible asset? What amortization schedule is used?

10. What prepayments are reported as assets? Secure a complete list.

11. If the balance sheet has a category or line item of "Other Assets," list and describe each asset and its valuation basis.

12. Describe any unconsolidated subsidiaries or joint ventures, their estimated value and income or losses from each.

13. Is management aware of any unrecorded assets such as written-off receivables, options, notes, assets received for defaulted receivables and patents?

14. Request a list of all vehicles, including trucks and trailers owned or leased. Determine their make and age.

15. Request a list of aircraft owned or leased. Estimate the market value of each.

16. Request a list of watercraft owned or leased.

17. Request a list of hunting, fishing or other recreational facilities owned or leased.

18. Identify all assets of significance essentially unrelated to the business's operations, including those acquired as a result of hobbies, interest or whims of past or present shareholders or executives.

19. Does the business have any assets segregated as "held for sale" or "discontinued operations"? If yes, list and describe circumstances and values associated.

20. Does the business have a security program to protect its assets and employees? Who is responsible? What has been the history of losses? Does management have major concerns over security matters?

21. Does the business utilize or store any assets it does not own or lease?

CHAPTER 35. LIABILITIES

1. Identify and list all liabilities not reflected on the financial statements.

2. Classify accounts payable by age. Confirm identity of major suppliers by reviewing accounts payable.

3. Is the business on a C.O.D. basis with any vendors?

4. If there are accrued liabilities, how were these calculated and are they adequate? Are there liabilities that should be accrued but have not been?

5. Are the systems and procedures such that liabilities are promptly recorded and the last balance sheet accurately reflects the level of liabilities? Is there any evidence that payables are held?

6. If there are "advances on contracts" or "billings in excess of costs and estimated earnings" or similar accounts, determine how these entries arose, how calculated and how relieved. Evaluate their accuracy.

7. If there are minority interests in subsidiaries, how are these valued and what is their history?

8. Have all monies required to be withheld by the business from employees or collected from customers for income taxes, social security, and unemployment insurance taxes and sales, excise and use taxes, been collected or withheld and either paid to the respective governmental agencies or set aside in accounts for such purpose?

9. Are liabilities recorded for underfunding of any benefit plans? Are there liabilities that should be recorded?

10. Is there a liability account established to offset income reported on an incomplete installment sale?

11. Are there any large contracts or commitments not in the ordinary course of business requiring future payments?

12. If the business has made any acquisitions in the past seven years, are there any continuing obligations to the sellers such as earnouts or note payments?

CHAPTER 36. BACKLOG AND INCOME RECOGNITION

1. What is the present backlog by product or service line of unfilled orders? Is this backlog normal, high, low, increasing or declining? Request copies of internal reports.

2. How much gross profit is in the backlog?

3. Can the backlog be produced immediately or is it spread over a period of time? When can the last 25 percent of the backlog be shipped and billed? How much is work in progress and how much is finished? Compare backlog by location to monthly revenues.

4. What was the backlog one year ago?

5. What are the policies, either formal or informal, as to when an order is considered firm and can be recorded into the backlog? Is there any evidence of sales being booked prematurely or reversed?

6. Describe the method for recognizing a "sale" when percentage of completed contracts accounting is used.

a. Describe in detail the method of taking up income. If a form or report is used, request a copy.

b. Describe the contingency reserves established for unknown variables.

c. Is there any profit "hold-back" or deferred profit? If so, when is it taken up?

d. Is "cost to complete" recalculated each month?

e. Review jobs in-house. Describe status as regards completion, profit taken, and profit remaining.

f. How are retentions recorded?

g. Are backlogs reduced as work is completed?

h. What has been the business's record for accuracy in estimating costs and percent of completion as jobs progress?

7. Does this business have a history of any of the transactions listed below? If yes, determine and verify how they were recorded on the financial statements. At what point were revenues, income or losses recognized?

a. Installment Sales

b. Customer Rebates

c. Returned Goods

d. Claims Against Customers

e. Contracts Subject to Renegotiation

f. Lease Purchase Revenues

g. Franchise Sales

h. Revenues Preceding Associated Costs

i. Anticipated Tax Refunds

j. Recording of Litigation Settlements Prior to Receipt of Cash

8. Have there been any unusual transactions or volume of transactions in the last days preceding the close of a quarter or year? If yes, identify the circumstances and impact upon reported income.

CHAPTER 37. COST OF SALES, SELLING AND ADMINISTRATIVE EXPENSES

1. Is the gross profit and percent of gross profit for each product line or profit center increasing, decreasing or remaining constant? What are the causes?

2. Determine, for the past year, the dollar amount of material, labor and overhead in cost of sales for each product line or business unit. Are the percentages of any changing?

3. What are the principal elements of cost included in overhead and the method of their calculation and allocation? Are the amounts allocated questionable as to fairness and/or controversial?

4. What cost-accounting systems are used to calculate components of cost of sales for each product line? Do variances result?

5. Is the gross profit the same percentage month after month?

6. Is the gross profit significantly higher or lower than the industry average?

7. What are the selling expenses for each product line and their percent of total revenues? Is the dollar amount and percentage increasing, decreasing or remaining the same? What are the causes for the changes? Are any selling expenses shared or allocated?

8. What are the amounts of general administrative expense and their percent of revenues for the past four years?

9. Determine the composition of each line item or account included in general and administrative.

CHAPTER 38. INTERCOMPANY TRANSACTIONS

1. What are the operational and financial relationships between subsidiaries, joint ventures, divisions, partnerships and internal profit centers? Review all intercompany transactions for the past year, and the amounts presently recorded on each income and balance sheet.

2. Describe in detail all types of intercompany sales and identify each account affected. What policies either formal or informal, govern intercompany sales?

3. Describe any transfer pricing designed to assign profits to one business unit over another. Does the business have defensible, written transfer pricing policies? Request copies.

4. Describe any management fees charged to subsidiaries or divisions. How are they determined? Is this a major source of controversy?

5. Are there any intercompany loans? If yes, determine origin, purpose and plans for their retirement.

6. Are there any intercompany investments?

7. Have there been any non-recurring or unusual transactions between subsidiaries or affiliated companies?

8. What are the methods of moving cash between units and the degree of financial independence of each?

9. Is cash managed centrally? If yes, describe system.

10. Do operating units have their own bank accounts? If yes, what are they? What is deposited and disbursed?

11. How does the parent company collect cash from the subsidiaries or divisions?

12. How does the parent collect cash from the less-than-100-percent-owned operations or investments, including joint ventures?

13. If the business being studied is a division or subsidiary of the larger company, determine what services are provided by the parent. How would these services be replaced after an acquisition?

14. Are there intercompany charges for use of intangibles such as technology, rights to know-how, patents, marketing rights, customer lists, trademarks and trade names? If yes, secure full details, amounts involved and copies of whatever documentation exists.

CHAPTER 39. INVESTMENT QUESTIONS AND ISSUES

1. Identify all third-party approvals necessary to complete this investment or transaction.

2. Identify all consultants or consulting organizations and their role or assignments during the past two years. What have they been paid and are there any continuing obligations?

3. Name any investment bankers or brokers retained. What fees have they been paid and what obligations exist to each?

4. Identify any accountants, lawyers, investment bankers or consultants who have strong influence on either the management or owners. If strong influence exists, explain.

5. Have any formal valuations of this business been conducted? If yes, request copies.

6. Identify and describe sales of businesses within the past three years that are comparable to this business or in the industry.

7. Identify any public companies comparable to this one and the latest book values, return on equity, earnings and market price per share.

8. Have any written reports or studies on the business, the industry's markets or specific problems been prepared by outside professionals during the past three years? If so, request copies.

9. What is the general business climate in the states and communities in which this business is located? How do these locations compare with competitors'?

10. What trade associations or societies does the business belong to? Secure membership lists. Are any employees officers?

11. Is management's vision of the future for the business and industry consistent with that of the investor? What revenue and earnings forecasts, either public or private, have been made by management?

12. What in management's opinion are probable good or bad events likely to occur that could materially affect the business?

Selected Bibliography

Arthur Anderson & Co. *Guide to Mergers and Acquisitions*. New York: Arthur Anderson & Co., 1988.

Arthur Young. Questions at Annual Meeting of Shareholders. Arthur Young, New York, NY, 1984.

Berger, Lisa, Donelson Berger, and William Eastwood. *Cashing In*. New York: Warner Books, 1988.

Bing, Gordon. *Corporate Acquisitions*. Houston: Gulf Publishing Company, 1978.

Blumberg, Paul. *The Predatory Society*. New York: Oxford University Press, 1989.

Bureau of National Affairs. *BNA Policy and Practice Series*. Washington DC: Bureau of National Affairs, 1994.

Cole, Robert. *The Death and Life of the American Quality Movement*. New York: Oxford University Press, 1995.

Coopers & Lybrand. *Checking into an Acquistion Candidate*. New York: Coopers & Lybrand.

Dobler, Donald W., David Burt, and Lamar Lee. *Purchasing and Materials Management*. New York: McGraw Hill, 1990.

Droms, William G. *Finance and Accounting for Nonfinancial Managers*. Reading, MA: Addison-Wesley Publishing Company, 1983.

Ernst & Young LLP. *Mergers & Acquisitions*. New York: John Wiley & Sons, 1994.

Ferris, Kenneth R., Kirk L. Tennant, and Scott I. Jerris. *How to Understand Financial Statements*. Englewood Cliffs, NJ: Prentice-Hall, 1992.

Fisher, Donald C. *Measuring Up to the Baldrige*. New York: AMACOM, 1994.

Fridson, Martin S. *Financial Statements Analysis*. New York: John Wiley & Sons, 1991.

Gibson, Cyrus F., and Barbara Jackson. *The Information Imperative*. Lexington, MA: Lexington Books, 1987.

Hansen, James M. *Guide to Buying or Selling a Business*. Englewood Cliffs, NJ: Prentice-Hall, 1975.

Harmon, Roy L. *Reinventing the Factory II*. New York: The Free Press, 1992.

Hendry, Mike. *Implementing EDI*. Nowood, ME: Artech House, 1993.

Kay, John. *Why Firms Succeed*. New York: Oxford University Press, 1995.

Lang, Hans, and Donald Merino. *The Selection Process for Capital Projects*. New York: John Wiley & Sons, 1993.

Mintzberg, Henry. *The Rise and Fall of Strategic Planning*. New York: The Free Press, 1994.

Moore, Peter G. *The Business of Risk*. New York: Cambridge University Press, 1993.

Naser, Kamal H. M. *Creative Financial Accounting*. New York: Prentice-Hall, 1993.

Rappaport, Alfred. *Creating Shareholder Value*. New York: The Free Press, 1986.

Research Institute of America. *Federal Tax Coordinator*, 2nd ed. New York: Research Institute of America, 1993.

Ricks, David A. *Blunders in International Business*. Cambridge, MA: Blackwell Publishers, 1993.

Rock, Milton L., ed. *The Mergers & Acquisitions Handbook*. New York: McGraw-Hill, 1994.

Rothchild, John. *Going for Broke*. New York: Simon & Schuster, 1991.

Schilit, Howard M. *Financial Shenanigans*. New York: McGraw-Hill, 1993.

Schonberger, Richard J. *World Class Manufacturing*. New York: The Free Press, 1986.

Siegel, Joel G. *How to Analyze Businesses, Financial Statements and the Quality of Earning*. Englewood Cliffs, NJ: Prentice-Hall, 1991.

Sperry, Paul S., and Beatrice H. Mitchell. *Selling Your Business*. Dover, NH: Upstart Publishing Company, 1992.

Thierauf, Robert J. *Management Auditing*. New York: AMACOM, 1980.

Trimble, Vance H. *An Empire Undone*. New York: Carol Publishing Group, 1995.

White, Gerald I., A.C. Sondhi, and Dove Fried. *Analysis and Use of Financial Statements*. New York: John Wiley & Sons, 1994.

Index

About the Author

GORDON BING is a Houston-based independent consultant specializing in multi-million dollar acquisitions and mergers in a wide variety of industries since 1978. Prior to 1978 he was vice president of a public company managing an international acquisition and divestment program, and earlier he was an executive specializing in industrial relations and labor relations management. He is the author of two previous books, *Corporate Divestment* and *Corporate Acquisitions*.

ISBN 1-56720-029-X

90000>

EAN

9 781567 200294

HARDCOVER BAR CODE